The fine art of repetition

Peter Kivy is the author of many books on the philosophy of art and, in particular, the aesthetics of music. This collection of essays spans a period of some thirty years and focuses on a richly diverse set of issues: the biological origin of music, the role of music in the liberal education, the nature of the musical work and its performance, the aesthetics of opera, the emotions of music, and the very nature of music itself. Some of these subjects are viewed as part of the history of ideas, others as current problems in the philosophy of art.

A particular feature of the volume is that Kivy avoids the use of musical notation so that no technical knowledge at all is required to appreciate his work. Thus, the essays will prove enjoyable and insightful not just to professionals in the philosophy of art and musicologists, or to musicians themselves, but also to any motivated general reader with a deep interest in music.

The fine art of repetition

Essays in the philosophy of music

PETER KIVY

RUTGERS: THE STATE UNIVERSITY OF NEW JERSEY

CAMBRIDGE
UNIVERSITY PRESS

Published by the Press Syndicate of the University of Cambridge
The Pitt Building, Trumpington Street, Cambridge CB2 1RP
40 West 20th Street, New York, NY 10011-4211, USA
10 Stamford Road, Oakleigh, Victoria 3166, Australia

© Cambridge University Press, 1993

First published 1993

Printed in Canada

Library of Congress Cataloging-in-Publication Data
Kivy, Peter.
The fine art of repetition : essays in the philosophy of music /
Peter Kivy.
p. cm.
Collection of essays written over the past thirty years and
published in various books and journals.
ISBN 0-521-43462-9 (hbk.) – ISBN 0-521-43598-6 (pbk.)
1. Music – Philosophy and aesthetics. I. Title.
ML3845.K583   1993
781'.1 – dc20   92-25274
                                                      CIP
                                                      MN

A catalog record for this book is available from the British Library.

ISBN 0-521-43462-9 hardback
ISBN 0-521-43598-6 paperback

For Arthur Danto:
Who taught my generation how to
make philosophy of art

". . . they say it is possible to select the best laws, as though even the selection did not demand intelligence and as though right judgement were not the greatest thing, as in matters of music."

Aristotle, *Ethica Nicomachea* (trans. W. D. Ross)

Contents

Preface   *page* ix

Introduction   1

PRELUDE: MUSIC AND US
I   Music and the liberal education   11

WORK AND PERFORMANCE
II   Platonism in music: A kind of defense   35
III Platonism in music: Another kind of defense   59
IV   Orchestrating Platonism   75
V   Live performances and dead composers: On the
     ethics of musical interpretation   95
VI   On the concept of the "historically authentic" per-
     formance   117

THE WORLD OF OPERA
VII   Opera talk: A philosophical "phantasie"   137
VIII How did Mozart do it?: Living conditions in the
      world of opera   160
IX   How did Mozart do it?: Replies to some critics   178

MUSIC AND THE HISTORY OF IDEAS
X   Mozart and monotheism: An essay in spurious
     aesthetics   189
XI   Child Mozart as an aesthetic symbol   200
XII Charles Darwin on music   214

vii

Contents

MUSIC AND EMOTION

XIII Mattheson as philosopher of art   229

XIV Kant and the *Affektenlehre:* What he said, and what
I wish he had said   250

XV Something I've always wanted to know about
Hanslick   265

XVI What was Hanslick denying?   276

XVII A new music criticism?   296

MUSIC ALONE

XVIII The fine art of repetition   327

XIX Is music an art?   360

Preface

The essays collected in this volume, written over a period of thirty years, and parceled out among a variety of journals and books, are addressed to an audience of philosophers, musicians, scholars in other disciplines, and whatever part of a general readership that might be interested in topics at the same time both musical and philosophical. It is not likely that any member of any one of these groups would have had access to more than a few of the places where these essays have appeared. I am delighted, therefore, that they are now together in one place, so as to be available to a larger audience than heretofore.

The earliest essay in this collection was published in 1959, the most recent is published here for the first time. It cannot be expected that essays written over so long a period of time will be entirely consistent with one another, or with my other writings on musical aesthetics, either in questions of philosophy or in points of historical interpretation. I know I have changed my mind on various issues since 1959, and I hope I have learned a few things as well. Nevertheless, rereading my essays, in the preparation of this volume, I have concluded that even at the outset I had, if not a core of fixed beliefs, at least some basic intuitions regarding what music is, and how one should talk about it.

Thus, in spite of the long period of time over which these essays were written, I think of them as an integrated body of work, and of a piece, as well, with the series of books on the philosophy of music I have published since 1980. And I am glad that now, with the publication of these essays in a single volume, my work on the philosophy of music to date can be viewed and (I hope) discussed in its entirety.

The original places and dates of publication are as follows:

I: *The Journal of Aesthetic Education* 25 (1991), pp. 79–93. II: *Grazer philosophische Studien* 19 (1983), pp. 109–29. III: *American Philosophical Quarterly* 24 (1983), pp. 245–52. IV: *Aesthetic Distinction: Essays Presented to Göran Hermerén on His 50th Birthday*, ed. T. Anderberg, T. Nilstun, and I. Persson (Lund: Lund University Press, 1988), pp. 42–55. V: *Human Agency: Language, Duty and Value*, ed. Jonathan Dancy, J. M. E. Moravcsik, and C. C. W. Taylor (Stanford: Stanford University Press, 1988), pp. 219–36. Reprinted by permission of Stanford University Press. © 1988 by the Board of Trustees of the Leland Stanford Junior University. VI: *The Monist* 71 (1988), pp. 278–90. Copyright © 1988 by *The Monist*, La Salle, IL 61301. Reprinted by permission. VII: *Cambridge Opera Journal* 3 (1991), pp. 63–77. VIII: Published here for the first time. IX: Published here for the first time. X: *Journal of Musicology* 2 (1983), pp. 322–8. XI: *Journal of the History of Ideas* 28 (1967), pp. 249–58. XII: *Journal of the American Musicological Society* 12 (1959), pp. 42–8. XIII: *The Musical Quarterly* 70 (1984), pp. 248–65. XIV: *Kant's Aesthetics*, ed. Ralf Meerbote and Hud Hudson, Volume I of the *North American Kant Society Studies in Philosophy* (Altascadero, CA: Ridgeview, 1991), pp. 63–74. Reprinted by permission of Ridgeview Publishing Company. XV: *Journal of Aesthetics and Art Criticism* 46 (1988), pp. 413–17. XVI: *Journal of Musicology* 8 (1990), pp. 3–18. XVII: *The Monist* 73 (1990), pp. 247–68. Copyright © 1990 by *The Monist*, LaSalle, IL 61301. Reprinted by permission. XVIII: Published here for the first time. XIX: *Journal of Philosophy* 88, 10 (October 1991), pp. 544–54.

Introduction

The earliest published essay in this collection was written while I was a graduate student in music history at Yale University, trying to decide whether I wanted to be a musicologist who loves philosophy or a philosopher who loves musicology. In the event I opted for the latter. The volume in your hands is one of the results, an interaction of music and philosophy.

The essays written before 1980 are all historical, and have as their sole reason for being historical curiosity. But in 1980 my career as a philosopher was drastically changed, although I did not realize it at the time, by the publication of my first book on the "philosophy of music," *The Corded Shell*. I had embarked on the writing of it as a pleasant interlude from my usual work in "analytic" aesthetics. Instead, I ended up devoting my philosophical career, if not exclusively, at least very significantly, to the working out of an extensive musical philosophy, which is still very much in process. All the essays after 1980, therefore, even the historical ones, deal with issues that have come up in the course of that work, and which are not dealt with, or not dealt with adequately, in *The Corded Shell* and the books that came after. It is not that my interest in historical questions in the philosophy of music waned during this period: The recent historical essays attest that it did not. But the contemporary issues just seemed to take over, and this is reflected not only in the proportion of analytic to historical subjects dealt with, but in the historical subjects themselves, and the way they are treated.

1

"Music and the Liberal Education" is my one attempt, ever, to write on the philosophy of education, or more specifically, what is called nowadays the philosophy of aesthetic education. The piece is the result of a very flattering invitation, tendered by Jay Bachrach and Barry Donahue, to give a public lecture before the student body and faculty of the William O. Douglas Honors College of Central Washington University in Ellensburg, Washington. The subject of music in the liberal education was chosen in an attempt to capture the interest of both students and their teachers by discussing a question that both parties might have asked, each from its own perspective: Why am I studying *this?*, Why am I teaching *this?* I was somewhat disturbed to discover, in writing this lecture, that I wasn't sure I knew the answer to either of these questions. Perhaps someone else does, although discussions on various occasions on which this lecture was given have failed to reveal anyone in possession of the secret.

The three essays on musical Platonism, variations on a theme, began with the simple idea of suggesting not that the universal-particular relation really would work as a proper model for the work-performance one, but that the reasons usually given for rejecting it just weren't very convincing. Perhaps I pursued it further and longer than I ought to have done. In any case, my foray into musical Platonism has received some heavy bashing in the literature. Notwithstanding that, one interesting idea that appealed to me in the beginning, and still does, is the idea that "discovery" rather than "creation" captures what composers do: I still think that point is worth developing further, and have done so in my book *Music Alone*. Certainly my Platonistic inclinations are weaker now than when these essays were published. But I wanted them to appear together, in one place, so that they could be evaluated as a whole. If someone wants to take another bash at them, I am resigned to it. Or perhaps there is someone out there who can make something more of my dabbling in Platonic metaphysics than I have done.

The two essays on performance practice are preliminary attempts to come to philosophical terms with the "historically authentic performance" movement. Currently I am writing a book on the subject, so this can be considered very much work in progress; the pieces reprinted here represent a fairly early stage of my thinking on the subject. Much needs to be done to get from these two rather different, but not inconsistent beginnings to a fully worked out analysis. Both, at least in idea, will play some part in the final outcome.

"Opera Talk" and "How Did Mozart Do It?" are a side effect of my 1988 book, *Osmin's Rage: Philosophical Reflections on Opera, Drama and Text*. The former has nothing directly to do with the book, except that my mind was still on opera when I wrote it. It is a fanciful attempt to characterize the way operatic personages express themselves in music, and was directly inspired by an essay of Edward T. Cone's on the same subject. And although it is certainly consistent with my general views on opera, as expressed in *Osmin's Rage*, it is not implied by them.

"How Did Mozart Do It?" is quite another matter. It came out of a symposium on character delineation in Mozart's operas that I proposed and subsequently organized for a conference on Mozart at Hofstra University to commemorate the bicentennial of his death. My plan was to develop further an idea about the nature of operatic characters that I had introduced toward the close of *Osmin's Rage*, but had not had time to deal with adequately there. I also wanted, in the process, to answer some criticism of it. To my surprise, and not quite according to plan, my co-symposiasts, Wye Jamison Allanbrook, Paul Robinson, and Mary Hunter found my paper provoking enough to criticize it quite incisively, for which I am very grateful. This criticism resulted in the second part of the essay, in which I tried to answer their main points. This is an ongoing project, for I am far from satisfied that my idea is fully worked out, although I still believe that it is in essential points correct, and that a good deal of pretentious nonsense is still written about how operatic composers portray character in music. It is that nonsense my idea was meant to combat.

The pair of essays on Mozart, although one is "early" and

the other "late," have much in common. Both deal with what I would call "curiosities" in intellectual history; neither deals with Mozart's music, in that regard, but rather with the "idea of Mozart," which, it seems to me, has replaced the "idea of Beethoven" as the dominating *musical* image of genius and creative intellect. I think this replacement of the "Beethoven idea" by the "Mozart idea," if I am right about it, must tell us something important about the difference between the way music, as a human enterprise, was viewed in the nineteenth century and the way it is viewed now. Indeed, I think it must tell us something about changing attitudes toward all the arts. I wish someone would take up this theme: It seems to me rich in possibilities for the history of ideas.

The essay on Darwin dates from my earliest attempts, while I was studying music history at Yale, to combine musical and philosophical interests. The whole thing started by sheer accident when I picked up, in a secondhand bookstore, a little volume of Herbert Spencer's literary and aesthetical essays, with his longish "The Origin and Function of Music" as the centerpiece. I soon discovered that Spencer's essay had stirred up a little hornet's nest of controversy among the "physiological aestheticians" and evolutionists of the time, including, indeed, the greatest evolutionist of all. And when I decided to take my M.A. degree in music history, I talked my advisor, the late William G. Waite, into letting me write on music and evolution for my Master's essay. "Charles Darwin on Music" came out of that research and was written to commemorate the centennial of *The Origin of Species*, which was the major intellectual event of my years at Yale.

At the time, music and evolution, and the "origin" of music in general, was a sideshow of intellectual history, and no self-respecting musicologist would have seriously considered the origin of music as a viable question. But times have changed, and I wonder if the current advances in evolutionary genetics, as well as interest in the study of a possible "deep structure" in tonal music might make such a question seem more tractable nowadays, and not mere airy speculation. In any event, I am surprised no one else has

4

become interested in the evolutionary theories of music, and, in general, that evolutionary period in the history of British aesthetics.

"Mattheson as Philosopher of Art," although a historical essay, is an instance of my concern for issues over history. For in getting clear my own views on "musical expression" in *The Corded Shell* (1980), I found the need to come to terms with my predecessors. And Mattheson, it seemed to me then (and still does) is closer to contemporary, "objectivist" views on music and the emotions, than anyone gives him credit for being. Musicologists, I think, consistently misread him on the fine points, and (perhaps for that reason) philosophers of art ignore him. He deserves better, and I hope he gets it here.

"Kant and the *Affektenlehre*" is a very recent piece of work, the result of an invitation of Ralf Meerbote to participate in a conference at the University of Rochester in 1990, commemorating the centennial of the publication of Kant's *Critique of Judgment*. Initially reluctant, not being a Kant scholar, I soon got "hooked," and, as in the case of Mattheson, tried to evaluate what Kant had said about music and the emotions not merely as an exercise in historical interpretation but in the light of my own work on the subject. Ultimately, I found what Kant had to say both enticingly original and forward-looking *and* a disappointing failure of nerve.

The pair of essays on Hanslick were written in close succession, the second a necessary result of the first. In the first, I assumed, but did not argue for, a particular interpretation of what Hanslick had said in his famous monograph, *Vom Musikalisch-Schönen*, about music and the emotions. On that assumption, I then revealed what I took to be a glaring and important inconsistency in his treatment of the relation between music and text. But was my assumption correct? Received opinion was against me, and so I felt impelled to argue carefully for my assumption – which I proceeded to do in the second of the essays. Alas, it didn't do any good: Received opinion *still* seems to be against me. But I satisfied myself. And it was important that I do so, not because I was particularly interested in Hanslick as a historical figure in music aesthetics, but because his monograph still lies at the core of all teaching and thinking about the "philosophy of music," where the vexed question of "music and the emotions" is being considered. Hanslick is still very much a "live" figure, to be either defended or refuted, but of necessity to come to terms with, one way or the other, by any serious worker in the field.

In completing my last book on the aesthetics of music, *Music Alone*, I became aware that I had been moving over a ten-year period, without really being aware of it, toward a version of musical *formalism*, unusual in that it countenanced in absolute music just those expressive properties – what I had begun to call the "garden variety emotions" – that from the time of Hanslick formalists are well known for dismissing. I am certainly not the only writer presently dissatisfied with traditional formalism in its rejection of emotive properties. But where others are, it appears to me, relapsing into a kind of neo-Romantic music analysis that makes what I take to be extravagant claims for musical "content," I have tried to make room for the emotive within a doctrine still recognizably formalist, that manages to reject musical "content" and other neo-Romantic baggage. "A New Music Criticism?" is an attempt to both criticize the new neo-Romantic analysis, and make some advances in a "new criticism" of my own that treats emotive properties "syntactically."

"The Fine Art of Repetition," the title essay of this volume, was born as a little germ of an idea, when I happened to ask a rather well known musicologist and musical aesthetician, who had just given the familiar characterization of symphonic music as "an evolving organism," how his account jibed with the obvious, indeed trivial, fact that symphonic expositions are frequently meant to be *repeated*, a very weird thing indeed for an "evolving organism" to do. I never got a straight answer to my question and vowed to consider the ubiquitous musical repeat seriously at some appropriate time in the future. That time arrived when I came to realize that the repeat is *not* a *trivial* fact at all about music but indeed something lying very near the heart of the matter. "The Fine Art of Repetition" is the result of that realization and a fitting title, I thought, to this collection: perhaps the closest to a "definition" of music that I will ever come.

The final essay continues, essentially, where "The Fine Art of Repetition" leaves off. For when serious consideration of the musical repeat led me inexorably to decorative models of music, rather than the traditional and still overwhelmingly popular literary or organism ones, the very status of music *as* a fine art seemed ready for a skeptical look. And when one realizes that, after all, acquiring that status in the Pantheon is a fairly recent event in intellectual history, a problematic one at that, the skepticism does not seem, at least on first reflection, completely misplaced. Moreover, viewing the whole question in its historical context seems an imperative, which is the reason I cast my argument in historical terms, although my history tends to be, at times, a bit speculative and "a priori." I trust the historical facts will bear me out or, at least, not contradict me.

I cannot omit mentioning, before I close, the special circumstances under which "Is Music an Art?" was written, and the very particular personal satisfaction these circumstances and the writing gave me. It is customary for the Eastern Division of the American Philosophical Association to invite, each year, a small number of philosophers to write papers specially for the annual meeting. These are published, just prior to the meeting, in *The Journal of Philosophy*. It has always seemed to me a singular honor to be recognized by one's colleagues in this way. To my utter delight, Robert Sleigh, on behalf of his program committee, invited me to write such a paper for the Eastern Division meeting in 1991. It is a recognition on the part of my colleagues in the profession, many of whom have a far stronger claim than I to the title of "philosopher," that is really very sweet to me. "Is Music an Art?" was my offering on that occasion.

It is a complete coincidence, but, I think, a serendipitous one, that the last essay in this volume has a title in the form of a question. This book *should* end with a question for two reasons. First, to suggest that it is not a finished project but a project in process. Second, to suggest that a philosopher who thinks he knows the answers, and says so in print is probably committing philosophical *hubris* and philosophical suicide at the same time. Indeed, far from knowing the answers, he very likely doesn't even know the questions.

Prelude: Music and us

Chapter I

Music and the liberal education

Suppose I were to play to an average audience of educated men and women, recordings, respectively, of Hamlet's famous soliloquy that begins, "To be, or not to be," and the opening measures of the *Eroica*. It is my hypothesis that almost everyone in such a group would know that the first excerpt I played was from a play by William Shakespeare called *Hamlet*, and that almost no one would know that the second was the opening of Beethoven's Third Symphony. This puzzling – some might say distressing – fact is the subject of my essay.

Three questions, I imagine, will immediately come to mind. Why *should* I be puzzled, one may well ask, by the fact that most people can recognize Hamlet's famous soliloquy but not the beginning of Beethoven's Third Symphony? Why, second, should I care about this, even if it is puzzling? And, finally, why should a philosopher be talking about Shakespeare, a poet, and Beethoven, a composer? Why doesn't he mind his own business, and talk about Plato, or Kant, or the meaning of life, or whatever it is that philosophers are supposed to talk about?

The answer to the third question will, I trust, just naturally emerge as this essay progresses. But the answers to the first and second I will get to right away, for these questions and their answers will serve, really, as the introduction to my subject.

It is fair to say that *Hamlet* is one of the acknowledged masterpieces of Western literature, perhaps the most famous play in the English language. It is equally safe to maintain, I would think, that being at least vaguely familiar with it – knowing who wrote it, approximately when, who Hamlet and Ophelia are, and so forth – is something we would expect any educated man or woman to know. If any of its liberal arts undergraduates were to leave a college or university without knowing a little about Shakespeare and *Hamlet*, I think their professors would see it as some kind of failure on *someone's* part.

Any musician, or musicologist, or just plain music lover will assert, quite rightly I think, that in the world of Western classical music Beethoven's Third Symphony occupies a place of honor and importance equal to that of *Hamlet* in the world of literature. As one eminent historian of music has characterized it, "one of the incomprehensible deeds in arts and letters, the greatest single step made by an individual composer in the history of the symphony and in the history of music generally. . . . [T]he *Eroica* simply dwarfs everything in its boldness of conception, breadth of execution, and intensity of logical construction."[1]

The puzzle, then, is this. Why should an average group of educated men and women almost all be able to recognize "To be, or not to be" is a line from Shakespeare's *Hamlet*, yet not be able to recognize what to lovers of music is an equally familiar and memorable passage from one of the "Hamlets" of the musical literature. And such a group, needless to say, would not be singular in this respect, but representative of the incontestable fact that educated people all over the English speaking world can recognize at least the best known passages from their literature, or such works as Michelangelo's Sistine Ceiling and the Mona Lisa, but not familiar passages from musical masterworks of equal stature and fame. Isn't that something to puzzle over? And isn't it scandalous? Hasn't the system failed as egregiously in producing graduates with a so-called liberal education who cannot recognize the opening of Beethoven's Third Symphony or the preludes

---

1 Paul Henry Lang, *Music in Western Civilization* (New York: Norton, 1941), p. 763.

and fugues of Bach as it would if it produced graduates who were not familiar, at least on a superficial level, with *Hamlet,* and the Sistine Ceiling?

But, you may well object, this is an unfair comparison. After all, music is a special sort of thing, for special sorts of people, like athletics, perhaps, or chess. Every person interested in sports will, of course, know who holds the record for hitting safely in consecutive games, and chess enthusiasts will be familiar with the greatest games of Capablanca. One hardly seems justified, though, in expecting everyone with a bachelor's degree to be familiar with the masterpieces, if I may so call them, of baseball and chess. And no more should we be embarrassed or disturbed to call ourselves educated and yet not know the opening of the *Eroica* or the finale of Mozart's "Jupiter" Symphony.

I think now we are getting close to the heart of the matter. And to bring us to the threshold, note, if you will, that the musicologist whom I quoted a moment ago referred to Beethoven's composition of the Third Symphony as a contribution to what he called "arts and letters." In so describing it, he put the work in just that class of objects that includes such things as Shakespeare's *Hamlet,* Michelangelo's Sistine Ceiling, the philosophical works of Plato and Aristotle, the novels of Jane Austen, the political and economic treatises of Adam Smith and Karl Marx, the histories of Thucydides and Gibbon, the essays of Montaigne – in a word, all those works one would expect to encounter in what we think of as a liberal education: a course in the liberal arts. One would hardly refer to Joe DiMaggio's hitting streak, or the best games of Capablanca as contributions to the field of arts and letters, as much as we might admire them. And so the response that it is no more surprising for a liberal arts student to be unacquainted with Beethoven's mighty Third Symphony than that he or she be unacquainted with Joe DiMaggio's unique contribution to Western civilization, and no more distressing, seems to run up against the powerful counterresponse that since Beethoven's Third Symphony is acknowledged on all hands to be squarely within the world of arts and letters, whereas accomplishments in sports and chess are excluded, one would surely expect it and not them to be familiar to educated people and find it both surprising and distressing if it were not, given its monumental significance in the history of music.

This would seem to be the end of the matter. What more is there to say? A liberal arts education should surely give one at least a passing acquaintance with the acknowledged masterpieces of arts and letters. Musical works like Beethoven's Third Symphony and (to take another example) the First and Fourth Symphonies of Brahms are such acknowledged masterpieces, yet it is a palpable fact that nine out of ten educated people would not be able to identify a theme from any of them. This is a distressing failure of our educational system that should be corrected; for it is – or ought to be – as embarrassing to us to send out into the world people whom we certify as educated in the humanities who cannot tell Brahms from Beethoven as it would be if we were to send them out not knowing Adam Smith from Karl Marx, or Homer from Virgil. Certainly many people in music whom I know feel this way.

But as much as I identify with the feelings of my colleagues and friends in the musical profession, and as strongly as I feel myself about the musical masterpieces, the defense I have suggested just now for the inclusion of music as a requirement in the liberal arts education seems far too facile and unconvincing. On the face of it, it is just going to seem absurd to most people – students and teachers alike – to maintain with equal force that it is unthinkable for someone to be considered educated in the liberal arts if he or she is not acquainted with the *Iliad* and that it is unthinkable for such a person to be considered liberally educated if he or she is not acquainted with Beethoven's Third Symphony. I do not say it *is* absurd. Indeed, I am much inclined to acquiesce in it. What I *do* say is that it is certainly going to seem absurd to others, and that if it is going to stand up to scrutiny it is going to have to have more of a defense than the argument that the Third Symphony, like the *Iliad*, is a contribution to the world of arts and letters, is of equal stature in music to the *Iliad* in literature, and therefore deserves equal consideration as a sine qua non for an education in the humanities. And now at last I have come to the true purpose of my essay, which is to investigate the possibility of such a defense.

Now if I do not think it sufficient for the inclusion of musical works in the required liberal arts curriculum merely that they be works of art of a sufficiently high order, then something important seems to follow: It is that there must be something *else* about a work of art *besides* its merely being a great work of art that I think justifies its inclusion in a proper liberal arts education. What can that be? In asking that question I am essentially raising the whole issue of why works of art are to be studied at all by the humanities student. If it is clear that the *Iliad* and *Moby-Dick* are to be on the curriculum, and less than clear, perhaps even doubtful, that Beethoven's Third Symphony should be, there must be something that the former possess, that the latter at least appears to lack, that rationally justifies such a serious judgment. What that something might be is a daunting question. And I cannot hope to give even the beginning of a satisfactory answer here. All I can do is make some exploratory probes.

I think it fair to say that two closely interrelated justifications are operative, either explicitly or, frequently, implicitly in our inclusion of works of art as objects of study in the humanities curriculum. To begin with, the Western tradition values knowledge perhaps above all other human goods. It is not surprising, therefore, that the most pervasive and influential defense of art as a necessary part of a humanistic education centers around the belief that works of art are sources of knowledge, that artists, like physicists or philosophers, biologists or economists, are discoverers and teachers of truths.

One must say straightway that this deep-seated conviction is far from being either clear or uncontentious, and has been questioned by philosophers since Plato, questioned by some, I should say, only to be reasserted and defended by others. Every Plato who has come along to cast skeptical doubt on the pretensions of the artist to wisdom has had his Aristotle to answer him.

What kind of knowledge does the artist possess? How does he or she acquire such knowledge? How is it conveyed to us? These questions have much bedeviled those philosophers and critical theorists who have perceived at least one of the values of art works to be their "truthfulness" or "insight." But as difficult as these questions have been to answer – and I doubt that we have generally accepted answers to them yet – faith in the artist's claim to be a seeker of the truth, and purveyor of it to mankind has refused to die out, particularly among those who read novels and look at paintings not as a profession but as a pastime: in other words, educated laymen.

Of course, the view that the artist is knower and educator has undergone evolution and change since antiquity, and has been, there is no doubt, particularly vulnerable to the inroads of the so-called scientific revolution. For as scientific discovery, theory, and verification have increasingly become our paradigms of the knowledge game, it has become increasingly difficult to see the artist as one of the players.

This has meant a certain retrenchment in the knowledge claims made for the fine arts. Where a Roman poet could claim to tell us the nature of the universe, we seek that information today from the physicist, astronomer, and cosmologist. And although we can learn a good deal about cetaceans from Chapter 32 of Melville's masterpiece, I doubt it is that kind of knowledge we seek there, nor would we be much distressed, or prone to give *Moby-Dick* a literary demerit, if we found that the author's zoology is inaccurate.

What the defenders of the knowledge claims of the fine arts tell us is that we can find in the fine arts something that we cannot find in the natural sciences, something called humanistic knowledge, or, better, knowledge about ourselves as human beings: self-knowledge, if you like. And that brings us to the second of the two interrelated justifications for the place of the fine arts in a liberal humanities education.

The Enlightenment dream of science as ameliorating the

human condition has brought along with it the Romantic nightmare of science as the de-humanization of human life; and the nightmare as well as the dream have, as we now know, both come true in our century. So if it is art, not science, that can tell us what it is to be human, what it is to be ourselves, then it is art that can bring us, through that knowledge, an essential part of the good life that science cannot. Science and its resultant technology can bring us physical well-being, and perhaps, as the *philosophes* thought, freedom from superstitious fears; and those surely are a part – a very important part – of the good and happy life. But they are not enough. They do not bring us human feelings, they do not soften the rough edges. More important, what scientific enlightenment fails to do is initiate us into our own culture, our own tribe. And such tribal identity we now know, as the *philosophes* perhaps did not, is a prerequisite not only for being happy, but, indeed, for being human. Rites of passage, then, are part of the function of art. In teaching us about ourselves, our symbols, the metaphors by which we live, art seems to humanize us in a quite literal sense of that word. It makes us human beings by helping us pass into our tribal identity.

How does art do these things? How does it teach and, in the process, humanize us? Plato's answer – which is the only even initially plausible answer that I know – is: by the dual process of representation and emulation. We see human beings and their ways of life represented in plays and pictures, or we hear about them in poetic recitations, and, as they are held up to us in such representations at least implicitly as examples, we follow as well as understand them. It is because he thought that people tend to emulate artistic representations, that Plato had such respect and, at the same time, fear of the arts. For what we emulate we *become*, on Plato's view, which means that in emulating the virtuous we become virtuous ourselves, but – and this is the ominous result – in emulating the wicked we become wicked ourselves, in emulating the cowardly we become cowards.

In any event, it is some modern transformation of this Pla-

17

tonic view that, I believe, constitutes the implicit justification of our inclusion of the arts, particularly the literary arts, in the humanistic curriculum. They impart, so many believe, a knowledge that the natural, and even the social sciences cannot; and that knowledge, far from being an end in itself, is one of the principal means of our acculturation, our initiation into our traditions, a principal means of our achieving truly human happiness.

If this is even a shadow of the truth, then we can see not only why, in general, the arts are considered an essential part of a liberal education but what principle of choice is employed in deciding which individual works are to have pride of place, which, that is, are to be considered *required* rather than merely optional for the liberal arts student. Of course the works chosen are those about whose outstandingly high aesthetic quality a general consensus has developed through time. But high aesthetic quality is not the only criterion. Confining my remarks here just to literature, I dare say that on any liberal arts curriculum, it is the "serious" literary works that will overwhelmingly predominate. Why is that? Clearly, because it is not just aesthetic quality that matters in these choices but subject as well. The works on the "required" list are those the consensus has determined not only to be literary masterpieces but, in a word, the "profound" ones, dealing with those questions of deep and abiding concern that have troubled mankind throughout its history: God, the problem of evil, human freedom, determinism, law, justice, love, knowledge, good and evil, life and death.

And where a comic work makes the grade, which is seldom, it is because a case can be made not only for its literary excellence but also for the "seriousness" of its intent, the comic elements notwithstanding. Only just so long as the people who make up the required humanities curriculum are convinced, for example, that *Candide* is about Leibnizian optimism and the problem of evil, and not just a comic romp, as some critics now seem to believe, will it remain part of the educated person's necessary equipment. And Sheridan's *School for Scandal*, or Oscar Wilde's *The Importance of Being*

Earnest, works of the highest aesthetic merit, will gain entrance to the Pantheon of essential reading only when someone comes along to convince them that beneath the frothy comedy of manners there lies some profound existential issue.

With this much said, the question of musical works, and *their* admission into the holy of holies can now be broached, with at least a tentative proposal in hand for what the ticket of admission might be. If Beethoven's Third Symphony is to make a valid claim on the humanities curriculum, as required reading (if I may so put it), it must be determined to be not merely a masterpiece, a perfect work of art, but a profound work into the bargain. It must reveal to us something about those questions of deep and abiding interest that we think of as vital to our understanding of the human condition, questions especially asked and answered by the humanities rather than the natural and social sciences, questions the consideration of, if not the answering of (which may in the event be impossible) eases our passage into the human tribe. All this Beethoven's Third Symphony must be, and must do if it is to lay valid claim to stand with Shakespeare's *Hamlet* and Dante's *Divine Comedy* as a necessary part of the liberal education. If so much cannot be said for it, then I have, it would seem, no more justification for clucking my tongue over the inability of a recent humanities baccalaureate to recognize Beethoven's *Eroica* than for his being unable to appreciate a stirring move in chess, or a well executed double play.

By this time I imagine you can suspect where this line of argument is leading. Not only is it difficult to see how Beethoven's Third Symphony could be about anything profound, it is difficult to see how it could be about anything at all. It is merely – if "merely" is the appropriate word for one of the greatest art works of the West – it is merely a magnificent, abstract structure of sound: one big beautiful noise, signifying nothing.

Of course, people have, over the centuries, made some extravagant claims about what music conveys to them, and they continue to do so. I do not know if it was in the nature of a satire of such claims, or merely another example of the genre, but in a passage toward the close of his novel, *Point Counterpoint*, Aldous Huxley has one of his characters say about the third movement of Beethoven's Quartet in A Minor: "It proves all kinds of things – God, the soul, goodness – inescapably. It's the only real proof that exists; the only one, because Beethoven was the only man who could get his knowledge over into expression."[2]

Now if Beethoven's music could do such things I don't think there would be any doubt as to its right to be considered essential for an education in the humanities. For it is just those profound questions that so many of the literary works on the liberal arts curriculum raise. But do I really need to play this music for you to convince you that it couldn't possibly prove "all kinds of things – God, the soul, goodness"? And if indeed it is true that, far from being able to speak to us of God and goodness, Beethoven's music, and music like it, is, as I have said, a beautiful noise, signifying nothing, it is difficult to see how it can fulfill the second function of such works as are acknowledged on all hands to be necessary for a liberal education, namely, the function of tribal initiation (as I have been calling it). For it is through the imparting of knowledge, the propounding of profound questions, the propagating of the metaphors and symbols by which we live that works of art can, so some people say, facilitate our rites of passage. If these latter things are totally absent from the Third Symphony, because it totally lacks for content, for subject matter, it hardly seems possible that it could serve the function of "cultural initiation" either. So we are left with the conclusion that Beethoven's Third Symphony, and works like it, are deeply satisfying amusements and nothing more. And though there is nothing against the notion that it is a good idea for the liberal arts curriculum to encourage and facilitate deeply satisfying amusements such

2 Aldous Huxley, *Point Counterpoint* (New York: Harper and Row, 1965), p. 433 (Chapter 37).

as chess, or baseball, or, as the argument seems to suggest, listening to classical music, there is absolutely no justification for making a particular one of those amusements, namely, listening to classical music, a requirement of the educated person. It would seem like mere snobbery to do so.

But perhaps I have rushed on too recklessly to this skeptical conclusion, in particular to the inference from lack of identifiable content to lack of what more generally might be called "humanizing influence." For it has long been thought that music does have special influence over the passions and emotions of men and women, in some kind of direct manner independent of any ability to do so by conveying psychological insights or prudential advice. "Music hath charms to soothe a savage breast" is the best known expression of a view widely held since antiquity that music exercises some kind of direct therapeutic influence over the emotional lives of human beings. It does so, many have thought, by actually arousing in the listener such emotions as love, hate, anger, fear, joy – what I like to call the garden variety emotions – and through that arousal, helping human beings, one way or another, to be better adjusted emotionally.

With the advent of the tradition of pure instrumental music in Western culture, beginning in the eighteenth century, such theories have had very tough sledding, however. Before that time, most music accompanied a sung text, and there was some plausibility to the claim that, for example, hearing someone sing sad words to the accompaniment of doleful melodies and harmonies, might make the hearer sad, by a kind of sympathetic reaction. To put the matter plainly, as I might be saddened by the plight of King Lear in the play, so might I be saddened by an operatic heroine singing in plaintive tones of her lost love, or by a choir singing the *Lamentations of Jeremiah*. But when it comes to pure musical sound, without any explicit or implied protagonist to identify with, it is very difficult indeed to imagine how such arousal of the emotions might take place. Since the middle of the seventeenth century, when the problem was just beginning to be perceived, a vast amount of philosophical ingenuity has been expended on the problem of how musical sound, pure and simple, without the aid of a text or dramatic representation, might arouse the human emotions. Yet no one, from Descartes and Leibniz, in the seventeenth century, to the best minds of our own, has come up with a convincing explanation. Indeed, at least so it seems to me, the more we know about the philosophy, psychology, and physiology of the human emotions, the less plausible seems to be the notion that pure instrumental music arouses them, in any interesting sense.

Nevertheless, the conviction that music does arouse the garden variety emotions, and in so doing makes us emotionally better adjusted and happier, is still abroad. And, after all, we do not need to know *how* music does this to justify putting the appreciation of musical works on the liberal arts curriculum. All we would need to know is *that* it does and we surely would have ample reason for insisting that our students study the great musical works of our tradition, as well as the great literary works. For if the reward of musical appreciation were, indeed, emotional health and stability, who would not want to encourage it?

But, alas, there is not a shred of real evidence that listening to music can achieve any such thing. Indeed, a modicum of common sense applied to this question will yield a very skeptical result. Think, for a moment, of what the implications really would be if music appreciation were, indeed, conducive to emotional health and well-being. Surely it would mean, among other things, that musicians and music lovers would be better adjusted than other folks. Is that what your experience has been? Are your friends who listen to classical music more agreeable, less strung out, better able to enter into "meaningful" relationships with others? Are the members of the music department on the whole more emotionally secure and better adjusted than the members of the physics department? Do musicians have a lower incidence of mental depression, divorce, or substance abuse? Are there fewer axe murderers among musicians than in the general population? Whenever such issues come up, it is usual to point out that the Nazi party was born in the cradle of the modern musical tradition and many of its leaders were music lovers. Of course, I am not suggesting that listening to Wagner can make you a sadist. Apparently, however, listening to Beethoven does not have any discernible tendency to prevent it either. Perhaps the safest conclusion is the one I began with: there is no evidence of music as conducive to emotional health and well-being. But if you are not completely disdainful of anecdotal evidence, a stronger conclusion is warranted: there is at least some evidence against it.

Now I am not denying that having relaxing hobbies and amusements is conducive to mental tranquillity and well-being. But one needs, as I have remarked before, a more powerful justification than that for singling out the appreciation of classical music above any of the other relaxing and harmless diversions that are available, like playing chess, or collecting stamps. Why should I insist that a liberal arts student be familiar with Beethoven's Third Symphony on the grounds that all work and no play is a bad idea? Isn't stamp collecting equally respectable? After all, a great president of the United States was an avid philatelist, and, as I recall, his favorite musical composition was "Home on the Range." Who am I to say he was badly educated? He was a Harvard man!

Thus, it seems, I have come again to the distressing conclusion that there is no real rational justification for requiring students of the humanities to be familiar with such masterworks of the Western musical tradition as Beethoven's Third Symphony. But why should I say that this is a "distressing" conclusion? Why should I not simply accept it with equanimity? Well, that is because I find myself confronted here with something in the form of a familiar kind of philosophical dilemma: a very strong inclination to believe that something is the case, and, not for lack of trying, no acceptable argument to *show* that it is the case. I am a very serious music lover, and a serious performer on a musical instrument; I have spent a good part of my career in philosophy writing on musical subjects. I am up to my ears in music. And the idea that a student should be *required*, for example, to read Voltaire's

Candide, before he or she can be granted a liberal arts degree, but not be required to have even a passing acquaintance with Beethoven's Third Symphony, seems to me utterly outrageous. I choose *Candide* as an example not merely because it is on everyone's humanities list but because it is a particular favorite of mine. I love the book and, indeed, have written about it. But to compare *Candide* with Beethoven's Third Symphony is to compare a pop gun with a cannon. Voltaire's classic is a sparkling ornament to the world of arts and letters. The mighty *Eroica* is a monument. And it must be deeply disturbing to someone steeped in the Western musical tradition to think that a student should have been required to know about Pangloss and Martin and Cunegonde before being accounted as educated in the humanities, and yet come out of the process without even being able to recognize the unmistakable opening chords and theme of Beethoven's Third Symphony, not to mention the unforgettable entrance of the French horn at measure 394.

So I have a very strong conviction, amounting almost to religious fervor, that an acquaintance with Beethoven's Third Symphony, and musical works of its caliber, is absolutely necessary for a well-rounded education in the humanities. Yet, so far, I have no rational justification for that conviction; and a philosopher who has not learned that the strength of a conviction is no argument for its truth ought to be summarily defrocked.

I confess that when I first began writing this lecture I could see no further than the conclusion I have already reached. And I thought merely to lay it out as a piece of unfinished business, badly in need of our attention as humanists: essentially a conviction in search of an argument. But the more I thought about this during the writing, the more I thought it would be a dirty trick to play on musicians to go to all this trouble to write on music and the humanities, only to state in the end that although I just love music to pieces, I cannot think of a single good reason to teach it to humanities undergraduates. With a friend like me, I don't suppose music needs any enemies.

Of course, we have all been taught to value no man above the truth. So I hardly need make an excuse for saying what I think is the case, even though we might all fervently wish it were not so. Nevertheless, along with my growing conviction that we do not have any properly worked out justification for demanding of the humanities student familiarity with the masterworks of the Western musical tradition has come at least the glimmering of an idea about how such a justification might be fashioned. For it has begun to press itself upon me that although we cannot look to the content of music, as we can to that of literary works, and even paintings, or to the somewhat naive and uncritical belief in music's direct influence on the emotional lives of human beings, to provide such justification, we can perhaps appeal to some function that it might perform in our social lives, related to its earlier history, before it entered the concert hall and, in our own times, the living room by way of the record player, a role analogous to the one literary works and works of the visual arts play in virtue of their content. Let me suggest briefly what I have in mind.

Now it is no very daring thing to assert that no culture is without what we would all recognize as music, and that in every culture, including our own, music has played various roles in our ritual and social activities: in our work, our dance, our religious rites, our public spectacles. And in all the instances in which music played a role in ritualistic activities, our relation to the music was not passive. In our work we moved to the music; in religious rites we sang; in social contexts we danced; in public events we marched.

This is in sharp contrast to music in the concert hall, of which Beethoven's Third Symphony has served as my exemplar. Concert going is a spectator sport. And the concert hall is the musical equivalent of the museum. As a matter of fact, both institutions, of fairly recent coinage, came into existence at the same time: toward the end of the eighteenth century. We go to the museum to gaze, and to the concert hall to gaze with our ears.

The music we listen to in the concert hall is, however, related to the music of our rituals. It grew out of those musics, and is, as it were, an aesthetic distillation. It contains, in stylized form, evocations of them: the dance, the march, the hymn, the dirge, and so on. As such, it has very deep reverberations in us.

But the performing of music is itself a ritual, a coming together, whether it is four members of a string quartet, coming together in democratic fashion, as equals, or the 100-odd members of a symphony orchestra, under what has been described as the military discipline of the conductor. And concert going, too, is a coming together. The community of performers, the musical work as the aesthetic distillation of ritual, the audience as a congregation of co-celebrants, all make, together, an experience that calls up deep responses from human beings beyond the enjoyment of music merely as a beautiful noise. It is, I want to suggest, somewhere within this ritualistic significance of the *whole musical experience* that the justification of music, as part of the humanities curriculum, must lie, if, indeed, there is to be any justification at all.

Two things should be remarked on that are relevant to this picture. The first is that the community of the concert hall is now in danger of being utterly destroyed by the isolation of the high fidelity sound system. For one can now get in one's own living room, not only a performance equal to that of a live performance in regard to quality of sound, but, in some respects, even a better one. Second, the audience for classical music, is, for the most part, no longer an audience of musically educated amateurs, capable of making music as well as listening to it, as Beethoven's audience, for example, still was, but an audience of completely passive spectators, not only passive in the sense of being, for the purposes of the concert hall, temporarily listeners rather than players or singers, but permanently so, with no musical activity in their lives apart from the passive one of listening. The result of the first development is that listening to music has become a completely asocial pastime, neither bringing people together in a sense of ritual participation, nor bringing them, in its fullness, the sense of cooperatively wresting order from chaos, society from anarchy that a live performance might convey. The result of the second development, far more harmful even than the first to the listening experience, is to deprive the audience of any real sense of what it is like to make music, what it is like to perform the ritual of bringing musical order out of the anarchy of noise.[3] For not only is the performing of music, in ensemble, a deep and rich communal experience in itself; it also enriches the experience of musical listening in ways hard to convey to the nonperformer. It literally makes one able to hear what to others is inaudible. In particular, I would conjecture, it renders more audible just those qualities of music having the deepest ritualistic, "tribal" vibrations, by a kind of sympathetic response to the performance that only someone who has experienced performance directly can have. At the risk of some exaggeration, let me say that to listen to music without having performed it at some level, as a singer or player, is like seeing *Romeo and Juliet* without ever having been in love.

Let me now try to draw these threads together in some kind of conclusion. There is some good news and some bad news.

The good news is that there may well be a viable defense for music listening not merely as a part of a liberal arts education, but as an essential part. That defense lies, I suggest, in the deep reverberations of tribal ritual that music, *in the complete institution of music making*, sets up. Participation in the musical experience has the effect, through these deep connections, of bringing people together: It has a culturally cohesive effect.

Unfortunately, of course, bringing people together, making them cohere in a tribe, is not an intrinsic good. For people can be brought together for wicked as well as for noble purposes, and music does not distinguish between them. The Nazis used music as a cohesive force for uniting the German people in one cause; and some of you may remember the

---

3 This image was suggested to me by Jacques Attali, *Noise: The Political Economy of Music*, trans. Brian Massumi (Minneapolis: University of Minnesota Press, 1987).

concerts that Toscanini conducted, during the Second World War, making use of much the same musical repertoire, to help unite us in another. We may not thoroughly understand it – indeed, I do not think we do – but music has always had, throughout the history of the human tribe, this enormous power of cohesion. There is no culture that does not use music to that end.

Thus, there would seem to be, in this enormous and unique socializing power of music, ample justification for our requiring the educated person not only to be acquainted with the literary totems of his or her tribe, but with the musical ones as well. That is the good news. Now for the bad.

The bad news is that, to the limited extent to which we try to teach music to the liberal arts student at all, we do it in a completely inappropriate way, with predictably negligible results. We have chosen the wrong paradigm. We pattern the teaching of what used to be called "music appreciation" on the way the English department, for example, would teach the nineteenth-century novel. But that is to make three crucial mistakes. First, it is to treat music as a "content" art, whereas I have been arguing that it is, rather, a "ritualistic" art, if you will. Second, it is to treat music as a "private" art, whereas I have been arguing, it is a "community" art. And third, it is to treat music, from the appreciation side, as a "passive" art, whereas I have been arguing that even where one plays the role of passive auditor, it is a "participation" art.

What I am getting at is this. If I were the kind of person who, on at least some of the nights he is at home, curls up with a good novel, becomes engrossed, reads it with pleasure and understanding, comes away having communed with fictional human beings and their problems, having gained emotional insight into the human condition, I think you would say that the English department of the University of Michigan, where I was an undergraduate, had done its work admirably well. And it did its work by giving me the works of the canon to read, requiring that I take them home to study, helping me understand and appreciate them, and, of course,

giving me the ability to read literary works after my gradua-
tion. They could do what they did, the way that they did,
because novels have meaning above and beyond their formal
and syntactical properties, because reading novels has its ultimate payoff in the privacy of the reader's own home, where
communion takes place, and because reading is, in a perfectly good and rewarding way, a passive activity, not, of
course, in the sense that the reader does not have to bring
concepts to his or her reading of a text, and do things conceptually to a text, but in the sense that the reader need not
be a writer or performer. To love, appreciate, and enjoy novels I hardly need also write them or read them aloud.

Music also has its canon. Where the English department
wants you to appreciate Jane Austen and Thomas Hardy, the
music department wants you to be familiar with Bach, Beethoven, and Brahms. And it proceeds in much the same way,
except, of course – and this is a crucial exception – that it has
no content to reveal, no message to decode. You will, of
course, be told about Beethoven's Third Symphony. But few
instructors, trained in the modern analytic and musicological
traditions as they are, will be tempted to attribute any *meaning* to it, or any of the other works discussed. Instead, you
will be told, with suitable musical illustrations, about the first
theme and the second theme of sonata form, what a minuet
and trio are, and a theme with variations, how to recognize
the subject and countersubject of a fugue, and so on. You
will, no doubt, be given one of the standard, analytically oriented appreciation texts to read; and, of course, you will be
expected to do your homework, that is to say, to listen to the
works either at home, on your record player, or plugged into
earphones, in the music department's technically up-to-date
listening room, just as you are expected to read the novels
assigned to you in English 235. If the instructor is successful,
and you cooperate in the process, you will be able to listen
to the first movement of a classical symphony and repeat the
litany of first theme, second theme, closing theme to yourself, or to your fascinated roommate.

But the sad fact is that you will not, thereby, have tapped

into the deep resources of musical culture that I have been talking about. If what I have said about music has any validity, then one cannot directly equate sitting at home reading *Pride and Prejudice* with sitting at home listening to Beethoven's Third Symphony. Something is missing here. Something has gone wrong. The modern musical conscience forbids us to burble on about deep and profound meanings in the great works of our musical tradition. We cannot see God and goodness in a Beethoven quartet; and we should not. So we teach music as pure, contentless abstract form, which, in a sense, it is. But we teach it in a way that is suited, instead, to works of art that have semantic as well as syntactic properties, meaning as well as form. Some, feeling how empty our teaching of music in the humanities curriculum really is, may well succumb to the temptation to fill the void by giving it a content it does not have. Their feelings are justified, their intentions good. However, we cannot substitute fantasy for content. It is just intellectually dishonest. What we can do is recognize that what is missing from our teaching of music as a humanistic subject is not a subject matter, which it never had in the first place, but a ritualistic dimension that has been forgotten, that we have allowed to slip away.

I fully believe, to again risk exaggeration, that the way we teach music to humanities students is much like trying to teach the nineteenth-century novel to people who cannot read. To be able to sing or to play is a necessary part of musical literacy. It is, as I have argued, a necessary part of the full listening experience. Literacy is best acquired, whether it is musical literacy or linguistic competence, before a student comes to college. But few students anymore will come to college able to sing, or to play a musical instrument, or to read musical notation. And so what I am saying is that we cannot teach music effectively in the liberal arts curriculum without teaching playing or singing, as well as basic musicianship, subjects traditionally given only in the conservatory. It is the only way that we will do justice to the ritualistic, communal, and participatory aspects of music that make it what it is, and make it so different from the literary and visual arts.

There is absolutely no justification at all, then, on my view, for insisting that well educated humanities students learn music in the way that music faculties today are required to teach it to them. But if they could teach it the way they all really know it should be taught, the justification is strong and compelling. To be able to rattle off "first theme, second them, closing theme" is a parlor trick not worth the trouble of acquiring. To have Beethoven's Third Symphony in one's blood and bones is a boon beyond compare, part of our rites of passage, part of our tribal identity, an important part, it seems to me, of what makes us human. Of course a *human* life guarantees neither a good life, nor a happy one. The best that we can hope from music, it seems to me, is that it help to *humanize*. Happiness and goodness we will all have to work out for ourselves.[4]

4 The present essay was delivered as a public lecture to the William O. Douglas Honors College of Central Washington University in Ellensburg, Washington, 11 October, 1989, and was written especially for that occasion. It appears here with minor revisions. I am grateful to Jay Bachrach and Barry Donahue for inviting me to speak, and to the audience of students and faculty that made it such a stimulating and memorable experience for me.

Work and performance

Chapter II

Platonism in music:
A kind of defense

The title of this essay is meant to suggest two things, obviously: that I offer here a defense of what I shall be calling musical "Platonism," and that I offer it in a far from confident tone. I have two reasons for wanting to defend it: first, because it offers a way to understand the relationship between musical works and their performances that, I believe, captures a great many of our intuitions and musical *façons de parler*; and, second, because I think some of the objections brought against the doctrine – those, in particular, that claim it is musically or aesthetically counterintuitive and contrary to the way we want to speak about music – are answerable. That I am neither confident, nor altogether happy in defending this Platonism is because, like any other well-brought-up student of philosophy, at least in the Anglo-American tradition, I have a healthy skepticism with regard to Platonic metaphysics, and the multiplying of entities (particularly problematical ones) beyond need.

I should also say, at the outset, that I have no intention whatever of presenting any arguments in favor of Platonism in music; I shall confine myself solely to defending it against some objections, and assume that my readers know the arguments in its favor, and the details of the position, in its various forms. As a result, I shall be keeping the concept of musical Platonism, for the purposes of this essay, open, and distressingly ill defined. I shall not, for instance, try to distinguish among such candidates for Platonic realism as universals, kinds, and types (assuming one wants to construe types

Platonistically at all). The critics that I will be considering will always make it clear which form of the doctrine they are belaboring; and I leave it to the reader to determine what other of its forms the objection in question might touch.

In the first section I will be considering what I take to be three of the most important "traditional" objections to musical Platonism, in the second section two of the newer ones. (None of them, actually, is all that old.) That the "traditional" objections keep cropping up in the literature shows, I think, that they are far from impotent with age, and still deserve an answer. That new objections continue to arise certainly is an indication, if any were needed, of how problematical Platonism of any kind will always be.

I

(1) Let me begin with a criticism that has been advanced by, among others, Joseph Margolis, in *Art and Philosophy*. Margolis claims that a work of art "cannot be a universal because [in part] . . . it possesses physical and perceptual properties."[1] And with regard specifically to music, and to Nicholas Wolterstorff's claim that musical works are "kinds," he says later on, "The essential difficulty with Wolterstorff's proposal is that we wish to say that we *hear* the music . . . , that the music *sounds sweet* . . . ; in short, we wish to attribute certain properties to the work itself and, on Wolterstorff's view, we literally cannot," because, Margolis urges, we cannot hear a kind nor can a kind (therefore) *sound* sweet.[2]

The obvious response to this is that to say "I hear the music" may be taken as short for, "I hear a performance of the music"; that, in other words, the performance might be the bearer of the properties that, Margolis insists, a universal or

---

1 Joseph Margolis, *Art and Philosophy* (Atlantic Highlands, N.J.: Humanities Press, 1980), p. 29.
2 Ibid., p. 75. See Nicholas Wolterstorff, "Toward an Ontology of Art Works," *Nous* 9 (1975), and his more recent *Works and Worlds of Art* (Oxford: The Clarendon Press, 1980), of which more presently. Margolis is criticizing the earlier view; but the criticism can be directed with equal force at the later version.

kind cannot be the bearer of. I mean here, of course, the performance taken to be the sound-occurrence, not the act of producing it, both of which can correctly be referred to in ordinary usage as the "performance."

The initial difficulty with this response is that there do seem to be properties of works that are heard properties of *them*, and cannot just be fobbed off on their performances. The unity of the *Goldberg Variations,* or the passion of Haydn's *Sturm und Drang* symphonies, are surely properties of those works themselves, whether or not they are properties of all (or any) of their performances. And, presumably, being *musical* unity and passion, they are audible properties.

The difficulty, however, may not be quite so heavy as it at first seems, if one does not forget what a Platonic construal of works and performances commits one to. It is said that there are statements one wants to make about works of music (as opposed to performances of those works) in which some heard property is predicated of the work; and since a universal or kind cannot possess heard properties, a universal or kind cannot be what we are referring to. But it should be noticed, in this regard, that when we say something like "The male lion has a mane," not in reference to a particular lion, we use the same locution; and we do feel we are making some sort of characterization of *the* lion, *as well as* of individual instances of it, without thinking that a "logical" entity can have a mane. When we say "The 49th Symphony of Haydn is passionate," we are, of course, saying that every properly formed instance – that is, performance – of it is passionate. But more: we are saying the work (kind or universal) is of such a nature as to be truly instantiated *only* by passionate performances. We are, then, saying something *about* the work (construed as a universal or kind): we are predicating passion of *it,* as of a universal or kind, even though we are not saying that it has the heard property of passion. This may be enough, it appears to me, to accommodate our intuition that when we say "The 49th Symphony of Haydn is passionate," we are not only saying something about correct performances of the work but something about the work itself, even though passion is (in this instance) a heard property, and universals or kinds not heard, or, rather, are heard through their instances, i.e. performances. It would be odd, would it not, to be charged with a logical howler for saying "The male lion has a mane," on the grounds that species or natural kinds cannot grow hair.

To talk about "a performance *of* a work" sounds very much as if one were talking about two things: the performance and the work, one of which is standing in for the other, as in "a copy of the original." But a lion is not a stand-in for the kind: he is an *instance* of it. Similarly, to hear a performance of a symphony *is* to hear the symphony: *is* to hear the work, not a stand-in for it. The performance is an *instance* of the work, not a substitute for it; and to make a statement about the work is to make a statement about its instances. It seems to me that once one lets musical Platonism really sink in psychologically, the gap between theory and intuition in this regard closes considerably. Not perhaps completely: but no matter what the theory, there will be a gap somewhere. So the question inevitably comes down to how wide a gap one will tolerate, and where. This is as good a place as any, and a more narrow gap than some.

(2) A second objection to musical Platonism, of more elaborate and searching a nature, can again be taken initially from Margolis, although I will go on, from there, to consider a more recent variation on the same theme. Margolis says that a work of art "cannot be a universal because [in part] it is created."[3] Later on, with specific reference to music, and, again, to Wolterstorff's views regarding it, he intimates that music cannot be a kind because "it is clear" that music is "actually invented," and, clearly, one cannot invent or create a kind.[4] I now want to spend a few minutes at the seemingly impossible task of convincing you that it would *not* be wildly counterintuitive to construe musical composition as a kind of "discovery" rather than as a kind of "creating" or "inventing."

---

3 Margolis, op. cit., p. 22.   4 Ibid., p. 75.

Let me talk just a bit about "invention." The Wright brothers invented the airplane. I suppose that is a paradigm of invention, if anything is. But in order to do that, they had, as we now know, to discover certain aerodynamic principles first. (They were not, it turns out, merely a couple of lucky tinkerers.) Every invention is part discovery. Edison had to discover the right material for a filament, and that it burned more properly in a vacuum, in the process of *inventing* the thing we turn on and off at night. The reason we call the end product of the Wright brothers' and Edison's activities *inventions*, and the activities *inventing*, is that the thing they are remembered for is something we think of as not having existed before they started work, and existing after.

But just as invention is part discovery, discovery is part invention. Michelson discovered the speed of light (if you will permit me to use the word "discovery" in this regard). To do this, however, he had to invent what is now called the Michelson interferometer – no small scientific accomplishment, as Einstein noted in recognition of Michelson's genius. Gödel discovered the theorem which bears his name. But he had to invent Gödel numbering to do it. Of course in mathematics our strong inclination to Platonize makes it unclear whether we don't want to say instead that he discovered Gödel numbering rather than invented it. In any case, we think of the speed of light, or Gödel's theorem, or permutation groups, or what have you, as discovered rather than invented because, of course, although inventions may have made their discovery possible, *they* were there all along, and were not brought into being.

I mention this to make it clear, first, that if Mozart discovered his music rather than invented it, there was just as much complexity to his discovery, just as much give and take between discovery and invention, as there was to the discovery of the speed of light by Michelson, or the incompleteness theorem by Gödel, or permutation groups by Galois and Abel. So I am not necessarily suggesting that Mozart was not, in part, an inventor or creator as well as a discoverer. What I am suggesting is that it may be more plausible to think of his works as Platonic objects of some sort and, therefore, things that could not have been brought into being. But just as inventing is not all making, so discovery is not all finding: A discovery, of any great complexity and significance, is invention, or creation, as well.

But surely, you will insist, this is not enough; for wasn't Mozart a *creator* in the paradigmatic sense of that word? Wasn't he a *creative artist*? Isn't music one of the *creative* arts? In calling Mozart a discoverer, am I not taking more away from him than intuition will allow?

Well, in one sense of "creator," there never has been one at all except the Lord God Jehovah himself. For even Plato's demiurge, a very creative fellow from all accounts, didn't create *ex nihilo*. So if Mozart must have been a creator, he was a demiurge and not the Deity. But what distinguishes him from any other sort of ordinary maker? Well, he was original. Or he made things that nobody else could make (if that doesn't come to the same thing). Or he made things of a certain kind better than almost anyone else has ever been able to do. But we can pack all of that just as well into Mozart the discoverer as Mozart the creator. The operative word here is not "creator" but "creative." Surely Mozart was creative if anyone was. He was as creative as, well, Galois, or Abel, or Michelson, or Gödel. Would you deny that *they* were creative? There are, after all, humdrum discoveries as well as creative ones. When Archimedes jumped out of the tub he had done more than just take a bath. It takes nothing away from Mozart's creativity, in the important sense (or senses) of the word, to think of Mozart as a discoverer rather than as an inventor or creator. His luster remains untarnished. In the company of Newton, after all, one is hardly slumming.

But perhaps we have moved too quickly. There may be more to the question than has yet been uncovered: In particular, we are perhaps giving up more, it may be felt, in construing the composer as discoverer rather than creator, than intuition will allow. Recently, in defending the view that "A piece of music is *some* sort of structural type,"[5] Jerrold Levinson has, nevertheless, made just this point, and insisted on what he calls the "requirement of *creatability*," to wit: "Musical works must be such that they do *not* exist prior to the composer's compositional activity, but are *brought into* existence *by* that activity."[6] His reason for insisting on this is worth going into. It is two-fold:

> The main reason for holding to it is that it is one of the most firmly entrenched of our beliefs concerning art. The whole tradition of art assumes art is creative in the strict sense, that it is a godlike activity in which the artist brings into being what did not exist beforehand – much as a demiurge forms a world out of inchoate matter. . . .
>
> A second, closely related reason to preserve true creation vis-à-vis musical works is that some of the status, significance, and value we attach to musical composition derives from our belief in this. . . . There is a special glow that envelops composers, as well as other artists, because we think of them as true creators.[7]

Levinson's first claim – that the artist as godlike creator is a firmly entrenched belief – is, to begin with, if not false, at least greatly exaggerated. In addition, even if it were true, without exaggeration, it would not be above being given up; for it is what it is supposed to *explain*, in my opinion, not its inherent plausibility of itself, that gives it what appeal it has – and what it is supposed to explain is in no need of that hypothesis at all.

First, as to its truth. As a matter of fact, the notion of the artist as godlike creator has a *history* – and not such a long one at that. Although suggested by Sir Philip Sidney in the *Apologie for Poetrie* (1595), it does not really come into its own until the end of the eighteenth century, partly through the influence on the Romantic movement, I imagine, of Kant's third *Critique*. It is, then, a gross exaggeration to suggest, as

5 Jerrold Levinson, "What a Musical Work Is," *The Journal of Philosophy* 77 (1980), p. 6.
6 Ibid., p. 9.   7 Ibid., pp. 8–9.

Levinson does, "that it is one of the most firmly entrenched of our beliefs concerning art." And it is just plain false that "The whole tradition of art assumes art is creative in the strict sense, that it is a godlike activity in which the artist brings into being what did not exist before." The "tradition of art" did without this assumption until barely two hundred years ago, and managed to produce without it the *Iliad, Odyssey,* the Greek plays, Gothic cathedrals, Shakespeare, the Italian Renaissance, Bach, Handel, Haydn, Mozart, and a good deal more. Bach did not think he was God; Wagner did, with dire results.

But more, it is at least in part to explain *another* common belief that the Romantic movement gave birth to (or at least nurtured to maturation) the concept of the artist as godlike creator. That is the belief in the *originality* of the great artist – another belief, it must be remembered, that has not always been with us, and has itself a distinctly Romantic aroma. Be that as it may, it is, in part, to explain what makes a work of art *original* that the notion of the artist as godlike creator is invoked. For what is the *original* but that which has never before existed, and is therefore unique? Then what but a *creation,* and who but a *creator,* can burgeon forth that which has never been before?

The playing off of these concepts against one another produced a hideous caricature of scientific discovery, already apparent in Kant's *Critique of Judgement,* and even more pronounced in Schopenhauer. For since, on the Romantic view, originality can only result from creation, and the scientist is a "mere" discoverer, the scientist, even of the stature of a Newton, can never deserve the epithet "creative," nor (therefore) "genius," the etymological connection between "genius" and "genesis" being too obvious to belabor here.

But once the Romantic circle connecting creation, genius, and originality exclusively together is broken, we can see that originality no more requires a godlike creator than does "creativity" itself, when understood in its full honorific sense. As Jack Glickman points out, "We say an activity such as painting, writing, or composing is creating if it achieves new and valuable results."[8]; and to that list we can add scientific and mathematical discovery as well, thus giving them their rightful place as "creative" enterprises. It is the achieving of "new and valuable results" that warrants the epithet "creative," and it makes no matter whether that achieving is "inventing," "discovering," or "creating in the godlike way." An "original," "creative" discovery is not, in the literal sense, the bringing into being of what has never before existed, for then, of course, it would not be a "discovery" in the literal sense. It is the revealing, needless to say, of what has always been there, but which no one has yet had the genius and creative imagination to see; and it is all one whether the discovery is a scientific or a musical one.

One further word about Levinson's first argument for the *creatability* requirement. I venture to assert, without documentation, for the documentation would require a book, that the language of "discovery" is as pervasive, throughout history, in discussions of what artists do, as is the language of "godlike creativity." That in itself, if it is true, should lay to rest the claim that the concept of the artist as godlike creator is either essential to the Western tradition in art (I will say nothing of the non-Western, non-"original" traditions) or that it is one of our most firmly entrenched intuitions about the enterprise.

Moving on to Levinson's second argument, we see that it too, like the first, makes a factual claim, from which the *creatability* requirement is supposed to follow, or which, at least, is supposed to strongly suggest its acceptance. The factual claim is simply that we would value the composer and the composition less if the composer were "merely" a discoverer, not a creator, and the composition a preexistent entity to be found out, rather than a creation that never before existed. This multiple fact urges on us, on Levinson's view, that we preserve the *creatability* requirement.

Assume, for the nonce, that the factual claim is true. Is this

8 Jack Glickman, "Creativity in the Arts," *Culture and Art,* ed. Lars Aagaard–Mogensen (Atlantic Highlands, NJ: Humanities Press, 1976), p. 136.

a very strong reason for maintaining the *creatability* requirement? I hardly think so. It may be the case, for example, that
an "instrumental" interpretation of scientific theories results
in a lower estimate of scientists and their "creations" than a
"realistic" interpretation would do. For, after all, on an "instrumental" account, scientists cease to be sages, and their
theories cease to be revelatory of "the nature of things": rather,
the former are now "merely" contrivers of artifacts for the
use of man; the latter, those artifacts. Indeed, it is sometimes
suggested that the transition from the medieval view of as-
tronomy as merely "the saving of the appearances," to a more
"realistic" interpretation of the enterprise, helped spur the
astronomers on to the great accomplishments of the scientific revolution, just because it made their work seem more
significant in their eyes. But it is difficult to imagine anyone
arguing for the "realistic" interpretation on the grounds that,
if it is accepted, science and scientists would get higher
marks.

In any case, however, the factual assumption – and that, I
think, is all it is, an unsubstantiated assumption – does not
seem to me to be true. Or, at least, the waters are far more
muddy than Levinson's rather artless claim makes them out
to be. Composers, as a matter of historical fact, have tended
to balk at the idea that they are mere makers or creators of
artifacts, no matter how original those artifacts might be. If
music were a mere created artifact, a kaleidoscope or arabesque in sound, to appropriate Eduard Hanslick's description, it would become, perhaps unjustly, lower in the estimation of most of its practitioners, as well as its audiences.
The composer *wishes* to be known for just what Levinson
seems to suggest would tarnish his reputation: he wishes to
be known as a discoverer and purveyor of truths about the
world, like almost everyone else in the Western tradition,
obsessed, as it is, with knowledge and the acquisition thereof.
Now, of course, the composer generally wishes to be known
not merely for discovering sound structures but sound structures that are somewhat revelatory of something beyond

themselves: the metaphysical will, the emotive life, the harmony of the spheres, or what have you. But "discovery" as opposed to "godlike creation" is not what is at stake here. There is no advantage in being a "godlike creator," rather than a "mere discoverer," if what one creates are "mere" structures in sound, although I suspect that discovery may, even here, have the edge over creation, since, in a funny Platonic way, one is at least finding something out about "what there is," rather than merely actualizing the trivial. Where there *is* an *unqualified* advantage, as most musical thinkers in the past have seen it, is in being a "discoverer" through music of something beyond "mere" musical structure: something out there in the "real world." It is this wish to puff up the composer and his works that has led to most of the extravagant theories of music in the past, and in the present as well. And it hardly bears out the claim that to call the composer a "discoverer" is to rebuke him either in his eyes or in the eyes of his public. It is only a rebuke if what he is alleged to discover is mean in his eyes; but in that case it is hardly less a rebuke to say that what is mean in his eyes he has created rather than discovered. For I take it that to discover trash is not more ignoble a thing than to bring it into being where it was not.

Surely though, it will be objected, our whole picture of how composition goes on is completely out of phase with the notion of composition as discovery. And, anyway, is it really plausible to think of an "object" as complex and metaphysically unwieldy as a Mozart opera or Mahler symphony preexisting its composition? In an incredibly short space of time, let me address these two objections at once.

You will all no doubt recall that dreadful relic of Victorianism, "The Lost Chord," poem by Adelaide Ann Procter, music by Sir Arthur Sullivan:

> Seated one day at the organ,
> I was weary and ill at ease,
> And my fingers wandered idly
> Over the noisy keys.

> I do not know what I was playing,
> Or what I was dreaming then;
> But I struck one chord of music,
> Like the sound of a great Amen.

Now surely this accidental discovery of a chord, in a fit of idle revery, hardly jibes with the realities of musical composition. Even a musician with the awesome mental equipment of a Mozart has to work at composing: He does not just fall into his discoveries. Discoveries in music, as elsewhere, are prepared for, even though there is an element of luck too. But what may not be so implausible in "The Lost Chord" is the notion that the chord was found, discovered, rather than invented or created; that that particular vertical arrangement of notes "existed," awaiting discovery, as did Kepler's laws, or permutation groups. Think of the *Tristan* chord. It seems to me quite plausible to regard it as a discovery of Wagner's rather than his invention, although, of course, the discovery of that chord required the labor of more than one lifetime. Nor does it stagger the metaphysical imagination to picture the *Tristan* chord – that particular relationship of four pitches – as preexisting its discovery, in the manner of a Platonic object. But, after all, the *Tristan* chord is part of a larger relationship of pitches called *Tristan und Isolde*. And if you grant that that small but vital part preexisted its composition, it seems to me you are on the slippery slope that must propel you into granting that the large composition of which it is a part also preexisted its compositional discovery by Wagner. I am told, in a recent issue of *Science News*, that the existence of "the sporadic Group F_1" requires a proof exceeding 5,000 pages in length. If logical space, or Platonic heaven, has room for *that*, surely it can find a niche for Beethoven's Ninth, or an itty bitty Wagner opera.

(3) Closely related to the uncreatability of universals or kinds is, of course, their obvious indestructibility. I will close this section with a necessarily brief discussion of that, and again take my departure from Margolis. He says that a work of art "cannot be a universal because [in part] it . . . can be de-

stroyed."[9] But when it comes to the particular case of music, he seems to waffle. He writes:

> Clearly, sculpture, architecture, painting, and etching *can* be destroyed . . . ; hence, they cannot be kinds. Music and literature cannot, in *this* sense, be destroyed, simply because their properly formed examples can be generated by reference to a notation *and* a notation is not a work of art. All the tokens of a notation may be destroyed, however, and the notation may cease to be remembered; in that sense, music and literature can be destroyed.[10]

It is not clear to me in *what* sense Margolis thinks music cannot be destroyed; whether, in fact, it might not be the sense in which I think it cannot. Clearly, I am committed to the view that the sense in which *The Art of the Fugue* or the *Tristan* chord cannot be destroyed is the sense in which permutation groups or that 5,000-page mathematical proof cannot be destroyed. Nor does it seem at all counterintuitive to me that that should indeed be the case. If you have already accepted the plausibility of the *Tristan* chord as a discovery rather than an invention, and hence as preexisting its composition, you will already have prepared yourselves for the conclusion that it cannot be destroyed (although as we know from the *Phaedo* the preexistence of souls does not of itself imply their immortality). But if the *Tristan* chord existed before it was thought of or notated, why should it cease to be when all notations, performances, and memories of it pass away? If it existed before anyone ever was aware of it, why should its existence be influenced by our ceasing to be aware of it? Once, I think, one is convinced that the preexistence of a musical work holds no terrors, its immortality will seem equally if not more benign. So I will tarry no longer over the question, but go on, as I said I would at the outset, to discuss some more current objections to the Platonistic move in music.

9 Margolis, op. cit., p. 22.   10 Ibid., p. 75.

47

II

(1) A recent criticism of the work–performance relation as the relation between type and token, advanced by R. A. Sharpe, is not without interest.[11] Sharpe points out, quite rightly, that "I can remove part of a token and replace it with part of another token and it remains a token of that type." For example:

> I could cut off part of a linen red flag and replace the missing part with the corresponding part of a plastic red flag of the same size. It is still a red flag, a token of that type.[12]

Suppose, now, that I try the same thing with two performances of the same musical work. The case, Sharpe argues, is not the same; for

> if I remove the last movement of Walter's *Das Lied* [*von der Erde*] and replace it with the last movement of Bernstein's my action does have aesthetic repercussions. For one thing we expect a conductor to present in performance a unified view of the work.[13]

If Sharpe's intention has been to establish by such examples that there is a logical disanalogy between the flag and the musical work, he has not, so far at least, accomplished that intention. Patching together a flag (token) from two separate flags (tokens) of the same type produces a flag (token) of the same type; but, it needs pointing out, a flag (token) of rather poorer quality: half linen, half plastic, with an unsightly seam. Likewise, a performance which two conductors share is going to be, in all likelihood, a poor performance, with its own musical seams, but it does not, on that account, fail to be a genuine, recognizable token (performance) of the type (work). For certain purposes, of course, we don't much care if a token is well or ill formed: we can rally round a tattered flag as

---

11 R. A. Sharpe, "Type, Token, Interpretation and Performance," *Mind*, 88 (1979). A criticism of Sharpe, along different lines, can be found in R. A. Dipert, "Types and Tokens: A Reply to Sharpe," *Mind* 89 (1980), and Sharpe's reply in "Performing an Interpretation: A Reply," *Mind* 91 (1982).

12 Sharpe, "Type, Token, Interpretation," p. 438.   13 Ibid.

well as a spanking new one. Whereas it will seldom be a matter of indifference to us that a performance-token of *Das Lied von der Erde* is poor. But so far as I can see, as long as we recognize that tokens can be well or ill formed, good or bad products, symphonies and flags are logically on all fours.

But there is more to Sharpe's argument than this; and it emerges in his summation of his position.

> The general principle is, then, that a token remains a token of a type when one part is replaced by the corresponding part of another token. Whereas a copy of a poem survives this transplantation, two performances of a single piece of music may not necessarily survive the exchange of their parts. Substitution is only possible when the two performances are performances of the same interpretation. Otherwise it will leave us with merely two parts of two different performances juxtaposed rather than a single performance.[14]

The argument here seems to be this. If all performances were tokens, and all musical works types, then since I can always get a token of any given type by piecing together two (or more) parts of other tokens of the same type, I should always be able to get a performance of any given work by piecing together two (or more) parts of other performances of the same work. But the latter, on Sharpe's view, is not the case. For if the performance parts that are pieced together are too disparate – not performances of the same interpretation – then, Sharpe claims, the result of the patchwork is not *a* performance of the work but, rather, *two* performance parts. This, presumably, is the "aesthetic repercussion" spoken of earlier, that prevents performances being well behaved tokens of types.

But this claim seems completely unfounded. Consider an occurrence (I will not beg the question from the start by calling it a performance) of *Tristan und Isolde*, the first act conducted by Leinsdorf, the second by Bernstein, and the third by Solti, each, we will assume, based on an entirely different reading of the score. What grounds are there for believing

14 Ibid., p. 439.

that this "occurrence" is not a "performance" of the work, but three different "performance parts?" No grounds at all, so far as I can see, just so long as one avoids slipping into an evaluative use of "performance," such that "performance" becomes "good performance," and being based on a single interpretation becomes a necessary condition of a good performance (I will assume that it is). As a matter of fact, I attended, some years ago, an "occurrence" of *Tristan und Isolde* at the Metropolitan Opera, which turned out to be very unusual indeed. As it happened, all three of the company's Tristans were sick. Each one, however, had enough to get through one act. And that was the expedient fixed on. The soprano sang three Tristans under the table (the death of number three being particularly convincing). Now the point is that no one, after the "occurrence" was ever tempted to call it anything but "that extraordinary *performance* of *Tristan und Isolde*." No one referred to it as "performance parts," or anything of that kind. Nor, I think, would anyone have been tempted to do so if, because of the illness of the Met conductors, a different one were to have undertaken each act. Neither intuition nor linguistic usage seems to support Sharpe's contention that in such cases we would not have *a* performance but many performance parts. That being the case, why should we accept it? Merely to support Sharpe's theory? Not, clearly, if we have a prior commitment to the work–performance distinction as an instance of the type–token one.

Surely, neither Sharpe, nor anyone else, would want to argue that it is analytic to the notion of *a* performance, as used in musical contexts, that *a* performance must be the act of *one* person. Were that to be claimed, we could not, of course, have *a* performance of a symphony, an opera, or even a string quartet, except in a keyboard arrangement, since they are all cooperative ventures. Even less does it seem analytic to the notion of *a* performance that it be based on *one* or *one person's* interpretation. The N.B.C. Symphony Orchestra, after the death of Toscanini, played for a number of years without a conductor at all. And although its performances might well have been criticized for lacking the unity or singleness of purpose that a conductor would have given them, there is surely nothing odd, logically or linguistically, in calling them "performances." No music critic, to my knowledge, ever called them anything else. Performances that produce an adequate number of the right notes, and fulfill an adequate number of the other requirements of a "correct" performance, may range in quality from great to terrible, unified to eclectic, but not from performance to nonperformance or performance parts.

The conclusion, I think, must be that Sharpe has not succeeded in showing any logical disanalogy between the type–token distinction and the work–performance one. Just so long as one bears it in mind that at least some types can have both well formed and badly formed tokens, it will cause no problem to discover that performance parts can seldom be joined together without deleterious aesthetic repercussions; for there is a world of difference between an ill formed token and no token at all. What Sharpe was obliged to show, to prove logical disanalogy, is that performance parts when not of the same interpretation cannot yield tokens – that is, correct performances – at all. But all he has shown, I think, is that they cannot yield good performances – and from that only those with ass's ears would dissent.

(2) By far the most logically rigorous and thoroughgoing musical Platonism to be found is in Part Two of Nicholas Wolterstorff's *Works and Worlds of Art*. But, ironically, Wolterstorff is willing to accept as a consequence of his Platonism a conclusion about music that, I think, any musician or musical scholar must count as a serious objection – perhaps even a decisive one – to the whole doctrine. It is this consequence that I want to examine here with some care. I think it must be answered if musical Platonism is to stand.

The process of composition, on Wolterstorff's view, can be described as a process of *selection*. "The composer selects properties of sounds for the purpose of their serving as criteria for judging correctness of occurrence."[15] The end result

---

15 Wolterstorff, *Works and Worlds of Art*, p. 62.

of this selection process is, of course, works of music, which Wolterstorff construes as "norm-kinds," being, that is,

> kinds . . . such that it is possible for them to have improperly formed examples. The Lion is obviously a norm-kind. The kind: Red Thing, however, seems not to be. For there can be no such entity as an improperly red thing, a malformedly red thing.[16]

That works of music must be *norm*-kinds is required, of course, by the fact that they can have improperly as well as properly formed examples: that is to say, "A symphony can have incorrect as well as correct performances."[17]

So far, nothing that Wolterstorff has said about the musical work, or its creation, is inconsistent with the views I have been expressing here: Composition as "selection" does not seem to me to be incompatible with composition as "discovery," as selection would turn out to be, on my view, a matter of choosing what discovery to record in a score, and thus make public. But there follows from Wolterstorff's position, so he supposes, what he refers to as a "corollary" concerning the art of improvisation which, although it conflicts with nothing said so far in this paper, is profoundly contradictory of deeply entrenched musical intuitions that I share with many others. It is this supposed corollary that I want to examine and dispatch, for I believe that it is neither true, nor a genuine consequence of Wolterstorff's "Platonism," and would, indeed, if true, constitute a serious objection to it.

The "corollary" is "that to improvise is not to compose." Wolterstorff goes on:

> That corollary is clearly correct. Suppose that someone has improvised on the organ. And suppose that he then goes home and scores a work of such a sort that his improvisation, judged by the requirements for correctness specified in the score, is at all points correct. In spite of that, the composer did not compose his work *in* performing his improvisation. In all likelihood he did not, during his improvisation, finish selecting that particular set of requirements for correctness to be found

16 Ibid., p. 56.   17 Ibid., p. 58.

in his score. Suppose, for example, that at a certain point in his improvisation he introduced a bit of rubato, with full consciousness of doing so. In so doing he has not yet decided whether to select rubato at that point as required for correctness of occurrence. One cannot uniquely extract a work from a performance.[18]

Let us look at a familiar historical case of improvisation. I think a bit of reflection on it will reveal how odd it would be to construe it as anything but composition. During his famous visit to Frederick the Great in Potsdam, which ultimately led to the composition of *The Musical Offering*, Johann Sebastian Bach was asked by the king to improvise a six-voiced *ricercare* (a kind of fugue) on a theme supplied by Frederick himself: the "royal theme." Finding Frederick's chromatic subject "unsuited" to the improvisation of so complex a composition, Bach improvised a three-voiced *ricercare* instead. Tradition has it that when he got back home to Leipzig, he wrote down, from memory, the improvised *ricercare* which we now know as part of *The Musical Offering*.

When did the composition of this *ricercare* take place? The obvious answer is: during Bach's visit to Potsdam, more exactly, as he was playing it for the king. Surely no musician would be tempted to say that he was composing it as he was writing it down. The composing was already done. Bach was merely (!) being his own copyist, recording in notation from his memory of what he had played: a prodigious feat, needless to say.

That this is the only intelligible way to look at Bach's improvisation, without ending up in absurdity, can be seen by altering the historical facts just a bit. Imagine, then, that Bach's great son, Karl Phillip Emanuel, who was undoubtedly present at his father's performance, was so taken by the piece that *he* wrote it down from memory and that Bach senior never did. Who, then, was the composer of the *ricercare*? Clearly not Karl Philipp Emanuel; and were he to claim he was, we would accuse him, quite rightly, of plagiarism. But

18 Ibid., p. 64.

if improvisation is not composition, then Johann Sebastian was not the composer either. There is no candidate, then, for composer of the *ricercare;* and we must conclude that it came into being without being composed at all.

Now there is nothing absurd about claiming that *some* music comes into being without being composed. Wolterstorff correctly observes that:

> There are works of indigenous folk music such that probably no one ever singled out the requisite properties in the requisite way for composing the work. The work just emerged from performances.[19]

But what is absurd, I think, is to claim that Johann Sebastian's *ricercare* is such a composer-less work. Surely three-voiced fugues are not the sorts of things that grow like "Greensleeves." And the one in question, improvised by Johann Sebastian, copied down by Karl Philipp Emanuel, owes its existence to the genius, originality, learning, and compositional choices of the former as much as do his other works. That its composition and first performance were the same act is something for us all to wonder at, but not an occasion for metaphysical conclusions even worse than musical Platonism requires.

What exactly has driven Wolterstorff to insist that improvisation is not composition? It is that "One cannot," on Wolterstorff's view, "uniquely extract a work from a performance," and that because we cannot distinguish, merely in the performance or improvisation, without the authority of the score, apparently, what properties are requisite for a correct performance, and what merely requisite for a good one; for if, for example, the performer introduces "a bit of rubato" into his improvisation, we have no way of knowing, prior to his preparation of an autograph, whether the rubato is "required for correctness of occurrence," is merely a performance choice of the moment, or perhaps a recommendation, to be written into the score, for what the composer takes to

19 I bid., p. 67.

be an optimal performance. That seems to be the substance of the argument.

The mistake, I think, lies in Wolterstorff's construal of musical scores as recipes for the realization of musical performances. It is not that this is wrong. Scores *can* be usefully seen as recipes for performances, and Wolterstorff is not the first to describe them as such. But if one *just* sees scores as recipes, one then comes to the conclusion, I think, as Wolterstorff has, that the conventions surrounding them only prescribe movement in one direction: from score to performance; cookbook to cookie. Such, however, is not the case, as a look at how students are taught to use scores – in what is called "ear training and dictation" – reveals. Every well trained musician has learned to write down in score what he or she hears: to, in other words, take down musical dictation, just as a shorthand secretary learns to "take a letter." And were there not conventions for doing this, for, that is, going from sound to score, the task would not be possible.

Now the major goals of such exercises in dictation are, of course, to enable the musician to read scores and to "hear" music "in the head," and to enable him or her to realize in notation what is "heard in the head" or worked out at the keyboard. The skill of "taking dictation," having served its educational purpose, tends to fall into disuse. But the fact is that one *can* do it, at least within certain practical limits; and when scores were rare and difficult to obtain, it might well have been a useful skill, as well as a musical parlor trick. (A famous eight-voice *Miserere* by Allegri was revered as a sacred object in the Sistine Chapel; parts and scores were not permitted to be made or circulated, on pain of excommunication. The fourteen-year-old Mozart, however, acquired a score for himself by listening to the work once, committing it to memory on the spot, and writing it down afterward.)

With this in mind, let us return to Bach's *ricercare:* the one, that is, improvised by Johann Sebastian, and written down by his son. Suppose that there is, in Sebastian's performance, a slakening of the tempo – a slight holding back – just before the entrance of the new triplet figure. Should Karl

Philipp Emanuel write "poco rit." at this place, thus enshrining the ritard in his score? or should he not? The question is not, after all, an unanswerable one. As a matter of fact, such things were far more often than not left to the performer in those days, and were seldom indicated by composers in scores. Musical convention, then, would have dictated that that ritard was an artifact of performance, and not a property of the work. And had Johann Sebastian, in fact, also made a score of the improvisation, and written "poco rit." at the appropriate place, he would thereby have produced a different version of the work, since he was under the implicit discipline of the convention, during the improvisation, which made the ritard simply a performer's choice. (The same would apply to trills, and other ornaments.) In other words, the improvisation was a version of the work in which the ritard was not a requirement of correct performance; and musical convention gives us reasonable assurance of that. Philipp Emanuel's autograph scores that version of the work, on the authority of the reigning musical conventions. Sebastian's autograph, with "poco rit." in the appropriate place, becomes a different, and more definitive version of the same work. It is true that Karl Philipp Emanuel cannot be absolutely certain, when he hears the improvisation, that the ritard is an artifact of performance, and not a property of the work. But no more can we be absolutely certain about a great many things in scored musical works. There are conventions for interpreting them, without which they would be useless, and we helpless. But the conventions are no more ironclad and beyond question than the one telling Karl Philipp Emanuel Bach that the ritard is not a part of the work.

What I think we can conclude from this is that in a loose sense of "uniquely," a score uniquely determines a correct performance, under a given set of implicit conventions for interpreting the score – conventions which may be quite different in different historical contexts – and a performance uniquely determines a score under a similar set of historically bound conventions for taking "musical dictation." In a logically strict sense of "uniquely," however, I doubt that a score uniquely determines a correct performance *or* that a performance uniquely determines a score. The "loose" interpretation has this very important point in its favor: It can accommodate the way musicians, musicologists, and, I think, the rest of us do in fact think about and talk about such things as composing, improvisation, scores, performances, and the rest. It seems to me this point is decisive.

III

I have tried to defend a Platonic interpretation of the musical work against some new and some familiar objections. But, it might well be asked, why bother? Why Platonize music?

I cannot answer this question here and now; and, quite frankly, I do not know if I could ever answer it any better than it has already been by such elegant practitioners as Wollheim and Wolterstorff. But this much I can say. When I think of the mode of existence of Bach's *ricercare* before he had time to write it down, and after he had composed it, I tremble as Darwin did at the thought of the human eye. Where did that *ricercare* exist? In Bach's head. But what is the cash value of that? What mode of existence "in Bach's head" did that *ricercare* have?

One suggestion, that seems to be implied by something Margolis says, bothers me. In a passage previously quoted, he remarks, you will remember: "All the tokens of a notation may be destroyed, however, and the notation may cease to be remembered; in that sense music . . . may be destroyed." Does Margolis mean to suggest that when a piece of music is remembered or thought about, it is the *notation* that is remembered or thought about? Did the *notation* of Bach's *ricercare* exist "in his head?" That seems wrong to me, although I do not wish to deny that a composer *can* visualize notation "in his head." To remember the *ricercare* that way is to remember it the way the "memorist" might do in *The Thirty Nine Steps*. A person with what used to be called a "photographic memory," or "absolute recall," might, indeed, commit the score of a musical composition to memory, being, all the while, tone-deaf and completely ignorant of music, just as I could memorize a paragraph of Urdu, a language I neither speak, read, nor understand.

I do not think *that* is the way Bach remembered or thought about the *ricercare*. Rather, it "ran through his head," when he wanted to think about or remember it, much in the way a melody "runs through the heads" of lesser mortals like me. Might we then think of Bach's *ricercare* "running through his head" as a mental "performance" of the work? Perhaps that *is* the right way to think about it.[20] One is reminded, in this regard, of the statement attributed to Brahms, on his being invited out to attend a performance of *Don Giovanni* (I think it was). "Why should I bother," he is supposed to have said, pointing to his score of the work; "I can have a better performance at home," meaning, of course, that all he needed to do to "hear" the music of *Don Giovanni* was to read his score. But if, at least when Bach was *conscious* of his *ricercare*, a "performance" of it was "running through his head," it makes perfect sense to ask: A performance (instance) of *what*? The work (kind or universal) of course; and before there was any notation of it. And here is where I feel impelled, wrongly perhaps, to take the Platonic pluge.

Margolis believes it no small advantage of his own way of thinking that it avoids "the extreme implausibility of platonizing with respect to art."[21] I hope I have succeeded in dispelling some of that apparent implausibility here. I am under no illusion that I have dispelled it all.

---

20 We should not be misled, here, by a widely circulated, but undoubtedly spurious letter in which Mozart is made out to say that he imagines music atemporally, the whole before him in one instantaneous synoptic view. The feat is impossible – perhaps even *logically*, as some have claimed of God's supposed atemporal perception of temporal events.
21 Margolis, op. cit., p. 22.

Chapter III

Platonism in music:
Another kind of defense

It may not be true for improvisations, and it may not be true
for certain kinds of electronic music. It may not be true in the
absence of a notational system. Indeed, it may not be true
for most of the world's musics. But for a great deal of the
most valued art music of the West, since the development of
a sophisticated musical notation, it seems to be true that there
are musical works, and that there are performances of them.
Some writers, taking a more or less Platonic line, find it plausible to say that musical works are universals, or types or
kinds, and the performances of them are particulars, or tokens, or instances. I am one of those writers, even though I
think of myself as a down-to-earth, sensibly empirical fellow, and the view about works and performances that I espouse has the reputation of being starry-eyed metaphysics.

I shall not try, here, to tout the advantages of musical Platonism, or to distinguish among its varieties. Rather, my object is to defend the view against two serious objections that
have been raised against it. The advantages of Platonism in
music seem to me to be obvious, the disadvantages highly
exaggerated. The present essay is part of an ongoing attempt
to chip away at the supposed disadvantages, and, in so doing,
to put the Platonic construal of musical works and performances in a more favorable light.[1] It is addressed to down-

1 For my previous foray into musical Platonism, see "Platonism in Music: A Kind
  of Defense, "*Grazer Philosophische Studien* 19 (1983), pp. 109–29. Reprinted in this
  volume, Chapter II.

to-earth, sensibly empirical (and somewhat musical) people like myself.

I

The first of these objections of which I speak is to be found in a recent article of Jerrold Levinson, where it is pressed with considerable skill and ingenuity. On the Platonist's view, as Levinson puts it, "A piece of music is *some* sort of structural type," to wit, "a *sound* structure – a structure, sequence, or pattern of sounds, pure and simple."[2] And it is, he goes on to point out, a consequence of identifying work with sound structure that "if two distinct composers determine the same sound structure, they necessarily compose the same musical work." This, Levinson argues, cannot be the case, because musical works possess essential aesthetic properties by virtue of being composed by particular composers at particular times in musical history: "the aesthetic and artistic attributes of musical works are partly a function of, and must be gauged with reference to, the total musico-historical context in which the composer is situated while composing his piece." Thus, it cannot be the case that the same sound structure, determined by two different composers, is the same work; for, "by Leibniz's law, the musical works themselves must be non-identical; if W_1 has any attribute that W_2 lacks, or *vice versa*, then W_1 does not equal W_2."[3]

Now Leibniz's law is very scary. How could there be any appeal from so magisterial a metaphysical principle? Yet it can easily be seen that it lays down a requirement for identity far too stringent in the present context, unless one is willing to sacrifice not merely peripheral intuitions and usages, but central ones as well, to some higher theoretical exigency – something which neither Levinson is willing to do, nor I. For Leibniz's law, notoriously, makes no distinction between

2 Jerrold Levinson, "What a Musical Work Is," *The Journal of Philosophy* 77 (1980), p. 6.
3 Ibid., p. 10.

essential and accidental properties, whereas common usage and ordinary intuition do. Nor do common sense and ordinary intuition stop where music is concerned (although I daresay there is more nonsense spoken and written about music than about almost anything else I can think of). On Leibniz's principle, *Don Giovanni* is a different work in a possible world in which Mozart was poisoned by Salieri from what it would be in one in which he was not, since there would be something true of it in the former case, not in the latter, namely, "*Don Giovanni* was written by the composer Salieri poisoned." No one, short of Leibniz himself, would be willing to accept such a conclusion.

So, pace Leibniz and his law, the only way we can decide whether Levinson's musico-historical properties of music are damaging to musical Platonism is to determine whether they are essential or accidental properties of works. Further, to do *that* we can only appeal to examples and ask ourselves where our intuitions go, in the absence of some theory "from above" to settle the issue a priori. Levinson does indeed provide some very compelling examples, of which I choose two for discussion.

[a] A work identical in sound structure with Schoenberg's *Pirrot Lunaire* (1912), but composed by Richard Strauss in 1897 would be aesthetically different from Schoenberg's work. . . . [I]t would be more *bizarre*, more *upsetting*, more *anguished*, more *eerie* even than Schoenberg's work, since perceived against a musical tradition, a field of current styles, and an oeuvre with respect to which the musical characteristics of the sound structure involved in *Pirrot Lunaire* appear doubly extreme.[4]

[b] The symphonies of Johann Stamitz (1717–1757) are generally regarded as seminal works in the development of orchestral music. They employ many attention-getting devices novel for their time, one of which is known as the 'Mannheim rocket' – essentially a loud ascending scale figure for unison strings. A symphony of Stamitz containing Mannheim rockets and the like is an *exciting* piece of music. But a piece writ-

4 Ibid., p. 11.

ten today which was identical in sound structure, with one of Stamitz's symphonies, Mannheim rockets and all, would not be so much exciting as it would be exceedingly *funny.*[5]

To be noticed, straightaway, about these examples, is that they are both wildly impossible, in the strongest sense of "impossible" short of logical impossibility. This is obviously true of the first: it is flat out impossible that Strauss could have composed a musical structure identical with *Pirrot Lunaire* in 1897. The impossibility of today composing a sound structure exactly like a Stamitz symphony is not quite so obvious because Levinson's story is open to two interpretations. John Cage could sit down and copy, note-for-note, a Stamitz symphony, and then have it performed as Cage's Symphony No. 1. (I don't mean that he would keep its origin a secret either.) In the craziness of the contemporary art world, this is no more crazy than Cage's piece of musical silence, and no less possible. But the question of what we would say about it has to do not with present concerns; it has, rather, to do with those problematic objects of the contemporary art scene that have been around since Dada, meant to test, twit, challenge, and perhaps to expand our concept of art itself. I see no reason to get involved with such questions here. I take it, instead, that Levinson is thinking of a case, like the Shakespearean monkeys, in which a composer sits down, in the usual way, to write, according to his own lights, an "original" symphony, and, by sheer, mad coincidence, comes up with a sound structure identical to a Stamitz symphony. And *that* is as flat out impossible as Strauss composing *Pirrot Lunaire*.

Now because these are impossible, "science fiction" examples (more about that in a moment), they, of course, stretch our intuitions to the breaking point, for our intuitions have been formed by the perfectly ordinary, eminently possible. It would be well, therefore, to test our intuitions first on a perfectly possible – indeed actual – musical case, and go on to the impossible cases from there.

5 Ibid., p. 12.

There is a little prelude and chromatic fugue in E flat, long thought to be an early work of J. S. Bach, which we now know, through the discovery of the autograph, to be a mature work of Johann Christoph Bach (1642–1703).[6] Do we want to say that we have discovered it to be a different work? Certainly we hear it differently as the mature work of an earlier, and lesser composer, than we used to as an example of the great Johann Sebastian's juvenilia. We "hear," in some sense very hard to pin down, "things" in it now that we didn't "hear" there before, and we don't "hear" things that we used to "hear." It somehow seems a more daring, more powerful, and of course a more mature piece and Johann Christoph a more imposing musical figure for having composed it. When we heard it as the work of J. S. Bach, the composer of *Well-Tempered Clavier*, it could only seem small and groping. It has "lost" certain sonic features, "gained" others. But are these features essential enough for us to say that it has lost its "identity" and gained another? Do we think of it as a different work or as the same work with a different history? (If it were discovered that Nicomachus were not Aristole's father, would we have discover that "Aristotle" wasn't Aristole?)

Our intuition here, I think, is firm. The pull of sound structure as a concrete identity criterion is too powerful for us to waver from it, far too paradoxical, at least for the musical mind, to think of disputes over authorship, or changes in attribution, as questions about changes in the identity of the work – where, that is to say, the cases are real ones, and not philosophers' nightmares. I recall a recent experience that, it seems to me, sums up the musician's way of thinking. At a chamber music concert, what was once thought to be an early work of Joseph Haydn's – and well known under that description – was being performed. The program notes, quite musicologically up-to-date (*de rigueur* nowadays), informed us that recent Haydn scholarship had proven the work spurious. But, the annotator added, perhaps to assure us that

6 See Karl Geiringer, *Music of the Bach Family: An Anthology* (Cambridge, Mass.: Harvard University Press, 1955), pp. 30, and 33–5.

we needn't stop enjoying the work, "Why shouldn't we hear it anyway, no matter who wrote it? It still is, after all, the same beautiful music." I have heard and read such sentiments frequently, as the ever vigilant musicologists turn up more and more misattributions of our old favorites. I submit that they reflect our ordinary intuitions about such common cases. It is the same "Sanctus" whether Mozart wrote it, or whether Süssmayer did. Knowing which will certainly affect the way we hear the movement, and the rest of the work of which it is a part, in some ways properly so, in other ways not. It is, however, the same thing we are hearing differently, not a different thing altogether. That, at least, is the way it appears to me, and the way, arguably, it appears as well to a lot of other people who are involved with music. Isn't that enough?

But what now of Levinson's impossible cases? What are we to say about these? To start with, it is not at all clear that some of the properties which Levinson's problematic works – Strauss's *Pirrot Lunaire* and the latter-day Stamitz symphony – have or lack, which the "originals" lack or have, are essential to work identity. It is murky, for example, exactly what Levinson is attributing to Stamitz' symphonies when he calls them "exciting." Manheim rockets were, no doubt, exciting to eighteenth-century audiences, but certainly no longer are to us, at least in Stamitz' versions, whether we are hearing them in eighteenth-century symphonies, or in miraculously composed twentieth-century clones. Thus, if the property of "excitement" Levinson is attributing to the Stamitz symphony is taken to be "excitement to its auditors," then it is a property that the work once may have had, but has lost over the passage of time. Does that mean the work has lost its identity? That seems hard to credit. And if the "genuine" Stamitz symphony has not lost its identity by losing its excitement, why should its clone not be identical to it, not having any to begin with? To treat the cases differently would simply beg the question in favor of the anti-Platonist.

Now, to be sure, the "genuine" Stamitz symphony does possess, in a timeless sense, a property of excitement that its clone does not, bestowed upon it by its peculiar history: its particular place in the history of music. It was exciting to its first auditors, and its clone was not; and we consider that musico-historical property a very important one. *How* important? Important enough to deny work identity to the clone? But here our intuitions give out. For we are up against one of those aspects bestowed upon these cases by virtue of their impossible character, and we have, therefore, no idea *what* we want to say. I am certainly not going to maintain that we are on a slippery slope leading from the identity of the little prelude and fugue, invariant under J. S. Bach's authorship, or under Johann Christoph Bach's, to the identity of a symphony invariant under Johann Stamitz' authorship and, per impossible, under the authorship of the little known American composer Johann Damitz, who resides in Ashtabula, and was born in 1929. I don't know *what* to say in such a case, and I don't think anyone else does either, unless they have a theory to tell them. Nor is this surprising. Why should we know what to say, since our intuitions are nurtured on the ordinary cases, the cases that really occur. Intuitions may, indeed, be a guide in possible worlds that are close enough to our own to fall under those intuitions in some convincing way. But where a "possible" world is wildly "impossible," as the world of Johann Damitz is, our intuitions fail us. And why should they not? They were made to fit just the kind of world that excludes Damitz and his relatives in the strongest sense short of logical exclusion.[7]

7 We had a similar situation a few years ago in ethics, when we were bombarded with bizarre examples against which to test our intuitions about the rightness or wrongness of abortion – Michael Tooley's serum for changing cat embryos into human ones, Judith Jarvis Thomson's kidnapped kidney helper – to all of them R. M. Hare finally replying, in something like exasperation: "The fantastic nature of his [Tooley's] example (like that of some of Professor Thomson's) makes it even more difficult to be certain that we are saying what we *should* say about it. Our intuitions are the result of our upbringings, and we were not brought up on cases where kittens can be turned into beings with human minds, or where people are kidnapped and have distinguished violinists with kidney failure plugged into their bloodstreams, as in Professor Thomson's example." R. M. Hare, "Abortion and the Golden Rule," *Philosophy and Public Affairs* 4 (1975), preprinted in James Rachels (ed.) *Moral Problems* (3d ed.; New York: Harper and Row, 1979), p. 161.

We might say that our intuitions go both ways, or we might say that they go nowhere at all. One might perhaps feel a strong pull toward the structure of the symphony, and the conclusion that Stamitz and Damitz wrote the same work, while feeling the pull, as well, of the wildly diverging histories of these two identical sound structures, and the equally compelling conclusion that they cannot, on that account, be the same work. On the other hand, one might, with justification, be completely baffled by the example: without intuitions at all. But however you want to describe the case as two equally strong intuitions pulling in opposite directions, or the engine just idling and out of gear, it is clear that our intuitions are not going one place or the other. The impossible stories are up for grabs: They are just as consistent with Platonism as with a position that rejects identity of structure as identity of work. There just is no clear intuition emerging here one way or the other. Where there are clear intuitions, as in the ordinary cases, like the Bach prelude and fugue or Mozart's *Requiem,* they are clear because the cases are just the ones that have nurtured the intuitions in the first place; and those intuitions point to sound structure as the only viable principle of identity. but when the philosopher's story begins, "if, *per impossible,*" the intuitions favor nobody; they simply haven't been honed to that task.

II

Per impossible! There's the rub! For the very impossibility of examples like Levinson's has itself been offered as an argument against musical Platonism. It is, it seems to me, the most powerful and most troublesome argument of all. I want to go on now to give it some serious thought, and, I hope, at least the beginnings of an answer.

The problem seems to be this. If musical works are Platonic objects – types, kinds, universals – then they are agreed on all hands to be eternal objects: they do not, cannot come into being; they do not, cannot pass away. They preexist the act of composition. But if that is the case, then composition cannot be, as most believe, an act of creation; rather, because the work already exists, it must be an act of discovery instead. This in itself has been thought to be a reductio ad absurdum of musical Platonism. I have argued elsewhere that it is not;[8] but it will not, perhaps, be out of place to rehearse the argument in rather a different way here, as prelude to another, more pressing objection to follow.

If the main reason for rescuing musical works from Platonic eternity is to avoid the conclusion that they are discovered rather than created, eternity holds no terrors for me. For it seems to me as much, if not more plausible to think of musical works as discoveries, rather than as creations. So let me, as briefly as I can, just suggest *one* of the considerations that has led me to this seemingly bizarre conclusion, so at odds with the intuitions of so many proponents as well as critics of Platonism in music. To this end, I would like to put before you, from my own private casebook, three examples of what I call "creative achievement," and recommend them for your consideration.

Case Number One. Pythagoras is walking across the Agora, assiduously avoiding the ingestion of beans, when, all of a sudden, he knows not how or why, the theorem that bears his name just pops into his head.

Case Number Two. Wolfgang Amadeus Mozart, quite unaware of Peter Shaffer's posthumous plot to have him poisoned, is playing a quiet game of billards with his friend Antonio Salieri, when, all of a sudden, he knows not how or why, the theme of the Allegro section of the overture to *Don Giovanni* just pops into his head, along with the wonderful countersubject that accompanies it at its second statement.

Case Number Three. Thomas Alva Edison is having his customary lunch of apple pie when, all of a sudden, he knows not how or why, the idea of putting the tungsten filament in an evacuated container just pops into his head. (Somewhat prematurely, we might say that a light bulb went on in his head.)

8 See Kivy, pp. 112–19.

All these, I think we would agree, are *creative* achievements; and I emphasize that just to foreclose on the obvious mistake of equating the creative with creation, at the expense of discovery. And I have called them *achievements* to avoid begging the question between creation and discovery, because that, of course, is the question I now want to raise.

As far as I can see, we know about as much about what psychologists rather knowingly call the "creative process" as Socrates knew after he had completed the interrogation of Ion: which is to say, nothing at all. Some people get bright ideas; most people don't. And the people who get them tell us they do not know how or why: they just pop into their heads. The ancients called it inspiration. I prefer that to the creative process. But in any case, the point I want to make here is this: whether we are talking about the bright ideas we get as creations *or* discoveries, the introspective reports of their comings are on all fours with one another; inspirations if you like, or just plain "poppings," as I prefer. In other words, nothing about the mental process that gives rise to a creative achievement can give us any clue to whether we want to call that achievement a creation or a discovery; or, for that matter, whether we want to call it a *creative* achievement, since dull as well as bright ideas can pop into our heads. (Of course, we are not likely to call a dull popping an "inspiration," since that is a value-laden term, in the positive direction.) It is the product, not the process that can tell us, if anything can, whether we are in the presence of a discovery or a creation, and whether that discovery or creation is *creative*. So let us run through our cases with that in mind.

I suppose it seems natural to say that Pythagoras discovered his theorem. Ordinary language seems to Platonize mathematics and geometry. But, I daresay, if one were leaning toward an instrumentalist account of the mathematical sciences, as Berkeley seems to have been in *De motu*, and elsewhere, one might prefer to say the Pythagorean theorem was a creation: a theoretical construct. (I will return to this subject later on.)

On the other hand, the invention of the incandescent bulb

seems like a paradigm of creation; it didn't exist before Edison invented it, and did afterward. But that is not altogether clear either. Might we not say, without doing any violence at all either to common sense or ordinary language, that Edison *discovered* a practical way of getting light from electricity? The *way* was there all along, leading a timeless Platonic existence; and along came Edison to ferret it out.

Finally, Mozart's theme and counterpoint. Creation or discovery? Let me tell you the rest of the story. As soon as these musical ideas popped into his head, Mozart dropped his cue and shouted "Eureka! I found it!" "Found *what*, my dear fellow?," the astounded Salieri asked. "The theme and counterpoint for the Allegro of that damned overture, old boy," Mozart replied; "and not a moment too soon, either: the thing has to be finished by tomorrow morning." Well, that sounds to me as much like the announcement of a discovery as of a creation – more so, in fact; for if it had been the latter, Mozart would surely have shouted "I *did* it!" which isn't what we usually say on such occasions (for whatever that is worth); and if he knew his Greek he wouldn't have said "Eureka!" either. I will just add that anyone who has ever wrestled with the demons of counterpoint knows how much like discovery that aspect of musical composition frequently is. And when your teacher gives you your assignment, he is very likely to say: "For next time, see if you can *find* a third species counterpoint for the cantus firmus." Indeed, I will go so far as to claim, although I do not have time to support my claim here, that talk about musical composition is thoroughly imbued with discovery words – as much, I suspect, as with creation ones.

So much, then, for the claim that having to construe composition as discovery rather than as creation *of itself* reduces Platonism to an absurd, intolerable extremity. However, even if the initial implausibility of construing musical works as discoveries rather than creations is removed, a further difficulty seems to follow hard by. For the same discovery, clearly, can be made by more than one person: the independent discovery of the calculus by Leibniz and Newton being the most frequently cited, but by no means solitary example. Whereas it seems widely implausible, indeed impossible, that both Haydn and Mozart (say) should both have "discovered" – which is to say composed – the sound structure of Mozart's 40th Symphony (or even the first five measures) or that a contemporary of Plato's should have anticipated Beethoven's "discovery" – which is to say composition – of the sound structure of the 7th Symphony by "discovering" it – which is to say composing it – in 399 B.C.

Now I have purposely used two examples here in order to distinguish two possible kinds of impossible cases: the kind in which two contemporaries, or near contemporaries discover the same thing and the kind in which a discovery is anticipated by someone of a much earlier time. I will treat them separately, as they raise distinctly different problems.

Let us take the case of "anticipations" first. I think it is the easier one, because it appears to me obvious that there is no disanalogy here between cases of scientific discovery and cases of musical composition. It is as flat out impossible for a contemporary of Plato's to have discovered (say) Kepler's laws of planetary motion, or Newton's gravititational laws as to have composed – that is, discovered – the sound structure of Beethoven's 7th, and for the very same reasons. A recent contributor to this debate, on the side of the anti-Platonists, writes that *"Tristan and Isolde* could not possibly have existed, say, at the time of Josquin, for its existence is contingent on human constructs developed centuries later – constructs such as equal temperament and the tonal system."[9] True enough; but surely the same is true of Kepler's and Newton's laws. they required for their discovery and very conceptualization a conceptual scheme in which to place them, completely unavailable to the ancient Greeks. (They were not only undiscoverable but unthinkable.) They required an accuracy of observation, indeed an attitude toward observation quite inconceivable before the seventeenth century. They re-

9 Renee Cox, "Are Musical Works Discovered?," *Journal of Aesthetics and Art Criticism* 43 (1985), p. 371.

quired, that is to say, the whole history of science up to Kepler's and Newton's time, as *Tristan und Isolde* required the whole history of music up to Wagner's. Clearly, then, if the impossibility of Archimedes discovering Kepler's and Newton's laws – he had the genius, after all – is not an argument against Kepler's and Newton's laws as discoveries, it hardly seems a better argument against musical composition as discovery that Socrates couldn't compose Beethoven's 7th when his voice told him to study and compose "music."

What really is troublesome, though, is the case of simultaneous discovery; for there does indeed seem to be no possible analogue in musical composition to the completely independent co-discovery of the calculus by Leibniz and Newton, or other cases of that kind, which are not uncommon in the history of science.

Suppose one were to reply (as I am about to do) that this only shows there are kinds of discoveries that can be shared and kinds that cannot, discoveries of musical structure (at least as exemplified by things like Beethoven's 7th) being one of the latter kinds? One's first reaction, no doubt, would be that the response is completely ad hoc. But I am not convinced of that, for the following reasons. There are, as is well known, those in the philosophy of science who maintain that theoretical terms like "quark" and "electron" refer to real objects in nature, and represent genuine discoveries by scientists of "what there is." There are also those who think, on the other hand, that quarks, electrons, and the like are not real objects in nature at all but, rather, "theoretical constructs" to save the appearances, and science, then, not a process of discovery but one of creation, of making or fashioning. Notice, though, it has never been thought (so far as I know) an argument *against* the latter view that it is impossible for two people to independently create the same thing, and so, since scientists do sometimes come up independently with the same theory, this must be discovery and not creation. What this perhaps shows is that *merely* being a creation, as opposed to a discovery, does not, *of itself*, imply that it cannot be the outcome of the independent efforts of

separate individuals, scientific "creations" being, on the instrumentalist's view, cases in point, and not at all counterintuitive. And, by parity of reasoning, it may well show that
merely being a discovery, rather than a creation, does not
imply the possibility of shared accomplishment. Therefore,
it becomes quite plausible, and by no means special pleading, to suggest that there might be a reason, other than their
being creations, that makes musical structures unshareable
outcomes of human endeavor – an explanation quite compatible with their being discoveries.

What more can we say? Can we perhaps say something
about this explanation – about why, that is, some discoveries
are shareable and some are not? Well, for starters, why
couldn't it be the case that some "objects" are so unique as
to be discoverable only by people uniquely constituted to notice them. The "creationists" often appeal to the intimate
connection between a work and its creator's personality: "the
essence of a musical composition is a personal expression,"
as one puts it.[10] A different personality from Beethoven's could
no more give forth with Beethoven's 7th Symphony than could
two different people have the same handwriting. This is
something of a cliché, to be sure; but if it contains a kernel of
truth within, I do not see why that truth cannot serve the
"discoverist" as well. If it is not the case that the possibility
of shared scientific "creations" (as the instrumentalist sees
them) is repugnant to common sense, I do not see why the
possibility of impossible-to-share discoveries – musical works,
for example – should be repugnant to common sense. I see
no reason why the discovery of so unique an object as the
sound structure of Beethoven's 7th Symphony should not be
thought every bit as much an "expression" of Beethoven's
personality (whatever that really means) as John Hancock's
signature is of his. Look at it another way. I do not think
there is a more intimate connection between personality and
work than that between the personality of Picasso and his
Head of a Bull (Paris, 1943). If there is a kernel of truth in the

10 Ibid., p. 373.

notion that sculpting and composing are "expressions" of "personality," then I see no less reason to think that this is an expression of Picasso's personality than that *The Thinker* is an expression of Rodin's. Yet it is far more plausible, in my view, to describe what Picasso did, in this particular instance, as "discovery" than as "creation." He "discovered" the form of a bull's head in a bicycle saddle and handle bars – that, you will recall, is all that the *Head of a Bull* is. There was nothing, really, to "create": the saddle and handle bars were already there. Here, then, is a discovery as unique, as personal as any "mere" creation can be thought to be. Only Picasso could have made it. We do not know why, but we are as intuitively certain of it as that only Beethoven could have been responsible for the sound structure we know as the 7th Symphony. We simply sum up our ignorance by saying that both are "expressions" of "unique personalities."

I am saying, then, that certain objects are so unique as to be discoverable only by a single individual. If that is to say that certain discoveries are "expressions" of "personalities," then so be it; it is harmless enough, since I see no less reason to think that discoveries can be "expressions of personality" (whatever that really means) than to think that creations can be. And there, I think, I will let the matter rest, except to add that the foregoing considerations, if they have not put musical Platonism in a more favorable light than its alternatives, have, at the very least, put Platonism on an equal footing vis-à-vis our musical intuitions. That must suffice for the moment.

III

Let me make an end with this curious observation. The greatest nominalist of our day has concluded that composers and scientists, contrary to the general view, are *both* of them engaged in the same endeavor, creating, or "worldmaking," as he calls it, even though the vulgar might describe the scientist's work as "discovery." Platonism, at the opposite (and to him detested) end of the metaphysical spectrum, implies that composers and scientists, contrary to the general view, are *both* of them engaged in the *same* endeavor, "discovery," even though the vulgar might describe the composer's work as "creation." There is, unexpectedly, some common ground here, and a valuable insight shared. But much remains to be done in understanding the implications of both these theories for our conception of what composers do, and what their doing does. If music be the food of love, our theories about it are still only half-baked.[11]

11 An earlier version of this paper was presented in London at the annual meeting of the British Society of Aesthetics on 21 September, 1986. I am most grateful to the members of that audience for valuable comment and criticism. I am also indebted to an anonymous reader for *The American Philosophical Quarterly*, who was of help in refining and improving one of my points.

Chapter IV

Orchestrating Platonism

There is certain music, namely, Western art music written since the development of a sophisticated musical notation, which we ordinarily describe in terms of "works" and "performances." We say, at least presystematically, that the *Eroica* symphony is one thing, the rendition *of it* by the Boston Symphony Orchestra last Thursday, another thing. What kinds of things are these, and what is their relation to one another? An answer that has been attractive to some, including myself, is the Platonic one: that works are universals, or types, or kinds, performances related to them as particulars, tokens, or instances.

The attractions of this view, however, seem to be offset by a number of serious objections and difficulties. Some of these I have sought to deal with elsewhere.[1] One, that I have not, and which I want to take up here, is to the effect that on the Platonist's view, instrumentation or orchestration is not an essential part of the musical work, whereas, manifestly (so it is claimed), it is, at least in the cases where it is specified by the composer. This objection is expressed with great vigor and cogency by Jerrold Levinson, and it is his version with which I shall deal. In order to do that, I will adopt his way of characterizing musical Platonism, which is as the view that "A piece of music is *some* sort of structural type," to wit, "a

1 For the essay to which the present on is the sequel, see Peter Kivy, "Platonism in Music: A kind of Defense," *Grazer Philosophische Studien*, 19 (1983), pp. 109–29. Reprinted in this volume, Chapter II.

sound structure – a structure, sequence, or pattern of sounds, pure and simple."[2]

With this piece of terminological business taken care of, we can now state Levinson's objection in its most general form. It is this:

> If musical works were simply sound structures, then they would not essentially involve any particular means of performance. But the paradigm musical works we are investigating in this paper, e.g., Beethoven's Quintet Opus 16 [for oboe, clarinet, bassoon, horn, and piano], clearly *do* involve quite specific means of performance, i.e., particular instruments, in an essential way. The instrumentation of musical works is an integral part of those works. So musical works cannot be simple sound structures *per se*.[3]

The crucial claim, here, is that "paradigm musical works," of which Beethoven's Quintet for piano and winds is an exemplar, "involve quite specific means of performance, i.e., particular instruments *in an essential way*"; that, in other words, "The instrumentation of [such paradigm] musical works is *an integral part of those works*." What are we to make of it? What is the nature of this claim? Is it a self-evident metaphysical principle of some kind? Is it a deeply felt intuition of Levinson's? Is it supposed to suggest how musicians talk or think? Is it the conclusion of an argument? Perhaps it is all of these things. There *are* some arguments, and I will consider them in a moment. But I will begin, simply, by presenting some cases, and giving some arguments of my own, meant to suggest that musical works of the kind Levinson and I are talking about do not possess, as *essential* properties, their instrumentation, or means of production, at least within certain wide limits.

Instrumental music as we know it – that is to say, music written specifically with an instrumental performance in mind, as opposed to vocal music played on instruments – began to be written at the end of the sixteenth century. One of the

2 Jerrold Levinson, "What a Musical Work Is," *Journal of Philosophy* 77 (1980), p. 6.
3 Ibid., p. 14.

best known composers of early instrumental music, as well as one of the best, was Giovanni Gabrieli. He wrote many pieces for instruments with the title *Canzona per sonar,* which means, simply, "song to be sounded" (which is where we get the word "sonata"), as opposed to "song" to be sung, i.e., "cantata," or "song" to be "touched," that is, to be played on a keyboard, a "toccata." Thus, a *canzona per sonar* was intended to be played by string, or brass, or wind instruments, or, one supposes, any combination of instruments capable of realizing its sound structure. *Any* combination of instruments? What about clarinets? Well, Gabrieli couldn't have had those in mind when he wrote the instruction *per sonar* since they hadn't been invented yet. So perhaps we should rule out clarinets. We will say, then, that it is an essential property of a Gabrieli *canzona per sonar* that it be played by any group of instruments of Gabrieli's own time: viols, or sackbutts, or cornetti, or recorders, or whatever. But now a problem seems to arise. Must we use valveless trumpets and wooden cornetti, or can we use modern brass instruments á piston (*including* the tuba, which didn't exist in any form whatever until the nineteenth century)? What is our intuition here? Would any musician or concertgoer think that when the New York Brass Ensemble "performs" a Gabrieli *canzona per sonar* on modern brass instruments it has not presented an instance of *that* work but of a different one? (Or is it enough just that the instruments have the same names as Gabrieli's?) What *is* our intuition? If we have any at all, surely it is that if the *sound structure* of the *canzona* is given to us more or less intact – more or less recognizable – we have been given an instance of the work. The only really firm footing for our intuition is the sound structure. Further, once you accept the performance on modern brass instruments, you are on the slippery slope that, so far as I can see, will propel you right into accepting a performance on clarinets (which, indeed, may sound more like cornetti than modern trumpets do), or saxophones, or any other combination of instruments that can present the structure of the piece. Indeed, wasn't Gabrieli playing just that piece when he tried out his latest *canzona*

77

per sonar on the organ of San Marco, to see if he liked it? I don't even think our intuition rules out a *canzona per sonar* being "touched," or, for that matter, sung by the Swingle Singers, and still being *that very piece*. And that is because there *is* something for our intuition to latch onto to preserve work identity: the sound structure. Notice, by the way – and I will return to this point later on – that I haven't said that a performance of a Gabrieli *canzona per sonar* on modern brass instruments, or on saxophones, or by the Swingle Singers, is a *good* performance, only that it *is* a performance of the work, a bona fide instance of that sound structure.

Let us now move forward a little. Until well past the death of J. S. Bach, much music was published with titles like: "Duet for flutes, violins, oboes, or other melody instruments," and so forth. If a duet with such a title, written (say) in 1725, were played on modern flutes or oboes, would it be a performance of the piece or not? What about if it were played on harmonicas? On electronic gadgets? Does it have to be played by two performers, or can I play it on the organ? Where does intuition go on this? The only intuition I have is that if the sound structure is preserved, we have an instance of the work.

As a matter of fact, until well into the classical era, people's concept of instrumental music was informed by just these kinds of laissez-faire attitudes toward instrumentation. If the era of instrumental music goes from the last quarter of the sixteenth century to 1986, at least half the era is clearly dominated by a completely *ab libitum*, nonessentialist attitude toward what instruments any given piece of music is to be realized on. If intuition is founded in practice, and not delivered from on high, then half the history of notated instrumental music practice embodies the intuition that, pace Levinson, instrumentation, means of production is *not* an essential property of the musical work. Whatever Beethoven's Opus 16 is a paradigm of, it is not, as Levinson falsely believes, "paradigmatic [of] musical composition in Western culture."[4] That is a historically biased view.

4 Ibid., p. 15n.

Let me turn to a third example, this time from Levinson, to help nail down this historical point, and work our passage to some of Levinson's arguments, and to the music which Beethoven's Opus 16 *is* paradigmatic of. Levinson is not completely unaware of the kind of music I have been discussing so far; the problem is, he grossly underestimates its historical and conceptual significance. Thus, he writes, anticipating the *kinds* of considerations I have been advancing, but hardly, I think, realizing their extent, "It is inevitable that someone will object at this point that certain composers, in certain periods, did not compose with definite instruments in mind and did not make specific instrumentation integral to their works." As an example, Levinson picks Bach's *Well-Tempered Clavier*, about which he writes:

> even in a case such as J. S. Bach, where controversy has long existed as to exactly what performing forces Bach intended, called for, or would have allowed in such compositions as *The Well-Tempered Clavier* . . . it is clear there are still more restrictions as to performing forces which must be considered as part of those compositions. Thus, *The Well-Tempered Clavier* may not be a work belonging solely to the harpsichord (as opposed to the clavichord or fortepiano), but it is clearly a work for *keyboard,* and a performance of its sound-structure on five violins would just for that reason not be a performance of *it*.[5]

Let us test our intuitions on this example. We won't need the whole *Well-Tempered Clavier,* just the C minor fugue from Book I, and to play it we will only need three of Levinson's five violins. So let us imagine the following performances of "it": on three violins, on a lute, on a modern Steinway, on a harpsichord with the buffer stop, on the organ, with oboe, English horn, and bassoon, on an electric keyboard, registered to play very dry, unsustaining "pings" (like a submarine's sonar, as depicted in Hollywood movies). What are we to say? If the relevant necessary condition for work identity is that it be played on a keyboard, then the performance on

5 Ibid.

79

the electronic piano, and on the Steinway are *echt*, in spite of the fact that Bach could not possibly have had such instruments and tone colors in mind as part of the musical content of the fugue, whereas the performances on lute and by woodwind trio would be ruled out, in spite of the fact that the former would be tonally indistinguishable from a performance on the harpsichord with the buffer stop, and the latter tonally indistinguishable from a performance on an appropriately registered baroque organ. Do we really want to say that the means of production has nothing essential to do with tone color but only with how the sound is physically produced, that is, that it must be produced by pushing levers but not blowing on pipes or plucking on strings? Whose intuitions go in *that* direction?

Well, suppose, then, we say that the relevant necessary condition for work identity of the fugue be that (a) it be played on a keyboard, and (b) the keyboard sound like one of the keyboard instruments of Bach's day. That, however, rules out a performance on the Steinway; we will have to say that Rosalind Tureck's much admired performances of Bach are not bona fide instances of his works. That seems monstrously implausible to me, and, I dare say, to a host of her admirers. And once we throw out the keyboard requirement, what principle of identity is left?

There is only one firm intuition here, and it is that work identity is preserved just so long as structural integrity is preserved. Indeed, so strong is that intuition that we do not even require *absolute* preservation of structure; that is to say, we only require that structural *relations* be preserved. That is why a song transposed from one key to another to accommodate a particular singer's voice is still considered *that song*, and why a performance of the C minor fugue on three violins would still be an instance of *it*, even though we would have to transpose it up an octave to preserve the structural relationships. This is the way composers and performers talk; this is the way they think.

But what of the kind of music that Beethoven's Opus 16 really represents: the kind for which instruments are specifically-stipulated, not merely suggested or left to the discretion of the performer? What are our intuitions here? As a matter of fact, Opus 16 itself exists both as a quintet for oboe, clarinet, bassoon, horn, and piano, and as a quartet (also by Beethoven) for piano and string trio.[6] Are these two works or one? There is no doubt about how musicians talk of such cases (which are numerous). It is one work, in two versions.

A few facts might help us to discern where our intuitions go. Music conservatories have separate courses for composition and for orchestration. Richard Rodgers composed the music for *Oklahoma*; it was orchestrated by someone else. As is the almost universal custom, Mozart composed the concerto for clarinet and *then* orchestrated it: we know this from one of his letters, and there is absolutely no doubt that he thought of the work as existing – as having its musical identity – before any of the instrumentation was in place (except, of course, for the solo clarinet part). Most composers compose in piano score, and put an orchestra work in full score during the orchestration process. Brahms frequently played his orchestral works to his friends, like Clara Schumann, for instance, before they were orchestrated. Most composers, from as far back as we have written documents to tell us, at least in the tonal tradition, have tended to think in terms of abstract sound, not in terms of instrumental sound. Mendelssohn continually tinkered, over the years, with the orchestration of the *Schöne Melusina* overture. Was he composing a new work each time he altered the orchestration? Mozart added clarinets to the 40th symphony without changing any of the notes; the original version had only the darker hued oboes for wind color. Two works or one? He arranged his oboe concerto for flute. Two works or one? *Valses Nobles et Sentimentales* was originally composed for piano; only later did Ravel produce the orchestral version that most of us know. Two works or one? The Ravel example is a particularly relevant one for our purposes, because it belongs to an era, and

6 See Alexander Wheelock Thayer, *The Life of Ludwig van Beethoven* (Carbondale: Southern Illinois University Press, 1960), vol. I, p. 208.

to a style of composition which we tend to think was intimately connected with tone color as an "essential property." (If Debussy and Ravel did not think in terms of timbre as well as structure, or, rather, in terms of "timbred structure," who did?) Yet it is clear that even here, the composer thought in terms of sound structure, and only later in terms of instrumentation.

None of this *proves* anything, I suppose; and anyone is free to insist that Mozart wrote two G minor symphonies with the same "K" number, alike but for the clarinets; that the clarinet concerto in his head was a different one from the one on paper, with the orchestration in place; that Richard Rodgers was co-composer of his shows; that there are two works by Ravel called *Valses Nobles et Sentimentales,* and so on. People in the music world don't talk that way, or think that way. But there is no compelling reason why a metaphysician shouldn't if there is some good metaphysical reason for doing so. So let us now see if Levinson provides us with any. He does give us four arguments; none, I think, is at all convincing.

(1) Levinson's first argument seems to me to be an appeal to an intuition that isn't there: a reductio ad non-absurdum. He begins: "Composers do not describe pure sound patterns in qualitative terms, leaving their means of production undiscussed."[7] This is quite true. The question is, What does it prove? He adds along the way: "The idea that composers of the last 300 years were generally engaged in composing pure sound patterns, to which they were kind enough to append suggestions as to how they might be realized, is highly implausible."[8] Well, Levinson tries to make it seem "highly implausible" by use of "loaded language" – "kind enough to suggest" – but if we phrase it in somewhat less prejudiced way, as a matter of fact from 1575 to 1775, instrumentation *was* more or less in the form of suggestions for performance, rather than requirements for it, as the notation of pitches would be. And thereafter, even though the instrumental re-

7 Levinson, p. 14   8 Ibid., p. 15.

quirements were stronger than suggestions, they were not, as I have tried to show, necessary conditions for work identity. True, there has never been a time, since the beginning of the Baroque era, when composers left the means of production of their works undiscussed. But it does not follow from this that the means of production was considered, at any time, to be definitive of the work. The "discussion" was not about that. What it was about I will get to in a moment.

(2) Levinson continues:[9]

> Scores are generally taken to be definitive of musical works, at least in conjunction with the conventions of notational interpretation assumed to be operative at the time of composition. It is hard to miss the fact that scores of musical works call for specific instruments *in no uncertain terms.*

That scores are definitive of works is a claim that I might well agree to, while not allowing that stupulations of instrumentation are part of the "score" properly so called, as Nelson Goodman would do. I would rather construe "score" more widely, as musicians do, to include not only notation (in Goodman's sense), but tempo markings, expression instructions, and instrumentation, too. On my view, then, *some* parts of scores are definitive of works and some are not. With this Levinson agrees, stating that

> This is not to say that *everything* found in scores is constitutive of musical works. Some markings do not fix identity of a work but are instead of the nature of advice, inspiration [?], helpful instruction, etc.

He adds – and here, of course, we are in disagreement – "However, the suggestion that instrumental specifications are of this [nonconstitutive] sort is totally insupportable."[10]

But with Levinson's admission that not everything found in scores is constitutive of musical works, whatever argument there is here completely evaporates. Levinson seems to be arguing as follows:

9 Ibid., pp. 15–16; italics mine.   10 Ibid., p. 16n.

Scores are definitive of works.

Instrumentation instructions appear in scores.

Therefore, instrumentations are (in part) definitive of works.

He admits, however, that merely being "in a score" does not make an instruction definitive of a work; so nothing follows from the claim that scores are definitive of works about whether instrumentation is definitive of works. Levinson tells us the suggestion that it is not "is totally insupportable." But the suggestion that it is remains totally unsupported in the above argument, when suitably amended by Levinson himself. He does say that "scores of musical works call for specific instruments *in no uncertain terms*," meaning to imply by that, I suppose, that these stipulations must be definitive of works. But, as a matter of fact, from 1575 to 1775, nothing could be further from the truth. Does it sound like "no uncertain terms" to prescribe that a duet be played on "flutes, or oboes, or violins, or other melody instruments," or that 48 preludes and fugues be played on a "keyboard"? The fact is that until the high classical era, instructions for instrumentation were, to a great extent, no more definitive of works than tempo indications or expression marks. They were, like the latter two, in large measure, suggestions for what, in the composer's eyes, would be a "good" performance of the work.

But what about the period for which Beethoven's Opus 16 provides a paradigm? What status do instrumentation instructions have here? Clearly, they are now more than mere "suggestions." It appears to me, however, that an entirely satisfactory answer can be given to this question, which will distinguish instrumentation instructions in the "ad lib" period from those in the "no uncertain terms" period, *without* having to construe the latter as definitive of musical works.

One thing about the growth of instrumental music in the late eighteenth century is quite clear. The musical structures became more and more complicated and expansive in ways that made greater demands on instruments. The range, for example, that was demanded in a violin sonata or concerto, or the doublestopping, made it impossible anymore to play such pieces on the flute or the oboe. Thus it ceased to be possible to advertise a sonata or conceto as "for violin or flute or oboe or other melody instrument," as had been the custom, simply because no other melody instrument could realize the structure of the work. In *that* respect, certain instruments became *essential*, but only temporarily, and if you will pardon the pun, *instrumentally*. That is to say, they were essential to the realization of the work because they were the only instruments capable, at the time, of realizing it, so were essential as a *means*, as a conductor is essential to the correct performance of a Verdi opera, not as the entrance of the main theme at measure 394 of the first movement of the *Eroica* is essential to a bona fide instance of that work. I say "temporarily," of course, because the development of new instruments, the technical development of old ones, and the development of instrumental technique, can make a sound structure realizable in ways other than those envisaged by the composer. In Mozart's time, his clarinet concerto could be played on but one wind instrument: the clarinet. And a large part of Mozart's fascination with the instrument had to do, no doubt, with its extraordinary range, as compared to any other woodwind of the day. But it can now be played on saxophone, for example, with no loss of sound structure. To take another example: Liszt could play, with the expanded piano of his day, and the technique to go with it, full orchestral works of the late eighteenth century that could not, at the time, have been fully realized on the pianos of Mozart and Haydn.

But range, of course, is not the only aspect of instruments relevant to sound structure realization. Technique is another: and the fact is that many musical figurations which composers of instrumental music began to exploit are playable on string instruments but not possible at all on winds or keyboard instruments, no matter how advanced the technique of the performer, or, if now possible on modern winds or keyboard, were not at some earlier time. That is why the strings have been so extensively exploited in the art music of the eighteenth and nineteenth centuries, as opposed particularly to the woodwinds. They present the composer with more structural possibilities. But where substitution is possible, *salve veritate*, it has occurred frequently, even in the concerto and solo literature, well into the "no uncertain terms" period of instrumentation, witness Beethoven's arrangement of his violin concerto for piano, and Brahms' "clarinet" sonatas, which were issued, right from the start, for clarinet *or* viola.

The point I am making here is that a good deal of interest in instrumentation in the period in which it emerged from the "ad lib." stage had to do not so much with "color" as "construction"; not so much with the timbre of instruments as with their capabilities of realizing sound structures; with, that is, their ranges, and the varieties of musically complex figurations they could, with advancing technique, produce. It was a period (needless to say) in which instrumental technique and technology were in an upward curve. Instrumentation and orchestration tend, I think, to suggest to the unwary only concern with the distinctive tone colors of the various families. This is a mistake. I do not say that they played no part. But what was uppermost, in the classical period, I suggest – and I include Beethoven in it – was instrumentation and orchestration as it related to structure. Instruments began to be "required" rather than "recommended" because structure was being pursued in ways that could be realized only by particular instruments.

But tone color did, of course, in the nineteenth century, come to have a far greater importance than theretofore. Gluck is frequently pointed to as the pioneer, in the eighteenth century, of this "modern" attitude toward orchestration, and was so thought of by the nineteenth-century pioneer, and systematizer, Hector Berlioz. What are we to say of this kind of attitude toward orchestration, so characteristic of the nineteenth and twentieth centuries?

It might be useful, in answering this question, to distinguish between timbre of tone color per se, and timbre or tone

86

color as musical means to some other musical end. That is to say, one wants to separate the kind of case in which the composer chooses some instrumental color to obtain a certain representational or emotive effect (say), and the kind of case where the composer "just wants that particular oboe sound there." The second kind of case requires no further explanation. Understanding what I mean by the first might benefit from examples. Here are two. Berlioz represented shepherds' pipes in the third movement of the *Symphonie fantastique* with oboe and English horn. In the last movement of the First Symphony, Brahms uses the French horn in measures 30 to 38 to achieve a "noble" quality.

Now what I want to bring out first is that timbre per se is pretty hard to imagine as being involved in compositional choices very often. Composers tend to think in structure, not color. Of course they *use* timbre and tone color to achieve or more exactly, help to achieve musical effects. But the effects have already been "written in" to the musical structure, the orchestration, which always follows composition, being employed to enhance effects already musically there. The noble quality is achieved by the melodic and harmonic structure at measures 30 to 38 of the Brahms – the horn merely adds to an already accomplished effect. Indeed, the nobility is still there if the passage is played on the piano, or, as in measures 38 to 46, where it is played by the flute, for variety and contrast. But it is a matter of degree – and where the emotive quality survives in sufficient degree, I would argue that musical structure, of which it is a part, has survived. And it is musical structure, so conceived, that makes an instance of the work. That is my contention.

As to representational qualities, it is perfectly true that some may not survive instrument substitution: Berlioz' sheperds' pipes might not be recognizable if played on violin and viola rather than oboe and English horn. That, however, is irrelevant to the present discussion. For the music under consideration in this essay is pure instrumental music, sans text or title or program. Representational music is no more pure musical structure than is an opera or a song. And as these kinds of music fall without the purview of the present essay, they need concern us no longer.

Finally, let us consider timbre or tone color per se. Suppose that there is a passage for flute, or oboe, or whatever, where we cannot see any musical reason of the kind discussed above why it was scored for that particular instrument raher than some other. We can assume one of two things: that the composer wanted just that timbre and no other right there or we may assume that it was a completely trivial, inessential choice. I say we may *assume* one or the other because there will be no third way to decide, (It is unlikely to the vanishing point that a composer would have documented his choice as one or the other. And if we must assume, then our assumption can be based on whether our intuitions do or do not lean toward Platonism.)

Let me just add, in concluding this section – which I take to be the one most crucial to my case – that there may indeed be instances where the playing of certain notes by a certain instrument is essential to something's being an instance of a work. I do not deny that. All I have insisted is that in the three-hundred-year or more history of instrumental music in the West, such cases are rare; that the *tradition* of Western music is one of musical works constituted by musical structure. In any tradition there are bound to be anomalies – particularly an *artistic* tradition. It is the tradition, however, not the anomalies that theory must fit. And it is the tradition, I am claiming, that Platonism is consistent with, when it comes to the question of orchestration and instrument specificity.[11]

(3) On Levinson's view, the "strongest reason why" means of performance cannot be divorced from the musical work's essence "is that the aesthetic content of a musical work is determined not only by its musico-historical context, but also in part by the actual means of production chosen for making that sound structure audible."[12] His major example of this is Beethoven's Hammerklavier Sonata, of which he writes: it

11 I am most grateful to Jerrold Levinson for forcing me to rethink the argument in this section.
12 Levinson, p. 17.

is a sublime, craggy, and heaven-storming piece of music. . . . However, if we understood the very sounds of the Hammerklavier Sonata to originate from a full-range synthesizer, as opposed to a mere 88-key piano of metal, wood, and felt, it no longer seems so sublime, so craggy, so awesome.[13]

We must remark, to begin with, that Levinson's argument leaves us in doubt about whether the sublime, craggy, awesome quality of the Hammerklavier results from our *believing* the sound structure is produced by a piano, or our *knowing* it is so produced, it apparently *not* being sufficient that it merely in fact be so produced. (I am taking "know that *p*" to imply "*p*.") The operative word is "understand," and the question is, when "we understand the very sounds of the Hammerklavier Sonata to originate from a full-range synthesizer, as opposed to a mere 88-key grand piano of metal, wood and felt," are we merely believing it or knowing it? Will the sublime, craggy, awesome quality be absent if we believe the work is being performed by a synthesizer, even though it really is being performed by a piano behind the scenes? Is it all merely a placebo effect? Will the sublime, craggy, awesome quality be there if we believe the work is being performed by a pianist when in fact it is really being produced by a synthesizer behind a screen? More important, will the sublime, craggy awesome quality be there if a person with no very definite beliefs at all about pianos, what they are made of, how many keys they have, how hard the Hammerklavier is to play, etc., etc., listens to it? This would describe most music lovers. Are we really to say that their beliefs – or lack thereof – preclude their being in the presence of the craggyness, sublimity, and awesomeness of the Hammerklavier, and, therefore, preclude their being in the presence of the work itself?

A second point to note is that Levinson merely says it will not be *so* craggy, *so* sublime, *so* awesome when played on a synthesizer than when played on a piano. And, by the way, it will not be *so* craggy, *so* sublime, *so* awesome when played

---

13 Ibid.

on "a mere 88-key piano of metal, wood, and felt" as when played on an even more "mere" fortepiano of Beethoven's time, for which it was written which had less than 88 keys, did not have a metal frame, had only two strings per note, a very weak treble, and contained no felt (the hammers being leather). Are we to understand from this that a performance by Rudolph Serkin on a Steinway grand piano would not be a performance of the Hammerklavier Sonata? Is there *any* instrument on which the Hammerklavier can be played correctly where *none* of its craggy, sublime, awesome quality will come through? I would be hard put to it to think of one. That is because Beethoven put that craggyness, that sublimity, that awesomeness into the sound structure itself. Where else? Any instrument that can realize that sound structure adequately will realize *enough* of the craggy, sublime awesome quality to qualify as an instance of the work: not necessarily an exemplary instance, but an instance nevertheless.

There may be a work in the standard repertoire, or on the fringes, that will lose *some* essential property when played on *some* instrument or other, even when the sound structure is adequately produced. *I* can't think of an example. But if the examples are so rare, I do not think musical Platonism need worry about the possibility. For it is not audacious enough, any more than are its rivals, to claim that every single thing in the world called "music" is in its mold.

(4) Levinson concludes his discussion of instrumentation with an argument about "artistic" attributes, as opposed to "aesthetic" ones. He does not tell us what the difference is, and I do not want to speculate on it myself. So let's just look at his examples. (a) A piece for violin might be *virtuosic* on that instrument, but not on some other instrument where "its sound structure might not be particularly difficult to get through." (b) A piece written for one instrument might have the artistic attributes of "originality" and "unusualness," but sound neither original nor unusual on another. (c) A composer might solve a problem of instrumental balance in a work, as Beethoven did in Opus 16, in which case, "solves the problem of instrumental balance xyz," would be, on Levin-

son's view, a property of the work lost if it were played on anything but xyz.[14]

These examples can, I think, be quickly dispatched.

(a) If, as Levinson believes, being difficult to play is a necessary condition for being virtuosic (sufficient, also, on Levinson's view?), then it is perfectly clear that being virtuosic is a property that a work can lose *without* losing its identity – without, that is, becoming a different work. For, I take it, Handel's concerto for oboe in G minor was virtuosic, that is to say, very hard to play, in its time – pushed the oboists of Handel's day to the limits of their technique on their instruments – but can be played quite easily today by any competent conservatory student. Surely, no one wants to say that a modern performance of that work, by Ronald Roseman or Heinz Holliger, is not "really" a performance of *it*? But if works can lose their virtuosity by becoming easier to play on the instruments for which they were written, or their modern equivalents, without losing their work-identity, there is no reason to suppose they can lose it by losing their virtuosity in some other way, like instrument-substitution, without simply begging the question in favor "instrument-essentialism."

(b) With regard to the original and the unusual, I am first going to assume that Levinson means "sounds original" and "sounds unusual": that is to say, I am going to assume that he means "original" and "unusual" to be sonic attributes, and not (say) art-historical ones. If so, it is clear that they frequently will not endure, where work-identity will. I take it that Mozart's clarinet concerto sounded both original and unusual to his contemporaries: original because it certainly expanded the dimensions of the woodwind concerto; unusual because the clarinet was still, at the time, a fairly new, novel and scarce instrument that Mozart was, in large measure, responsible for "domesticating." Played on the clarinet today, it sounds neither original nor unusual in these respects; not original because the large-scale woodwind con-

14 Ibid., pp. 18–19.

certo is old hat to us now, not unusual because the clarinet is a well known and familiar friend. I take it, though, that the identity of K 622 endures. Its originality, if we mean "sounding original," we cannot restore. Its unusualness we might restore by playing it (say) on the rather little known heckelphone, instead of the tired old clarinet, unless one thought, like Levinson, that *that* would make it a different work.[15] If originality and unusualness both "naturally" dissipate in the passage of time, where work-identity endures, I see no reason at all to think that if they are made to dissipate "unnaturally," by substitution, as in Levinson's example, a familiar instrument for an unusual one – the example is of a flute playing flute-sounding violin passages – work-identity should not endure here as well, just so long as sound structure is preserved.

But suppose, instead, what Levinson means by a work's being original is that it possesses, in a timeless sense, "originality" as an art-historical property. In that case, the *work* would remain original even if it didn't sound original, for originality would not be a sonic property: would not be one of those properties that works and their performances or instances share. Not every property of a work is shared by its performances or instances. A performance or instance can be too fast, but the work cannot be. A work can be original, but not one of its performances or instances, at least in the same respect (although a performance might be original, in tempo or phrasing or whatever, in that the performer played the work in a way not thought of heretofore). None of this, of course, would cause the least problem for the view being put forward here. As a sonic property, originality does not always survive in performance, but that does not deter us from saying that we have heard a correct instance of the work. And as an art-historical property, not a sonic one, it is a property of works, not their performances: so that sound of the work, when played on instruments other than those called

15 The heckelphone is a baritone oboe, named after its inventor, the bassoon maker, Heckel. Richard Strauss calls for the instrument in *Elektra* and *Salome*. I doubt if one *could* play Mozart's concerto on the thing; but we live in hope.

for by the composer, cannot in any way alter or diminish the work's originality.

(c) The artistic attribute of *solving a problem of instrumental balance* is surely an esoteric one; and there is very good reason to think that its perception plays a role in few people's musical experience, at least if perceiving it implies *perceiving that* a composition solves the problem. But if it *is* an essential property of Beethoven's Opus 16, then the recording that Levinson listens to does not preserve *it*, nor, on Levinson's view can it, therefore, preserve the identity of the work. For Beethoven solved the problem of instrumental balance for a wooden and leather fortepiano with only two strings to a note, an oboe, clarinet, and bassoon with no keys to speak of, a different construction, and reeds quite unlike their modern counterparts and a valveless, natural horn. Indeed, players on modern instruments have to "re-solve" the problem of instrumental balance to play Beethoven's work successfully. Musical scruples may lead one to think that a performance of Opus 16 on modern instruments is not a good one; but only metaphysical scruples of the most austere, theory-laden kind could lead one to think that it was no performance at all. Surely musical intuition does not that way tend.

It appears to me that the only really stong intuition we have about the relation of instrumentation to work-identity is that there is no relation at all; and I think an examination of the way musicians talk and think fully bears this out. But if that is not the case, at the very least our intuitions go in *both* directions, are mixed, and musical Platonism is no worse off in this regard than a theory that construes instrumentation as essential to work-identity. Certainly, then, that composers call for their works to be performed on specific instruments cannot be used as evidence against the musical Platonist; and that is sufficient conclusion for my purposes here.

A concluding note: I have argued that the way in which instruments and instructions for instrumentation function in Western music of the early modern and modern eras is perfectly compatible with a Platonistic construal of works and their performances. But I would like also to advance my account of these matters as an independent one: that is to say, as holding whether or not Platonism stands up, in the end, as a viable analysis of works and performances. For it seems to me that however we construe works and performances, the nonessentialist account given here of means of musical performances is the correct one. Performing a Bach fugue with a choir of kazoos may, of itself (although not necessarily), make it a very bad performance; of that there can be no possible doubt. But it cannot, of itself, make the performance a performance of something else. This will be surprising to no one in the world of music. It will only be news to the metaphysicians.[16]

16 An earlier, and abridged version of this essay was read at the Central Division meeting of the American Philosophical Association, in Chicago, 1 May, 1987. I am most grateful to my commentator on that occasion, Jerrold Levinson, for his careful and constructive criticism. The many disagreements I have with Professor Levinson on matters musical have never diminished my great admiration for his work.

Chapter V

Live performances and dead composers: On the ethics of musical interpretation

If Bach were alive today, he would be rolling over in his grave.

Anonymous

Early in his well-known and influential book *Aesthetics: Problems in the Philosophy of Criticism*, Monroe Beardsley reaches the conclusion that "intention . . . does not play any role in decisions about how scores . . . are to be performed."[1] And to the familiar belief that a primary function of the musical performer "consists in determining how the composer intended the music to sound . . . and then realizing that intention," Beardsley replies: "No doubt some performers operate upon this principle, but it can easily be shown that most of them do not."[2] It appears to me that this is false: that composers' intentions *do* play a substantial role in decisions about how scores are to be performed; that *most* performers, as well as musical scholars, *do* operate on the principle of determining and being governed by the intentions of composers, although they labor under the expected quantity of self-deception about which intentions are the composers' and which their own. I propose to argue this case in what follows. In the first section of my paper I will counter what I take to be two distinct arguments that lead Beardsley to his conclusion

1 Monroe C. Beardsley, *Aesthetics: Problems in the Philosophy of Criticism* (New York, 1958), p. 24.
2 Ibid., p. 22.

95

about composers' intentions. In the second section, having urged that, Beardsley's arguments to the contrary notwithstanding, considerations of composers' intentions *do* play a major role in performers' realizations of scores, and, as a matter of fact, weigh very heavily in their decisions regarding them, I shall argue that there are rational grounds for this: that is to say, that intentions not only *do* play a major role but *ought to*. First, then, to Beardsley's arguments.

Beardsley's first main objection to composers' intentions as a criterion of correct or optimal performance – a special case of a more general argument advanced in his earlier article with W. K. Wimsatt – is that the composer's intentions are, for the most part, inaccessible to us and, therefore, *cannot* figure in the performer's decision procedures. He writes: "Since [the performer] must choose among possibilities left open by the score, the criterion he uses must be something besides intention, or in most music he would never be able to decide upon a way of performing it at all."[3] The claim seems to be something like this. Most of the decisions a performer must make regard just those places in the score where the composer has not made his intentions clear. Bach marked the third number of the *Magnificat in D* "adagio," and it is fair to assume that that is the tempo at which he intended it to be performed. But except for this and one other place, the work is (as is usual with Bach) completely devoid of tempo markings. The rest of the tempi, Beardsley would conclude, cannot, therefore, be determined on the basis of what Bach *intended*, for Bach did not make his intentions known in the score. Scores contain some such indications of composers' intentions, but not very many; and the performer's real work starts just where these few indications of intention leave off.

To this the performer and musical scholar would most likely reply that Beardsley has unduly restricted the sources of our knowledge of composers' intentions – particularly with regard to what Leonard Meyer has called the "secondary parameters" – to just those *direct* indications that are most ob-

3 Ibid.

vious: tempo markings, phrasing, dynamics, and the few other directions such as "espressivo," "marcato," and the like, that occur with increasing frequency in scores of the nineteenth and twentieth centuries, and only rarely before that. But that hardly scratches the surface of our sources of knowledge of these secondary parameters and much else that is relevant to the intentions of composers. We possess now a vast and growing knowledge of the historical background, performance practice, and musical instruments of earlier periods, all of which together gives us a far wider and more substantial, albeit indirect, inferential knowledge of the composer's intentions than the obvious indications that Beardsley seems to suggest exhaust the possibilities. As an authority on the performance of "early" music has recently put the point:

> The best performance of, say, a motet by Ockeghem, is only a representation of what someone, the director of the singers, thinks Ockeghem meant [i.e., intended], but any information that we have about how Ockeghem and his contemporaries sang, or in the case of later instrumental music, what the instruments were like and how they were played, cannot but help to make that representation clearer. To my mind this presents the performer with an absolute injunction to try to find out all that can be known about the performance traditions and the sound-world of any piece that is to be performed, and to try to duplicate these as faithfully as possible.[4]

Needless to say, Beardsley is not unaware of the historical research of the last hundred years or more on the performance practice of early music. But he insists that this does *not* constitute a revelation of composers' intentions.

> To restore Bach's cantatas to the way they were heard when his singers and players performed them . . . we must investigate the techniques of performance, vocal and instrumental, that were used in his day. But in conducting these investigations, we are not seeking for the intentions . . . of Bach. We are asking what the music sounded like at a particular time,

4 Alejandro Enrique Planchart, "The Performance of Early Music in America," *Journal of Musicology*, 1 (1982):21.

> not what sounds the composer heard in his own mind. . . .
> [T]he customs of baroque performance were public conven-
> tions, historically discoverable, at least in principle; they did
> not depend upon the intentions of a particular individual.[5]

A number of points can be teased out of this passage, none,
I think, conclusive against the relevance of the composer's
intentions.

First, the performer and musicologist might well agree with
Beardsley that one of the things we want to know, when we
conduct research into the performance of Bach's cantatas, is
how the music sounded in Bach's day. But how does this
preclude the desire also to know Bach's intentions? And surely
one of the ways we can find out how Bach intended his music
to sound is to find out how in fact it sounded. We can reasonably, though not of course infallibly, infer how Bach intended the instrumental obbligato of the third number of the
Magnificat in D to sound by finding out how the two-and
three-keyed oboe d'amore of Bach's day sounded. Why we
should perform it the way Bach intended is of course another
question; and I shall get to that in the following section. But
why we should perform it the way it sounded in Bach's day
is also another question. And it is no more obvious that we
should make a piece of music sound as it would have sounded
in the composer's lifetime than that we should make it sound
the way the composer intended, when there is a divergence,
as sometimes there of course is. (Berlioz complained that most
European orchestras of his day played out of tune: that is
obviously not the way he intended his music to be played.)

Second, Beardsley seems to think that to know what the
composer intended, we must know what sounds the composer heard in his head, and that in doing historical research
"we are asking what the music sounded like at a particular
time, not what sounds the composer heard in his own mind."
Beardsley is correct in believing that there is a connection
between finding out what sounds the composer heard in his
head and what sounds he intended to be heard. But again, I

5 Beardsley, p. 24.

do not see how the desire to know "what the music sounded like at a particular time" precludes the desire to know "what the composer heard in his own mind." Indeed, as before, the one is a means to the other. If a composer hears a piece of keyboard music in his head in E major, what he hears will be different if the keyboard instruments he is used to are given a mean-tone rather than a well-tempered tuning; and we are helping ourselves to know, therefore, what sounds the composer heard in his head when we do historical research into the tuning of keyboard instruments of the seventeenth century. Likewise, the oboe sound Bach heard in his head was doubtless the oboe sound of the instruments he customarily heard. So if we want to know what Bach heard in his head when he composed and orchestrated the third number of the *Magnificat in D*, we had better know what the two- and three-keyed oboe d'amore of Bach's time sounded like. Of course a composer may have an "ideal" sound in his head that exceeds the capabilities of the instruments of his day in certain respects; and that is what encourages instrument makers to improve their products. No doubt Bach would have preferred better intonation from his oboes than he got. But in general, the orchestral sounds Bach heard in his head were those of the instruments he heard in his world. So, clearly, when we do research into the way the instruments of Bach's orchestra sounded, we are, at the same time, doing research into the way music sounded in Bach's head; and, to generalize from the special case, when we "ask what music sounded like at a particular time," we are, ipso facto, asking what the composers of that time heard in their heads.

Finally, Beardsley here, as in "The Intentional Fallacy" and elsewhere, seems much concerned about the "privacy" of intentions, for he contrasts them unfavorably with the public, "discoverable" nature of past performance practice, which, he insists, "did not depend upon the intentions of a particular individual." But for a third time Beardsley seems to be representing as incompatibles things that are quite comfortable with one another. There is nothing necessarily private about an intention: We can, after all, make our inten-

tions known. And the public conventions of baroque performance practice *are* the products of individual intentions of
composers, performers, and audiences. Of course baroque
performance practice is not just the product of J. S. Bach.
Nor, however, are Bach's intentions unconnected with the
conventions of baroque performance practice. Bach ac-
quiesced in a great deal of the performance practice of his
day. Indeed, he made a substantial contribution to it: it was
in fact part of his artistic life's blood. He did not acquiesece
in *all* of it, and he did not leave it unchanged. But taken as a
whole, it is part of the public documentation of Bach's intentions, just as what I write in this essay, and where I publish
it, are public documentation of mine. And just as one can
make reasonable, if not infallible, inferences about my intentions by reading this essay, one can make reasonable, if not
infallible, inferences about Bach's intentions by examining
the historical artifacts of his day, both the written ones and
the others. Intentions are revealed amply by what the inten-
ders leave behind.

The second main objection that Beardsley makes to the relevance of composers' intentions is that we frequently decide
first how the music is to be performed, and then infer the
composer's intentions from *that*. Thus, for instance, in deciding where the accents should be placed in the scherzo of Beethoven's Fifth Symphony, Beardsley writes, "There can be
no appeal to Beethoven; the conductor is after the intensifi-
cation of some quality, a blend of playfulness and sinister-
ness, which it seems to him is best brought out in one way
or the other." His conclusion from this and other instances
is that "we don't decide what should be done after deciding
what Beethoven wished, but the other way around."[6] That
is to say, first we decide what the best or right or proper way
is to perform a piece, on internal, musical grounds, and then
we infer that *that* is what the composer's intention was.

Now as a matter of actual practice, performers do often, at
least when they can, determine the composer's intentions

6 Ibid., p. 23.

about how a piece is to be played, and then comply with them. Often, that is to say, we go *from* intentions *to* performance. But Beardsley is quite right that often – perhaps more often – things go the other way around. We may then ask, in the latter kind of case, what role the composer's intentions play in the process. The obvious answer is none at all. But I am not sure the obvious answer is correct.

Anyone who, as either an amateur or professional, has taken an active part in a practical discussion of how a passage is to be rendered, will recall the following kind of comment being made: "At measure 49 you must bring out the triplet figure in the bass so that it can be recognized as an echo of the main theme. If you don't, the movement just won't hang together. Surely Beethoven must have intended the triplet figure to be played forte, and the right hand somewhat subdued." What I am trying to suggest is that performers generally operate on some kind of principle of "charity" to the effect that the best way is the intended way. But the question is, What finally determines how the music is to be played: that it is the best way or that it is the composer's way? Such comments as the one just fabricated at least *suggest* – although I admit that is *all* they do – that it is the latter. If it were not, then the reference to Beethoven's intentions would be superfluous.

A test case would, of course, be a case in which the composer's intentions and the best way to play the piece diverged. In such a case, what would be decisive, the best way or the composer's way? Common sense would say, perhaps, the best way. But the answer is not so clear. To begin with, performers and musicologists have an almost unconquerable aversion to admitting that the best way could possibly not be the composer's way. No one performs Beethoven's symphonies at the tempi that *Beethoven's* own metronome markings indicate, because they are impossibly bad tempi. But no one is likely to admit, without a fight, that those really are the tempi Beethoven intended – some explanation is always invented of how the markings got fouled up. Thus it is hard to get a real case where "best" and "intended" are believed by musicians to diverge. All we can do is conjecture. But anyone who knows the way performers and musical scholars talk and behave will not find my own conjecture beyond belief: It is that the composer's way would more often than not win out; and even if it did not, it would nevertheless not be easily overridden.

To sum up, it seems to me that nothing Beardsley has said, in arguing against the claim that composers' intentions play a major role in decisions about how music is to be performed, has really dislodged the claim. Further, it seems a palpable fact that composers' intentions weigh heavily – perhaps even are decisive in such decisions. The question I want now to ask is *what* justification, if any, there really is for this.

Let me begin with some distinctions, made recently by Randall R. Dipert, which I want to adopt. There are, Dipert points out, at least three kinds of intentions that a composer might have. "His intentions concerning means of production of sound will be termed *low-level intentions,* which include the type of instrument, fingering, etc. *Middle-level intentions* are those that concern the intended *sound,* such as temperament, timbre, attack, pitch, and vibrato." Finally, we have *"high-level intentions,* which are the effects the composer intends to produce in the listener."[7]

Now as Dipert makes clear, it may well be impossible to realize *all* of a composer's intentions in any one performance, simply because his low-level, middle-level, and high-level intentions may have been, or may have become, incompatible. In such cases we will have to decide which of his intentions we are most anxious to realize and, presumably, high-level intentions take precedence. Thus, Bach's low-level intention, in the third number of the *Magnificat in D,* was to have the instrumental obbligato played on the oboe d'amore of his day, to achieve a certain tone quality (middle-level intention) that, in turn, would have a certain expressive effect on his audience (high-level intention). But *that* tone quality

7 Randall R. Dipert, "The Composer's Intentions: An Examination of Their Relevance for Performance," *Musical Quarterly* 66 (1980):206, 207.

and, hence, the effect Bach wanted, *might* be better achieved today, given the conditions of modern musical performance, by the modern French oboe d'amore, rather than the two- or three-keyed instrument of Bach's day. That being the case, we cannot serve Bach's middle- and high-level intentions most fully without going against his low-level ones. So when, from now on, I talk about the justification for taking intentions of the composer as decisive or powerful considerations in regard to manner of performance, this complication of the notion of composers' intentions, and its implications, should be borne in mind. They are assumed throughout.

It might also be well here to distinguish between a *strong* and a *weak* sense of what a composer does *not* intend, to be borne in mind in what follows. In the strong sense, Bach did *not* intend the instrumental obbligato in the third number of the *Magnificat in D* to be played on the flute or violin of his day; and in the weak sense, he did *not* intend it to be played on the modern French oboe d'amore. Perhaps we could make this clearer by saying that Bach intended the obbligato *not* to be played on the flute or violin of his day, but on the oboe d'amore; whereas he did not intend the obbligato to be played on the modern French oboe d'amore. I would call the former the *strong* sense and the latter the *weak* one, because Bach chose between the flute, violin, and oboe d'amore of his day, and rejected all but the oboe d'amore; whereas he was, of course, in no position to choose between the oboe d'amore of his own day and the modern French instrument. Bach positively did *not* want his obbligato played on the flute or violin; simply by default he did not intend it to be played on the modern French oboe d'amore. This complication, too, will be assumed wherever there is talk about what composers have and (especially) have *not* intended.

Dipert suggests that there are three possible answers to "the question of why we should want to play a piece the way a composer intended to be played."

> The first asserts that we have a moral obligation to the composer to play his music according to his intentions. The second holds that music, like other artifacts of a time and place,

embodies the *Zeitgeist* of that period, and to understand the period properly, the historical artifact (in this case, a performance) must be correctly reconstructed. The third answer – and the one to which I am most sympathetic – claims *generally speaking* that we are likely to perform a piece of greater artistic merit if we follow the composer's intentions than if we do not.[8]

I shall have nothing to say here about the urge for historical accuracy per se; historical accuracy as an intrinsic value will appeal to few. The more compelling argument among performers, musicologists, and concertgoers alike is that historical accuracy, if a value at all, is an instrumental value merely, an avenue to the best performance of the music. Nor will I have anything to say about the argument that realizing the composer's intentions will usually result in a better performance. I too, like Dipert, am very sympathetic with this claim, and I believe it provides *one* very compelling reason for honoring the composer's intentions. Anyone who has ever heard Handel's oratorios or the *Mass in B Minor* performed something like the way they were intended to be will never again wish to hear them performed with booming contraltos, pious tempi, a choir of trombones, and a cast of thousands. But this defense, clearly, does not recognize composers' intentions as *decisive*. They are only sought for the purpose of gaining an optimal performance, on the assumption that, generally speaking, music sounds better when played the way the composer intended it to be. And if some piece sounded better performed in a way not intended by the composer, either in the weak or the strong sense, that would be decisive against the intention.[9] But, as I have said, I think

8 Ibid., p. 212.

9 One might, perhaps, argue after the manner of a rule utilitarian that although some pieces of music sound better in some respects if the composer's performing intentions are ignored, in general following the composer's intentions come what may will decrease the chance of ignoring them where observance would make the music sound better. Ignoring them on occasion, even when the occasion is propitious, will in the long run tend to encourage ignoring them when the occasion is wrong, thus making on the whole for more bad performances than good. Even here, however, where following the composer's intentions is made a hard and fast rule, it is the result, not the rule, that decides the issue after all.

there is a strong urge on the part of musicians to honor composers' intentions per se, an urge so strong that they will often, if not always, honor them over all considerations of musical aesthetics. And the conventionalist sulk, common among musicians, to the effect that "It can't be the composer's intention, because the other way sounds better," only reinforces the impression that there is an almost unconquerable urge to bring performance into compliance with intention, if not at the expense of aesthetics, then at the expense of logic. There is an almost missionary zeal here, something that can only be described as a moral imperative; and that, as well as the process of elimination, points of course to the only alternative left: a defense of honoring the composer's intentions on moral grounds. That, indeed, is the defense I want to give.

My model for this defense will be the familiar one of morals as, at least in part, a system of (perhaps conflicting) duties and obligations. I shall say, then, that along with such obvious duties as telling the truth, keeping promises, not causing unnecessary pain, and so on, we have an obligation to honor when possible the wishes and intentions of the dead, a special case of this last being the obligation to honor the performing intentions of dead composers.[10] We can think of the composer's score, in this regard, much as the dying words or written will of the deceased. That this is not such a bizarre suggestion can be seen from, among other things, the fact that we often refer to the body of a composer's work as his musical or artistic "testament." Just as we feel a strong obligation to honor the wishes of the dead, even when prudence and convenience recommend that we ignore them, and are quite convinced that the dead are beyond feeling the pain of disappointment that thwarted wishes and desires cause to the living, so we feel a strong obligation to honor the dead composer's intentions as to how his music is to be per-

---

10 I should point out that expressing my view in terms of possibly conflicting moral duties and obligations is not essential to the main argument of my essay. *Any* moral theory will do, *just so long as there is allowance made in it for duties and obligations to the dead.*

formed, whether indicated directly in his score or indirectly in some other way, even when musical prudence, in the form of a better way to perform it, might beckon us. At considerable expense and inconvenience to herself, a confirmed atheist, with no belief whatever in an afterlife or the immortality of the soul, will travel from Peking to Peoria with the corpse of a loved one to grant a dying request. And for what *other* reason than a strong moral commitment to honoring the wishes of the dead? It is no more surprising, I submit, that the same commitment might cause us to make a far less painful and costly sacrifice of an aesthetic kind to honor a composer's wish that his piece be played adagio, when a slightly quicker pace sounds right to us.

But at this point a serious objection to my argument is likely to be registered. Granted, it will be argued, that many (or perhaps most) of us do feel strong obligations to honor the wishes of the dead, this by no means implies that such obligations in fact exist. The belief that such obligations exist may, indeed, provide a psychological explanation of why the lady from Peking took all that trouble to get a corpse to Peoria, why a performer feels such reverence toward a composer's intentions that he might perform a piece adagio even though he really thinks it goes better a little bit on the andante side, or why I feel such outrage when one of the *Leonore* overtures is stuck in between the last two scenes of *Fidelio*, no matter how grand and moving it is. If, however, there is no justification for these moral beliefs, then the thing to do is not to continue to be governed by them, at considerable trouble to ourselves and to others; rather, we must give them up as basically misguided – relics of a superstitious belief that the dead watch over us. And, surely, the argument continues, there *is* no justification for them: we have no obligations to the dead, but only to the living (and perhaps to those who will be the living at some time in the future). In dismissing the moral defense for honoring dead composers' performing intentions pretty much out of hand, Dipert indeed relies heavily on what might appear to be the out-and-out absurdity of thinking that we can have very much of a duty, if any at all, to the dead, and refers us, in passing, to a passage in Aristotle.[11] It would be instructive here, as always, to see what he has to say.

In *Nicomachean Ethics* I.11, Aristotle writes: "That the fortunes of his descendants and of all those near and dear to him do not affect the happiness of a dead man at all, seems too unfeeling a view and contrary to the prevailing opinion." But he concludes that

> if any good or evil reaches them at all, it must be something weak and negligible . . ., or at least something too small and insignificant to make the unhappy happy or to deprive the happy of their bliss. The good as well as the bad fortunes of their friends seem, then, to have some effect upon the dead, but the nature and magnitude of the effect is such as not to make the happy unhappy or to produce any similar changes. [12]

Aristotle does not draw the expected moral conclusion from this, and for good reason, as we shall see in a moment; but surely we can do it for him. If the effects of our actions on the dead are vanishingly small, then so must be our duties and obligations to them. And if, as I and many others believe, our actions have no effect at all on the dead, who are beyond happiness or unhappiness, then how can we have any duties or obligations *at all* to them? How can good or evil reach them at all, if they can *experience* neither? I have duties to the living because they are in a position to experience the results of my moral observances and omissions. But what can be the moral or immoral cash value of a broken promise to the dead? What inconvenience can it cause? What disappointment arouse? Surely, just as the dead are beyond thinking and feeling, perception and pain, happiness and unhappiness, they are beyond wickedness as well.

As persuasive as this argument might seem, readers of the essay "Death," by Thomas Nagel, will have what seems to

11 Dipert, p. 213.
12 Aristotle, *Nicomachean Ethics* 1101a22–b9, trans. Martin Ostwald (Indianapolis and New York, 1962), pp. 26–7.

me to be an even more persuasive reply. For consider the assumption on which the argument is based. That we have no duties to the dead, because they cannot experience the results of our actions toward them, is simply a special case of the precept that "what you don't know can't hurt you." But think of what this means.

> It means that even if a man is betrayed by his friends, ridiculed behind his back, and despised by people who treat him politely to his face, none of it can be counted as a misfortune for him so long as he does not suffer as a result. It means that a man is not injured if his wishes are ignored by the executor of his will, or if, after his death, the belief becomes current that all the literary works on which his fame rests were written by his brother, who died in Mexico at the age of 28.[13]

Or, we might add, if his oratorios are reorchestrated by every well-meaning composer and conductor entrusted with their performance.

But this cannot be right. Nor did Aristotle believe that it was, which is precisely why he did not draw the moral conclusion one might have expected him to draw from the passage in the *Nicomachean Ethics* quoted above. For in the preceding chapter, in fact, he had already expressed the view that "to some extent good and evil really exist for a dead man, just as they may exist for a man who lives without being conscious of them, for example, honors and disgraces, and generally the successes and failures of his children and descendants."[14] And that perhaps explains why, as Leibniz put it, "in man there is a certain concern for dignity and propriety which . . . leads us to look after our reputations, even beyond the point where this serves our needs and beyond the end of life."[15]

It is an injury to a man, then, to betray him, even if he never knows, and hence never experiences the pain of be-

---

13 Thomas Nagel, "Death," in James Rachels, ed., *Moral Problems*, 3d ed. (New York, 1979), p. 453.

14 Aristotle, 1100a18–21, trans. Ostwald, pp. 23–4.

15 G. W. Leibniz, *New Essays on Human Understanding*, trans. Peter Remnant and Jonathan Bennett (Cambridge, England, 1981), pp. 93–4.

trayal or its discovery. And it does not matter whether the betrayal is never known because his friends keep the secret during his lifetime, or because it is committed after his death. To quote Nagel again: "Someone who holds that all goods and evils must be temporarily assignable states of the person may of course try to bring difficult cases into line by pointing to the pleasure or pain that more complicated goods and evils cause. Loss, betrayal, deception, and ridicule are on this view bad because people suffer when they learn of them." But, Nagel points out, "the natural view is that the discovery of betrayal makes us unhappy because it is bad to be betrayed – not that betrayal is bad because its discovery makes us unhappy." Further, and much to the present purpose, "if this is correct, there is a simple account of what is wrong with breaking a deathbed promise. It is an injury to the dead man."[16] That the reason a man does not know, or therefore suffer, from the breaking of a promise to him is that he is *dead* is irrelevant. This broken promise is an injury to a living man, irrespective of his finding out or not. The inability of a dead man to know or suffer from the breaking of a promise cannot, therefore, make it benign. And if we can injure the dead, then we surely have the obligation to refrain from doing so when we can.

That the concept of obligation to the dead may still seem paradoxical, in spite of these considerations, is only to be expected; and perhaps the most paradoxical part of all arises from the difficulty in identifying just *who* it is we owe the obligation to, and *who* will be harmed by its nonfulfillment. For death is not just another state or condition that a person finds himself or herself in: it is no condition at all. Death is the total annihilation of the subject; no "person" remains after death for us to harm or have obligations to.

One way, perhaps, to get around this metaphysical problem of the lack of a subject, suggested by Joel Feinberg, "is to think of all harm done to men and women as convenient elliptical references to, and identification of, the interest that

16 Nagel, pp. 453–4, 455.

was thwarted or set back." Adopting this notion of harm: "Although *he* [the dead person] no longer exists, we can refer to his earlier goals (as a matter of identification) as *his* interests, and *they* were the interests directly harmed by his death," and, more relevantly, the interests that remain to be harmed or forwarded after his death by those who survive him. And so: "When death [or an event after death] thwarts an interest, the interest is harmed, and the harm can be ascribed to the man who is no more, just as his debts can be charged to his estate."[17]

Of course, not *all* of a person's interests survive his or her demise. "The interests that die with a person are those that can no longer be helped or harmed by posthumous events. These include most of his self-regarding interests, those based, for example, on desires for personal achievement and personal enjoyment." But Feinberg continues: "Because the objects of a person's interests are usually wanted or aimed-at events that occur outside of his immediate experience and at some future time, the area of a person's good or harm is necessarily wider than his subjective experience and his biological life." It is clear, then, that although some of a person's interests perish with that person, others endure. "These include his publicly oriented and other-regarding interests, and also those 'self-centered' interests in being thought of in a certain way. Posthumous harm occurs when the deceased's interest is thwarted at a time subsequent to his death." And Feinberg concludes, as do Aristotle, Nagel, and, I think, common moral sensibility, that for posthumous harm to a person's interests to occur, "the awareness of the subject is no more necessary than it is for harm to occur to certain of his interests at or before death."[18] It cannot, then, be an argument against the moral defense of honoring the dead composer's performance intentions that we cannot have obligations to the dead because the dead cannot suffer or rejoice, are, in fact, beyond all experience whatever. Thus, it seems

17 Joel Feinberg, "Harm and Self-Interest," in *Rights, Justice and the Bounds of Liberty* (Princeton, 1980), pp. 61, 62, 64.
18 Ibid., pp. 65, 68.

to me, the most serious objection to the belief that we have an at least prima facie obligation to honor the dead composer's performance intentions is defeated.

But showing that we can and *do* have obligations to dead people does not, ipso facto, show that we have obligations to honor the intentions of dead composers concerning the way their works are to be performed. Perhaps we just don't in fact have such obligations to composers, for reasons other than that the composers are dead. I do not have the time here to canvass this proposal fully. I will conclude my defense, however, by briefly considering two further arguments by Dipert, each of which, I take it, is meant to be a reductio ad absurdum of the claim that we have duties or obligations to honor the intentions of dead composers. They are as follows. First, "there are many composers whose music we rarely or never play. Certainly they had intentions to have their music performed . . ., intentions which we guiltlessly ignore." And second, "there are intentions of even great composers which we have disobeyed, or would disobey if we could; for example, composers' often-expressed wishes to have scores destroyed."[19]

Now the answer to both of these supposed reductios is the same; and it is, in fact, the same answer one would give to the objection that we cannot have a prima facie obligation to tell the truth, since we would then have to tell Simon Legree that Eliza is hiding in the attic. The well-known answer is that duties can be overridden by other and stronger ones; but this does not show, even at the time they are overridden, that they are not real obligations. Let us look, in turn, at our obligation to perform the works of Johann Stamitz, as well as those of Joseph Haydn, and at our predecessors' obligations, if the respective stories are true, to destroy the manuscripts of Virgil's *Aeneid* and Mendelssohn's *Italian Symphony*.

Johann Stamitz labored long and hard at the practice of musical composition. Were it not for his pioneering efforts

19 Dipert, p. 213.

toward the development of what we now think of as the classical style, Haydn could not have done all of the things that
he did that we justly revere above the works of Stamitz the
elder. Surely we *do* owe it to Stamitz to give his music a hearing from time to time, and we do the man an injury by ignoring him. There is nothing whatever absurd in the suggestion, as Dipert seems to think. But *of course* we are not obliged
to perform his music as frequently as Haydn's, any more
than we are obliged to spend as much time and money finding a cure for the common cold as on cancer research. A half
hour of Stamitz is pleasurable and enlightening; three hours
is a mind-deadening experience. On purely utilitarian
grounds, if for no other reason, our obligation to Stamitz's
intention to have his music played is overridden – but it exists as a real obligation nonetheless.

As for the alleged intentions of Virgil and Mendelssohn
that the manuscripts of the *Aeneid* and the *Italian Symphony*
be destroyed our ancestors had an obligation to both of them
to comply, as would anyone receiving a deathbed declara-
tion concerning the disposition of the testator's property. But
they had another obligation as well to refrain from injuring
us, their posterity, by depriving us of those wonderful works,
and to refrain from injuring Virgil and Mendelssohn by di-
minishing their reputations in ill-considered and irrevocable
acts of vandalism. In short, the obligation to honor the intentions of dead composers is *defeasible*. But that should not be
very surprising. So is the Sixth Commandment. I do not suggest, by claiming that we have an obligation to honor the
performance intentions of dead composers, that we must
honor them come what may. Handel intended many of the
parts of his operas to be sung by castrated men, and they
will never sound the way they should without the castrati.
We quite rightly ignore Handel's intentions on moral grounds.
Beethoven *apparently* intended his symphonies to go at
"strange" tempi. There is some dispute about what Beethoven's metronome markings really mean – the device was,
after all, in the early stages of its development. But if indeed
it turns out that the numbers don't lie, and if those tempi

really deprive us of truly enjoyable and musically satisfactory performances, then Beethoven's intentions are defeated on moral as well as on aesthetic grounds: on aesthetic grounds because the musical price we must pay to honor his intentions is too high; on moral grounds for the obvious reason that we owe *some* consideration, at least, to the maximization of musical pleasure in the auditors of these works.

Now it may seem to some that, in claiming our obligations to the intentions of dead composers are defeasible, I have given with one hand only to take away with the other. But that would only be the case if I permitted the overriding conditions to be so numerous and trivial as to render the obligations impotent. if I were to say that we have an obligation to refrain from doing *x*, but that that obligation could be defeated by, among other things, my simply feeling like doing *x*, then I have indeed completely emasculated, for practical if not theoretical purposes, the concept of obligation in this particular case. That is not my intent, however, in the present instance. I am *not* saying that our obligations to honor the performance intentions of dead composers are very easily overridden. Indeed, just because performers and musicologists believe they are not easily overridden, they resist the suggestion that the performance intentions of composers be overridden or ignored with a passion hard to explain if the *only* thing at stake were how the music will sound. It does not nullify our obligation to obey the Sixth Commandment to admit that it is defeated by our right to kill an assailant in protecting our lives or the lives of others. Likewise, it surely does not reduce to nothing our obligations to the performance intentions of dead composers to maintain that *sometimes* – how frequently and under what circumstances I will not venture to say – they are overridden by aesthetic considerations, or moral ones, or a combination of the two. As Ruth Barcan Marcus has forcefully argued, "Wherever circumstances are such that an obligation to do *x* and an obligation to do *y* cannot as a matter of circumstance by fulfilled, the obligations to do each are not erased, even though they are unfulfillable. Mitigating circumstances may provide an explanation, an excuse, or a defense, but . . . this is not the same as denying one of the obligations altogether."[20]

To sum up, then, I claim that we have a strong obligation to honor the performance intentions of dead composers. This is a special case of our obligation to comply, where we can, with the wishes and intentions of the dead; and this obligation has its source in our duty to refrain from injuring the interests of others. Arguments to the contrary notwithstanding, it *is* possible to injure the interests of the dead. Our obligation to honor the performance intentions of dead composers is defeasible; but, nonetheless, this obligation is usually strong enough to justify our honoring the performance intentions of dead composers even when doing so will make the music sound worse than if the intentions were ignored. Finally, the peculiar zeal with which performers pursue the performance intentions of dead composers even when the music may be the worse for it, as well as their extreme reluctance to admit the possibility of intentions diverging from optimal performance, can best be explained by their strong belief in an ethical calling vis-à-vis the performance intentions of the composers whose works they interpret.

I have said nothing so far about the very important and sticky question of how we are to interpret the wishes and intentions of the dead in light of posthumous contingencies that they cannot, of course, be aware of. It is frequently suggested that one fulfills one's obligations to the wishes and intentions of a dead person if one does what he or she *would have* wished or *would have* intended were he or she now alive and cognizant of present conditions. And this kind of argument is frequently appealed to by musical performers who take liberties, both small and great, with the musical text. Thus, conductors have insisted that they are indeed honoring Handel's wishes and intentions by reorchestrating the oratorios, because it is what Handel would have done him-

20 Ruth Barcan Marcus, "Moral Dilemmas and Consistency," *Journal of Philosophy*, 77 (1980): 126.

self had he been alive to know and appreciate modern musical instruments.

Such considerations are important, and open up areas of discussion that cannot be pursued here. It must suffice to point out that the form of the argument itself is perfectly consistent with what I have urged in the preceding pages. I have not suggested that we cannot reinterpret the wishes and intentions of dead composers in light of present musical conditions. On the contrary, I think that we have to do so, as in any other situation in which we feel an obligation to the dead, and must determine what exactly that obligation is, or how best to fulfill not just its letter but its spirit. The practical pitfall in such counterfactuals, I need hardly say, is that they can easily become irrefutable apologetics for doing anything you please. If the composer said *p* in 1720, who can prove that he wouldn't have said not-*p* in 1988? So if you want to play the *Art of the Fugue* with a quartet of kazoos, why not? Surely Bach *might have* – which easily slips into *would have* – intended his work for those instruments, had he only lived long enough to hear and fall in love with them. Nevertheless, that there are unscrupulous ways of applying a principle does not render the principle either useless or invalid; nor can we, I think, dispense with the present one without rendering the whole notion of honoring the wishes and intentions of dead composers (or anyone else) completely nonsensical. Bach could not have intended his *Art of the Fugue* to be played on a modern replica of a Baroque organ; yet some of us do think we are carrying out the spirit of his intentions by doing so today.

In any event, what these considerations indicate – what I have been arguing all along – is how deeply entrenched in the interpreter's thinking composers' intentions really are: so much so that, no matter what route he or she takes to the right performance, we seem to arrive, either by logic or illogic, at the composer's intentions as a criterion of great, and sometimes decisive, significance.

And if we can, at least in principle, think of the composer's way and the best way as logically distinct, my conclusion is that sometimes we owe it to a dead composer to play his music as he intended, rather than in what we may think is the best way possible, because we have real obligations to the interests of the dead. Perhaps that conclusion may seem eccentric. Nevertheless, each time I hear the third movement of the *Magnificat in D* going even slightly more briskly than adago, even though I have a nagging feeling that it sounds better that way, I see the stern visage of the Cantor of Leipzig before my mind's eye, and think to myself: "If Bach were alive today to hear *this,* he would be rolling over in his grave."

Chapter VI

On the concept of the "historically authentic" performance

What has knowledge of the history of music to do with its performance? Not so long ago the answer would have been "Nothing." And not so very long before that the history of music was a non-subject.

Today the situation is radically altered. As Joseph Kerman writes in his recent, and refreshingly irreverent survey of the current musicological scene,

> Musicology . . . has a whole long catalogue of music to contribute to the repertory and a definite theory as to how it should be performed. The catalogue consists mostly of "early music" – early by comparison with that of the so-called standard repertory – but also includes later works . . . which never got into the repertory or else dropped out. All this music, according to musicological doctrine, should be presented – as far as this is possible – according to the reconstructed performing traditions and conditions of its own time and place.[1]

This performance idea, nurtured by the theory and practice of modern musicology, has come to be referred to generally as the concept of "historical authenticity" in performance.

Two questions have quite naturally arisen, in the musicological and music-critical literature, with regard to the historically authentic performance. *What* is it? And, of course, *why* is it; that is to say, *why* should we want a "historically authentic" performance, whatever we may construe it to be?

---

1 Joseph Kerman, *Contemplating Music: Challenges to Musicology* (Cambridge, MA: Harvard University Press, 1985), p. 184.

These questions are, needless to say, intimately related, and, regrettably, all too often inadequately distinguished by those who ask and attempt to answer them. I shall be dealing here primarily with the first question. I want to examine closely the concept of the authentic performance – this for two reasons. First, because I believe that too little attention has been paid to its logical niceties by all concerned. And, second, because by going too quickly from the former question to the latter, the attempt to find reasons for the authentic performance, or against it, being based on an inaccurate idea of what an authentic performance implies, ends in an entirely unsatisfactory conclusion which, in turn, leads to renewed, inevitably futile dispute.

Insofar as it is possible, then, this essay will be concerned exclusively with the question of what it might mean for a musical performance to be historically authentic, and I will ignore, insofar as it is possible, the question of whether or not a historically authentic performance is a musically desirable goal to attain. But the rider, "insofar as it is possible," is meant to give fair warning that the two questions cannot be prised entirely apart; and so, at least in a tangential way, the *why*, as well as the *what*, will have to be present.

AUTHENTICITY AND INTENTION

It may not seem obvious why, on first reflection; but often the concept of historical authenticity in performance is identified with the realizing of the composer's intentions. Richard Taruskin quite correctly observes that "the usual answer" to the question of why we should (as Wimsatt and Beardsley put it) "consult the oracle" "is that we want our performance to be authentic."[2] I will not enter here into the haze of problems and perplexities that surrounds the concept of compositional intent, for I want, rather, to explore a

2 Richard Taruskin, "The Musicologist and the Performer," in *Musicology in the 1980s: Methods, Goals, Opportunities*, ed. Claude V. Palisca (New York: Da Capo Press, 1982), p. 106. I am not, by the way, suggesting that Taruskin endorses that answer: He does not.

different approach to historical authenticity, and do not want to get involved with irrelevant considerations, interesting though they certainly are. But it might be useful to point out, in passing, two distinct advantages that accrue to the identification of authenticity with intention.

It is frequently advanced, as a reductio ad absurdum of the "authentic performance" movement that it endorses "bad" performances by endorsing, to use Kerman's description, the reconstructed performing conditions and traditions of the music's own time and place. For, as Charles Rosen observes, in his article, "Should Music Be Played 'Wrong'?," the title of which just about sums up the argument,

> Like most things, music is generally badly played. . . . I have heard a tape of a new composition in which most of the rhythms were at least slightly wrong, the players were rarely quite together, and often they forgot to come in at all. The composer lamented that if this tape were exhumed in the twenty-second century, students would conclude that it represented the performance practice of the twentieth century. As a matter of fact, they would be quite right.[3]

Rosen's point, of course, which is reinforced by an impressive bill of particulars, documenting the more horrendous practices of *outré temps*, is that if we are committed, without qualification, to the reconstruction of the performance practice of any period whatever, we are committed to the perpetuation of what is bad in that practice as well as what is good, under the quite reasonable assumption that, on *any* reasonable standard of good and bad, *any* performance practice will contain both.

What this points up is that the reconstruction of performance practice, like any purely historical reconstruction, is non-normative, value free. But the concept of compositional intention is not; and that is what allows it to circumvent Rosen's objection. For, I take it, we have a right to assume that the composer intends, among other things, the best possible

3 Charles Rosen, "Should Music be Played 'Wrong'?," *High Fidelity* 21,5 (May, 1971): p. 55.

performance of his or her work. Indeed, that is what, presumably, all of the specific intentions add up to. If, therefore, we construe the historically authentic performance to
be identical with the performance intended by the composer
(to the extent that the composer had specific intentions in
this regard), we need not include any "bad" performance
practice. We need not play Berlioz' music out of tune, if that
was the practice of his times, for we can reasonably assume
that he did not intend it to be played that way. Nor, to take
a more interesting case, need we conduct eighteenth-century
music by "beating a rolled-up sheet of music paper on the
desk to keep the orchestra in time," even though, as Rosen
points out, "this practice was traditional and part of the immediately audible experience of eighteenth-century opera."[4]
Indeed, we may even assume that the eighteenth-century
composer intended the music to be conducted this way; for,
of course, this was an intermediate intention, serving the
primary intention of keeping the orchestra in time, in the
most effective possible way. And if we can think of a better,
more effective way, we *are* realizing the composer's intention
more fully, under the methodological assumption that the
composer intended his or her music to be played as well as
possible.

A second objection to the historically authentic performance, even more obviously avoided by identifying authenticity with intention, is that it is a mistake to assume composers acquiesce in all aspects of the performance practice of
their time, even when it is not obviously bad practice, and,
therefore, that in being authentic, we are violating the composers' intentions and wishes as to the performance of their
works. As Taruskin correctly surmises, "performance styles
in the past, no less than in the present, had their proponents
and their detractors,"[5] and it is surely likely that at least some
composers were among the detractors. Authenticity and intention, then, may frequently be at cross purposes; and it is

4 Ibid.
5 Richard Taruskin, Daniel Leach-Wilkinson, Nicholas Temperly, and Peter Dow-
  ney, "The limits of authenticity: a discussion," *Early Music* (1984): p. 12.

intention, so the argument goes, that should be honored. But, needless to say, if authenticity and intention are identified, this conflict cannot occur, and the objection to authenticity is quite blunted.

Recognizing, then, these distinct advantages of authenticity as intention, let us briefly touch on some of the supposed difficulties. The mere mention of the word "intention" in regard to any art-critical or art-theoretical question is liable to elicit, these days, the most violent reaction, as if one had just dropped a snake in a crowded room, so discredited has the concept become in some circles, where it is deemed as metaphysically suspect and closed to human scrutiny as the will of God or the *Ding an sich*. Let me just state what seem to me to be some simple, and reassuring truths about intentions in general, composers' intentions in particular. We all have intentions; and so did our ancestors, as far back as we wish to trace the history of homo sapiens. Intentions are not mysterious or inaccessible, either in principle or in practice. They are inferred, or known directly, through actions, documents, circumstances, both present and past; through art works, artifacts, fossils, and ways of living. If the intentions of dead composers cannot, at least some of them, be known, then the intentions of dead kings and ministers cannot be known, or the intentions of dead philosophers and scientists; so a good deal of what we think of as political and intellectual history goes up the spout along with what we think of as a legitimate part of the history of music. But this is a reductio ad absurdum. Unless we are raising the kinds of doubts about other minds that are raised in epistemology seminars, we should be no less comfortable with knowledge claims, or at least well-founded conjectures, about the intentions of Bach or Dufay than with similar claims or conjectures about the intentions of Newton or Archimedes, Henry VIII or Solon. And if we are raising such skeptical doubts, then we might just as well give up music history, or the history of anything else, across-the-board. Because skepticism about the external world is bound to follow, on similar grounds, in the wake of skepticism about the existence of other minds, so soon after

Beethoven loses his intentions, he is going to lose his sketch-books as well. What I am suggesting, then, is that just so long as the musicologist puts no more constraints on the concept of knowledge, or well-founded belief, when it comes to the intentions of composers, than he or she puts on these concepts when it comes to any other factual question in music history, or anywhere else, for that matter, composers' intentions will be seen to be neither metaphysically nor epistemically suspect.

For the rest, the specific problems that seem to bother musicologists and critics about the concept of the composer's intentions seem to me to be a mélange of non sequiturs and misunderstandings, many of which devolve on the mistake of confusing what I would call a "regulative" concept with what they seem to take to be a singularly impractical "practical" one. But, as I say, I do not want to get caught up in the intention muddle here. Rather, I want to make out what I think are some important points about historically authentic performance that would only be obscured by the flap over intention, and are better explicated using another concept of authenticity.

AUTHENTICITY AND RECONSTRUCTION

Let us revert, then, to Kerman's way of putting it: the reconstructed performing traditions and conditions of the music's own time and place. How can we cash that out as a description of the historically authentic performance? To begin with, we are faced immediately with the problem, avoided, as we have seen, by authenticity as intention, of playing the music "wrong." We must assume, therefore, that any attempt to reconstruct a performance tradition of the past, for the purpose of playing real music to real audiences, and not just as a scholarly exercise, will be an attempt to reconstruct only the "optimal" one. We do not want to reconstruct an incompetent performance – at least not one incompetent by the standards of *its* time as well as ours.

For starters, let us say, then, that a historically authentic performance of a musical work will reproduce, as closely as possible, how an *optimal* performance of the work would have sounded in its time. (If we stick literally to this, by the way, it would mean, paradoxically, that the modern players of old instruments, even if they managed to play them "better" than anyone could play them in the period in which these instruments were used, would have to play them only as well as the best players of that period.)

A second consideration is this. We will have to ask, when we state our formula, about whom we are talking when we talk about a performance sounding the way it would have at some historical period: that is to say, we will have to ask, *to whom* it sounded "the" way it did. For, clearly, a performance will sound different to different auditors: different to an educated listener than to an uneducated one; different to an Italian than to a German; and, most important different to *me* than to a contemporary of the music. For *I* can hear a piece of music (say) as anticipating the harmonic techniques of Brahms or Wagner; and Bach could not. No matter how hard I try to reproduce the "sound" of an eighteenth-century performance, it will, it seems, never be the "sound" of an eighteenth-century performance in a way that is so musically deep and significant that even after the last treatise is perused, the last instrument reconstructed and mastered, the last notation deciphered, we will still be light-years away from an "historically authentic performance."

Imagine the following extreme science fiction example. With the help of H. G. Wells and Stephen Spielberg, I return, via time machine, to eighteenth-century Leipzig, just in time to hear a performance of the *St. Matthew Passion* under the direction of the master himself. I think this is the kind of conceptual ideal that many perpetrators of "authentic historical performance" have. But this does not, for the reasons rehearsed above, give me the opportunity of hearing an authentic performance in the sense of one that would sound the way it sounded in Bach's time, *if* we mean by that the "sound" that was in the ears of Bach or his contemporaries. Undaunted, however, I obtain, this time through the good offices of Robert Louis Stevenson, a drug that completely obliterates my twentieth-century self and provides me with an eighteenth-century one, "memories" and all. Back again I go; now I am an "eighteenth-century" man hearing Bach performing the *St. Matthew Passion*. The trouble is, in a quite obvious sense, I am no longer myself. *I'm* not finding out how Baroque music sounded to Baroque ears because I have turned myself into someone else: into a Baroque man.

Not to worry, though; I have anticipated all of that. The drug is of a temporary kind, and wears off soon after my time machine returns me to 1986. So although I can't hear Baroque music with Baroque ears, I can *remember* what Baroque music sounds like to Baroque ears, since I was so recently a Baroque bloke. (*Recently?*)

However, it should be clear that that stratagem is not going to work. Because all I will be doing when I *remember* hearing Bach's performance is what I would be doing if I were remembering any other performance: that is to say, hearing the music running through my head, as best I can. And I will be mentally "hearing" it through twentieth-century ears of the mind. I am up against a metaphysical stone wall.

I have gone through this little exercise in musical science fiction partly for the sheer fun of it – but partly, too, to keep it very prominent before our minds that "historically authentic performances," whatever they are, are for twentieth-century audiences, and there are times when, it seems to me, people who talk up authentic performance say things that imply something else. Be that as it may, perhaps I should conclude this train of thought with some consolation, if consolation is needed. It is *not* a misfortune not to be able to hear Bach with the ears of his time. If it is even *intelligible* to conceive of it as a goal, it is a goal that no sensible music lover should want to achieve. For what Bach or Josquin means to me, in terms of appreciation and greatness, neither could possibly have meant for his contemporaries. Were I a contemporary of Bach, chances are I wouldn't enjoy his music much at all, let alone see it as one of the deepest and most sublime experiences music has to offer; for we all know, if only from Nicholas Slonimsky's *Lexicon of Musical Invective*, that contemporary audiences, with few exceptions, have trouble appreciating the music of their times that later achieves the status of "masterpiece." This, just to remind us again that it is the performance that is supposed to be reconstructed, not us. With that in mind, let us see if we can get a better handle on "authenticity."

AUTHENTICITIES

If we understand the necessary limits, and inherent logical absurdities of the time travel model of the historically authentic performance, we can safely use it, I think, as some kind of ideal, or regulative principle, that really does capture, conceptually, what at least one very pervasive notion of historical authenticity is. So I shall assume, for purposes of argument, that what we mean by a historically authentic performance of a given piece of music is one sonically like a performance we would hear if we were transported by Wells, Spielberg, et al., to the right time and place.

Again, though, we must ask who the "we" is in our formula. It is not a person of that time and that place; that we have already established. But *who?* Clearly, the sounds that Leonard Bernstein would hear if he were our time traveler, would be different from those a completely untutored music lover would hear: that finely tuned, superbly educated ear would hear far more than the average concert goer's. For argument's sake, I will simply stipulate the "we" as *me:* somewhat more musically perceptive and educated than the average concert goer, some orders of magnitude less so than Leonard Bernstein. I shall mean, then, by a historically authentic performance of a musical work, a performance sonically like one I would hear if I were at the right historical time and place for performances of that particular work, and were hearing an optimal performance of it. I should also add the necessary rider that we mean to exclude from our notion of "sonically like," nonmusical sounds that might accompany such a performance: the squeaking of eighteenth-century buckleshoes, or the sound of a bassoon player scratching underneath his wig. There certainly may be an area of uncertainty here, of sounds that on one view might be musical, and on another not. Robbins Landon, to instance a case in point, thinks that the sound of the harpsichord continuo is a musical characteristic of late Haydn symphonies, when performed "authentically," whereas Rosen thinks it is merely an unmusical artifact, produced by a method that Haydn needed to keep his orchestra together, and that we do not need because we have found a better way to do it.[6] This is, from the musical point of view, a nontrivial question; but it is a question of historical fact, and musical judgment, best left to musicians and musicologists to answer, *if they can*. It raises no point of principle about the *concept* of the historically authentic performance.

However, there certainly is another question, of real substance and principle, about our phrase "sonically like." Do we mean *exactly* like? If we do, the quest for authenticity is certainly vain. For even if there were no reason, in principle, why we could not achieve a performance that was sonically "exactly like" a period performance, in practice it is, of course, a will-o'-the-wisp. So, surely, if we are to reasonably construe our phrase "sonically like," we must construe "like" as "approximately like," "something like," or something of the kind, and allow, therefore, for *degrees* of authenticity. We will want, then, to say that some performances are more authentic, historically, than others. We will want to say in what respects some performance is historically authentic and some other not. A most important implication of all this is that we will come to see authenticity, for all practical purposes, as a trade-off: that is to say, one will have to choose in which respects one wants one's performance to be authentic, because, in practice, various authenticity-producing features are incompatible with one another. When one realizes this, it seems to me to be liberating, and to redeem the notion of "historical authenticity": to rescue it from what some per-

6 See Rosen, "Should Music Be Played 'Wrong'?," p. 57.

forming musicians see as pedantry without discrediting it as a viable performing concept.

Clearly, the time travel model of historically authentic performance throws the doors wide open to every kind of historical research into the way music was performed in any given period, and the kinds of physical means at the disposal of performers. It sanctions the use of old and reconstructed instruments, the following of instructions about how to phrase, ornament, articulate, and so forth, that can be culled from treatises and documents of the period. It licenses, indeed, the whole institution that has come to be called the "early music movement," loudly trumpeted (on valveless trumpets, of course) by its supporters as the only way to perform, just as stridently put down by the so-called musical establishment as the work of pedants and philistines (although it is beginning to be a real question these days as to which group has the right to "establishment" status: Steinway and Co. may be running scared).

But before we throw away our Steinways, and tear the keys off our clarinets and oboes, it might be well to think a little bit more carefully about just what, *exactly*, our musical time traveler will hear if he or she returns to the scene of the crime. Let's go back, then, to Leipzig, for that performance of the *St. Matthew Passion*. What will we hear? Well, certainly we will hear oboes and (wooden) flutes without keys, short-necked fiddles, and all the rest of it. We will hear the ornaments played in whatever way they really were, the phrasing and articulation likewise, and we will, or won't hear vibrato, double-dotting, *notes inégales*, little *sforzandi* at the beginning of phrases, a pause before the final chord – depending on which, if any, of the students of these things are right. We will hear, in short, all those things that the early music enthusiasts try to reproduce in their carefully researched, original-instrument performances. To the extent that they succeed – to the extent that their research is sound and its realization accurate – their performances will be historically authentic: more or less sonically like what I would hear if I had that musical time machine.

But what else would I hear? To introduce my answer to that question, let me call attention to two frequently voiced objections to what its critics call "authentic" performance. The first objection is that authentic performances are dull, pedantic affairs, in which the performers have substituted rule-following and calculation for aesthetic sensibility and imaginative musicality. The authentic performance movement, they charge, has tried to transform the art of performing into a science of the thing, with dire, mind-deadening results. Second, so the critics believe, true, live, convincing musical performance must come out of a living musical tradition, a laying on of hands; but, it is argued, authentic musical performance is the vain attempt to revive a dead tradition, on dead instruments, rather than to carry on a live one with the living tools of one's trade.

With these objections in mind, let us imagine once again what our musical time traveler will hear at Bach's performance of his *St. Matthew Passion*. Will he hear a dull, pedantic, scholarly performance where rule-following is substituted for musical imagination and artistic spontaneity gives place to "musicological" calculation? Will there be the absence of a living musical tradition that some feel at a historically authentic performance today? The answers are so obvious that the questions need hardly be put. Bach was not reproducing an eighteenth-century performance of his work, he was giving one. Bach was not reviving a tradition, he was living one. He was not "following the rules": he was in the dynamic process of making and breaking them. And those that he was "following" he was not following in the sense in which I follow Mattheson's instructions for ornamentation, or Heinechin's for realizing a figured bass, but in the sense in which one follows rules when they have been internalized and are part of one's blood and bones. Bach was not an outsider to a tradition he was trying to reconstruct, but part of the living tradition that *we* are trying to reconstruct. Thus, what our time traveler would hear in Leipzig would be a performance full of the spontaneity, vigor, liveliness, musicality, aesthetic imagination that critics of the "early music" movement find lacking in its "authentic" performances.

The lesson to be learnt from this *gedankenexperiment* is that we are creating a false dichotomy in contrasting *the* historical authenticity of (say) a musicologically correct performance of a Mozart sonata on one of Mozart's fortepianos with the historically *inauthentic* performance by Rudolph Serkin on a Steinway grand. And the question, remember, is not which is better, but which is historically authentic. The answer is, *both* and *neither*, not in some metaphorical or attenuated sense of "historically authentic" but in the rich, full-blooded, and quite literal sense that the time traveler model is intended to convey. The musicologically correct performance on a period fortepiano is indeed historically authentic in ways in which Serkin's is not. The instrumental sound is more like the sound of Mozart performing it than the sound of a modern concert grand would be. And, let us assume, the phrasing, articulation, dynamics, ornamentation, balance, and "expression" are more like a Mozart performance too. In all these ways, then, the performance on the fortepiano by the musicologist-performer is more historically authentic than Serkin's on the Steinway. But in (at least) two very important ways, which result in a host of sonic features, Serkin's performance, on the modern piano, is more historically authentic than the musicologist's on Mozart's fortepiano. For, like Mozart, Serkin is giving a performance based not on historical judgment but on musical imagination, and all the rest of those "good things" that the great performer brings to the art of musical interpretation, on the instrument to which he was born. And, like Mozart's performance again, and unlike the musicologist's "reconstruction," Serkin's performance comes out of a living musical tradition, a laying on of hands, that gives such performances qualities of vibrancy and spontaneity that musicologically "correct" ones are felt to lack. Whether these qualities of sound that the "living tradition" performer gives are musically desirable or not, remember, is not the question at issue: only whether they are part of "authenticity," and that, I claim, they are.

It is in this sense that, I suggested earlier, historically authentic performance involves a trade-off. We cannot have it entirely both ways. For there are historically authentic features of the musicologist's performance that I simply cannot have if I want the "living tradition" performance; but, contrariwise, there are, in the true, literal sense, historically authentic features of the "living tradition" performance that I cannot have in the musicologist's. If I am giving myself over entirely to the "archaeological" reconstruction of Mozartian performance (and I mean no disparagement of that enterprise), then I *must* renounce the kind of musically imaginative spontaneity that the "living tradition" performance relies on and throw myself into the arms of "scientific" historical judgment; and in so doing I lose those historically authentic features that the "living tradition" performance bestows — historically authentic because the Mozartian performance that the musicologist is trying to "reconstruct" was itself a "living tradition" performance, not a "reconstruction." But if I am after the historical authenticity of the "living tradition" performance – the spontaneity of imagination, artistic judgment, laying on of hands, etc., etc. – that a Mozart performance had in Mozart's day, then I must abrogate my "scientific," historical judgment (if I have any) and throw myself into the arms of musicality, intuition, aesthetic sensibility, and all those good things that a "living tradition" performance is supposed to have. In a word, I cannot serve two masters at the same time. I can, indeed, give a "mixed" performance (as all performances to a certain extent will always be): serving one master here, the other there. What I cannot do is have it entirely both ways, at least in practice, if not in principle as well.

To all this the musicologist-performer might reply that the bestowal of the title "historically authentic" on the "living tradition" performance is a trivial victory: a mere debater's point. True, he might reply, there are these two respects (let's assume, for the sake of the argument, there are only two) in which Serkin's performance of a Mozart sonata on the Steinway grand is historically authentic and the musicologist's is not. However, the question is, Which performance is *more* historically authentic? And in that contest, the musicologist's performance wins hands down. For, after all, he continues, Serkin's performance has only these two features of histori- cal authenticity, whereas the musicologist's carefully re- searched, cunningly calculated one has dozens of them. It is a simple accounting problem in which the musicologist's performance comes out in the black.

But the obvious answer to this objection is that *it is not a simple accounting problem.* For criteria of historical authenticity have various weights; they are not indistinguishable atoms that can just be counted and summed, like pennies in a piggy bank. And the criteria of historical authenticity that musical imagination, aesthetic sensibility, and a live performance tra- dition represent are, doubtless, going to be weighted very heavily indeed. An analogy will help. The thing is much like asking which of two drawings of an elephant is more "au- thentic," Rembrandt's sketch, which does the business with three or four boldly executed lines, that give an uncanny impression of the creature's creased and leathery skin, or the zoological illustrator's minutely detailed engraving. It is no good to answer by adding up points. Clearly, there are many more "elephant features" in the textbook plate than in Rem- brandt's superbly economical drawing. But for all of that, the few bold strokes of Rembrandt's pencil, in spite of the pau- city of features (or, in part, because of it?) may well give a more authentic idea of the elephant than the illustrator's minutiae can do.

In sum, then, there are aspects in which the musicologi- cally reconstructed performance is historically authentic and the performance by the "establishment" performer, on a modern instrument, is not – this needs no arguing, and pro- vides ample justification, if it were needed, for musicological research into performance practice and the construction of "ancient" instruments. What has apparently escaped notice, and what I have argued for here, is that in a literal, full-blooded sense of "historically authentic," the "establishment" per- formance is historically authentic in ways that the musicological performance cannot be. What weight may be given to the various features of these performances that are seen to lend historical authenticity to them is a question of real interest and depth; but I shall not attempt an answer here. Rather, I want to conclude by explaining what significance this distinction between historical authenticities has for the ongoing debate between defenders and antagonists of the "historically authentic performance movement."

AUTHENTICITY AND EVALUATION

The assertion that a performance is not "historically authentic" is never offered, or taken, as value-free: it is offered, and taken as implied criticism of an adverse kind. For this reason, the recipient of the charge of inauthenticity seldom responds with "authenticity be damned, long live inauthenticity," but, rather, tries to reach out for some distant or attenuated sense of "authenticity," as an answer.

Students and readers of the late Charles Stevenson will know full well what is going on here. For it was largely through Stevenson that we first became aware of how deeply value-laden words like "authentic" are – he used to draw little diamonds next to them, on the blackboard, to indicate it – and how easy it is to slip into using them evaluatively while seeming to be doing otherwise. It is because of this aura of positive value that surrounds the concept of "authenticity" that no one dares admit to lacking it; and so, if one cannot be "authentic" in the obvious way in which the musicologist is when he or she is playing on a period instrument, with carefully researched phrasing, dynamics, embellishments, and so forth, one claims to be "authentic" in quotation marks, authentic in some attenuated but, of course, deeper, finer, truer sense than that of the poor benighted musicologist-performer, banging away on a rinky-tink fortepiano, or trying to play in tune in E major on an oboe without keys. This sense of "authentic" usually cashes out in terms of sincerity, to which the musicologist's authenticity is, of course, supposed to compare unfavorably.

Well, what my main conclusion here suggests is that the charge of "inauthenticity" emanating from the scholars' camp is as musicologically unsound as the claim of the "living tradition" performer to an inauthentic, quotation-mark authenticity, superior to the musicologist's, is logically and morally disreputable (and quite unnecessary into the bargain). But this much can be said for the forgers of inauthentic "authenticity": they have the right intuition that authenticity is not merely the property of the scholars; no one owns it all, and no one can. What they have not seen, and what I hope to have shown, is that they have no need to settle for some shabby, back-stairs authenticity, and a logical fallacy to try to make it respectable; for they have as much claim on the real article as do the musicologists. They are authentic in a different, but no less authentic way, and need not give their critics the satisfaction of their settling for debased or counterfeit coin. On their side, the musicologists can rest assured that their authenticity is no more shallow, or unworthy than anyone else's.

The debate between defenders and critics of historically authentic performance becomes, at its worst, largely a matter of self-congratulation and name-calling, with "authentic" and "inauthentic" as the epithets of choice, the parties to the debate doing no more than biting their thumbs. Where the debate is real and interesting, it seems to me it is either over a matter of historical fact or critical evaluation. In the former case, the issue is whether or not a performance has come close to duplicating what, given the present state of knowledge, the musicologist construes as the historically correct performance. In the latter case, the issue is whether the "authentic" performance was a good one. Where the debate collapses into rhetoric is just where "good" collapses into "authentic." It is my hope that the present essay will help to prevent that collapse, which is to say, help to keep the debate about authenticity authentic.

The world of opera

Chapter VII

Opera talk: A philosophical "phantasie"

> Every utterance and every gesture that each one
> of us makes is a work of art.
>
> R. G. Collingwood

The train of thought that I wish to pursue here was initiated by Edward T. Cone's recent essay "The World of Opera and its Inhabitants."[1] To the extent that my views diverge from his I suppose I may be taken for a critical adversary. But I prefer to think of the present effort as more a continuation and development of Professor Cone's ideas than an attempt to refute or criticise them. It is in the spirit of ongoing research rather than the more common one, in my profession, of philosophical confrontation that I offer remarks on the general questions, as posed by Cone: "How does the world of opera differ from other dramatic worlds? Who are the people that inhabit it, and what sorts of lives do they lead there?"[2] More particularly, *my* question is: What is the nature of operatic utterance? *How* are operatic characters "saying?"

In the first section of my essay I will present Professor Cone's answers to these questions. In the second I will go on what will appear, no doubt, to be a completely tangential excursion into R. G. Collingwood's philosophy of art. But in the final two sections I will try to weave these two seemingly

1 Edward T. Cone, "The World of Opera and its Inhabitants," in Edward T. Cone, *Music: A View from Delft*, ed. Robert P. Morgan (Chicago: 1989), pp. 125–38.
2 Ibid., p. 125.

disparate strands together into an answer of my own to the questions that Professor Cone has so insightfully raised. Perhaps "an answer of my own" is too strong a phrase to use, implying something more like disagreement than is actually the case. So a better way of describing my whole enterprise, and the final sections especially, is "variations on a theme by Cone."

1

Cone begins his argument proper by distinguishing between what he calls "realistic song" and "operatic (or conventional or expressive) song." In a play, where the playwright calls for a character to sing a song – as, for example, the many such instances in Elizabethan drama – we have a case of "realistic song:" The character really does sing, after which we lapse back into the normal medium of speech. (More accurately, someone represents a person singing a song by really singing a song.) But: "Unlike incidental song, which occurs in situations calling for realistic singing, true operatic song replaces what in a more naturalistic medium would be ordinary speech."[3] That obvious distinction is retained even in opera, where the "natural" mode of expression is singing as well:

> Of course realistic song can occur within opera too – as when Cherubino presents his "Voi che sapete," a song he himself has written. One apprehends the character in such circumstances as "really" singing, as opposed to other occasions (such as Cherubino's first aria) when he is "operatically" singing.[4]

Cone asks: "Does the rigid distinction between realistic and operatic song hold up?"[5] The answer, which he develops by way of example, is that it does not. And it is this answer that, in its development, constitutes Cone's answers to the other questions about opera with which his essay begins, and par-

3 Ibid., p. 126.   4 Ibid., p. 126.
5 Ibid., p. 126.

ticularly *my* question of what the nature of operatic utterance is.

A pretty good idea of what Cone is up to here can be got from his first example: the musical interaction between Violetta and Alfredo in Act I of *La Traviata*, in particular their recitative and duet, Violetta's aria closing the act, and its interruption by Alfredo, singing under her balcony. The recitative and duet one assumes, on first reflection, to be not realistic but operatic song. "If you should ask the principals what they are now doing, they would respond 'We are talking to each other.' "[6] It seems difficult, however, not to construe Alfredo's interruption, heard from afar, as anything but realistic song, Cone argues:

> If a lover, under a balcony, wants his plea to be heard, what does he do? A Stanley Kowalski may shout, but the well-bred Alfredo has to rely on a more elegant tradition. Saying to himself, "Even though she has refused my love, I shall not let her forget me," he sings – realistically sings, for Violetta is too far away to hear normal speech.

Thus Cone concludes: "I submit that the only way we can make dramatic sense of the scene is to take it at face value: as an example of a familiar romantic situation – the serenade under the window."[7]

Now there is nothing at all paradoxical here until one recalls that Alfredo's "serenade" uses some of the same thematic material employed previously in what was taken to be operatic colloquy: "his serenade depends on a crucial transformation: the musical motif that we assumed originally to be not realistic but conventional song (representing normal speech) now appears in such a way that it must be taken as 'really' sung." And therein lies the paradox: for "in that case, it must have been 'really' sung – in some sense – the first time, else there would be no actual music for Alfredo to recall or for Violetta to hear."[8]

6 Ibid., p. 127.   7 Ibid., p. 127.
8 Ibid., p. 127.

What Cone concludes from this example – and other examples like it – is that "the rigid distinction between realistic song on the one hand and conventional or operatic song on the other cannot be sustained;" that "the categories cannot be hard and fast."[9]

Now one might at this point attempt to evade the "paradox" of Alfredo's "serenade," and the conclusion Cone draws from it, that the distinction between realistic and operatic or conventional song must break down – itself a somewhat paradoxical conclusion – by simply demurring from Cone's description of Alfredo's performance outside Violetta's window as realistic song. If the only argument for construing it that way is that "speaking" would not be audible to Violetta, whereas "singing" would, an appeal to operatic "convention" might well suffice as an answer. After all, considering the many other startling departures from reality that one readily accepts in opera, it is hardly asking much more to accept that "speaking" voices carry a little further there than elsewhere.

This response is by no means despicable; and although other responses would have to be fashioned, piecemeal, for the rest of Cone's examples meant to blur the distinction between realistic and operatic song, there is no a priori reason to believe this could not be done in a convincing manner. And although such responses would necessarily be ad hoc, they would not be so in any pejorative sense of that expression.

But it is not my purpose to explore this possible avenue here. For I wish rather to pursue the distinction-blurring strategy further, in order to bring out the general and altogether fascinating conclusion that Cone educes from it, and with which, for somewhat different reasons, I tend to be sympathetic. To that purpose, then, let us have a look at another, more elaborate of Cone's examples: this one – or more accurately, this collection of examples – from *Carmen*.

Why *Carmen*? Well, perhaps we should begin at the begin-

9 Ibid., pp. 127–8.

ning – the beginning of opera, that is. It is no coincidence, as has been frequently pointed out, that the first operas – Peri's, Caccini's, Monteverdi's – had as their subjects the Orpheus legend. It was a "natural" for easing people into the unfamiliar conventions of a drama in which characters sing rather than speak. For there is no doubt that audiences then (as thereafter) had difficulty accepting the "absurdity" of conversation in song; and a singing hero – that is to say, a hero who in Cone's terms could frequently, if not always, be interpreted as engaging in realistic rather than operatic song – considerably reduced the instances of what might be thought of as prima facie absurdity.

But the Orpheus legend did not exhaust itself as a subject for sung drama in the early "experimental" years. It persisted. Further, what it so quintessentially represents, a person who, *characteristically*, sings rather than speaks, became an operatic mainstay. And no operatic character besides Orpheus more fully embodies that trait than does Carmen. Indeed, she could well be thought of as his female operatic counterpart. As Cone remarks, "Carmen's natural musicality is evident. In her first two acts she loses no opportunity for singing and dancing."[10] Indeed, throughout the opera, no opportunity is missed for realistically sung set pieces. And where it is not obvious that realistic rather than operatic song is intended, the situation is frequently ambiguous and can go one way or the other. Or, more perplexing still, the situation may be such that neither characterisation, realistic or operatic, is completely consistent with all of the relevant features:

> Is the Toreador's Song expressive or realistic? In Act 2 it is the primary vehicle by which Escamillo reveals himself; yet its recall at the end of Act 3, as he sings the refrain offstage, serves realistically to inform both Carmen and Don José of his presence nearby. The choruses, too, contribute to the ambiguity: almost every one of them, whether sung by soldiers, urchins, smugglers, or spectators at the bullring, can be taken as real or as conventionally symbolic.[11]

10 Ibid., p. 131.   11 Ibid., p. 131.

Now Carmen and Orpheus – and one could name others – are, one might say, the extreme cases: the cases in which the character and the realistic singer almost entirely coalesce, with little left for operatic song to do. But it is Cone's view that, in a real sense, they stand for all:

> What Carmen knows is what all operatic characters must know, although not always so patently: that they live in a world of music, and that they express themselves and communicate with one another in song. If it is often impossible to demarcate expressive from realistic song, that is because they interpenetrate each other.[12]

But further, it turns out that if the operatic character is a singer, in the realistic not the operatic sense, he or she is a *composer* as well: a composer of the songs he or she (realistically) sings. And this is something of a surprise. For in ordinary life one usually sings what somebody else has composed. Not, however, in Cone's view, in the life of opera, where "a song, whether realistic or operatic, is so intimately connected with the character who sings it that he or she is usually to be accepted as its composer."[13] And thus, "the evidence suggests that Orpheus is not the prototypical operatic hero for historical reasons only: his role as composer-singer symbolizes what it means to be an operatic character."[14]

Cone's views are put forward not in the form or spirit of a philosophical disquisition; rather, as a more informal progression of observations and ideas. But if one wanted to find, or to construct an argument here, I think it might go something like this.

1. There is a distinction, in ordinary life and in spoken drama, between talking and singing.

2. On first reflection, there would appear to be an analogous distinction in opera, even though no one in an opera *literally* talks: thus, Cherubino *sings* "Voi che sapete," a song he himself has written, to Susanna and the Countess; but he *speaks* to Susanna of his amorous feelings in "Non so più."

12 Ibid., p. 132. 13 Ibid., p. 129.
14 Ibid., p. 135.

3. But Cherubino is not a singular or unusual case in opera in that he has composed his own song. In many other cases it is made specific that the singer and the composer are one and the same, as when Alfredo improvises a drinking song, in the first act of *La Traviata*, at Violetta's request. But, further, and this of course is a crucial (perhaps doubtful) point, we must assume that all operatic characters who realistically sing songs or otherwise realistically perform music have composed the music themselves; for these set pieces, serenades, drinking songs, dances, music lessons, and so forth are so intimately expressive of the inner feelings of the characters themselves that their own authorship of them is the only reasonable explanation.

4. But, as we have seen, the distinction in opera between "speaking" and "singing" will not hold: the edges are too blurred to be clearly made out. We might conclude, then, that we are on a slippery slope. Which way shall we slide, though: in the direction of "speaking" or "singing?" If we slide in the direction of "singing," we get the altogether intriguing notion that, since all realistic operatic singers are also composers of their songs, and the distinction between realistic singing and "talking" is blurred enough to be declared null and void, all operatic characters, in all of their utterances, turn out to be composers: singer-composers. This is the conclusion one must assume Cone has been aiming at all along – and the only interesting conclusion for the understanding of opera to be reached from the contention that the distinction between "singing" and "talking" in opera will not stand up.

But though intriguing and worth pursuing, the notion of the operatic character as composer suggests two related difficulties straightaway. Opera, as we all know, is problematic just because it seems so remote from "reality" – so remote as to seem absurd to many, because it substitutes singing for speech and adds the accompaniment of an orchestra into the bargain. Cone's proposal widens that gulf even further. For now we must think of operatic characters not merely as singing counts and countesses, generals and queens, barbers and barmaids, but *composing* counts and countesses, and so on, as well. And, further, we must give up, in doing so, a perfectly commonplace distinction, that exists both in real life and in spoken drama, between singing and speaking. For giving up that distinction is one of the premises of Cone's argument, necessary for reaching the conclusion that operatic characters are composers. Perhaps the price is too high to pay.

Yet the suggestion that we see the characters in opera as composers of what they sing has an intuitive feel of rightness about it. Yes, one wants to say, that's the way it is. That's the image that fits the strange world of opera best: a world in which, when the chips are down, singing surges forward in its most exuberant and extravagant forms. That's what makes opera make some kind of sense.

What I wish to do is to suggest another way of arriving at Cone's conclusion, one that will close the gap Cone's way has opened between the world and the world of opera. And to do that I will first, as I said at the outset, go on a seemingly irrelevant excursion into R. G. Collingwood's philosophy of art; as that excursion progresses, its relevance will begin naturally to emerge. So on, then, to irrelevancy.

2

Collingwood's philosophy is as interesting, perhaps, for what it says art is not – is not craft, not amusement, not magic, not representation – as for what it says art is: *expression*. But it will be neither possible nor to the point to go into these niceties here. And for the most part it will not be advisable, either, to dwell very much on Collingwood's arguments. What is relevant is the position itself: a bare outline of what Collingwood means by calling art "expression." With that minor task of exposition I now proceed.

We may logically begin this brief discussion of Collingwood by saying what the concept of expression is for him. And, again, it is as interesting to see what it is not as what it is. We are, it must be made clear from the start, dealing only with the expression of *emotion*. But we are not to think that the relation of an emotion to its expression is like that between something one recognises in one's self, and then finds the means to express. Rather, and this is very important to Collingwood, expression is a process in which one comes to be aware of what the emotion is one has felt the need to express and has, in the event, expressed. One does not know the emotion before its expression but only afterwards. Here is a reasonably full statement of the idea.

> When a man is said to express emotion, what is being said about him comes to this. At first, he is conscious of having an emotion, but not conscious of what this emotion is. . . . From this helpless and oppressed condition he extricates himself by doing something which we call expressing himself. This is an activity which has something to do with the thing we call language: he expresses himself by speaking. It has also something to do with consciousness: the emotion expressed is an emotion of whose nature the person who feels it is no longer unconscious. It also has something to do with the way in which he feels the emotion. As unexpressed, he feels it in what we have called a helpless and oppressed way; as expressed, he feels it in a way from which this sense of oppression has vanished.[15]

The expression of emotion is put here in terms of what we would normally call language: in this case spoken language, although the characterisation applies, *pari passu*, to written language as well. And it applies also to what we normally call art. Art "proper" is the expression of emotion. "The artist proper is a person who, grappling with the problem of expressing a certain emotion says, 'I want to get this clear.' "[16]

But what is the strength of the "is" in the assertion that art *is* expression? It would appear that it has the strength of if and only if: expression if art; but, somewhat surprisingly, art if expression. Somewhat surprisingly because it then turns out that the person who, in perfectly normal circumstances, succeeds in expressing his or her emotion in ordinary lan-

15 R. G. Collingwood, *The Principles of Art* (Oxford: 1938), pp. 109–10.
16 Ibid., p. 114.

guage is, in so doing, an artist, and the written or spoken utterance art. "The aesthetic experience, or artistic activity, is the experience of expressing one's emotions; and that which expresses them is the total imaginative activity called indifferently language or art."[17]

Now Collingwood is not saying that every example of what we presystematically call "language" is an example of art, and the user therefore an artist (nor, of course, is he using the word "language" in its ordinary presystematic sense). For Collingwood, there is no such thing as literally "bad art." There is art and that which does not succeed in being art. If we fail to express, we do not express badly; we do not express at all. And if we fail in making art, we do not make art that is bad. Sometimes we do not even try to express, but do make something artlike in some respect: the painting of sailboats in the dentist's office, the "academic" fugue, the shilling shocker. This is what Collingwood refers to as "art falsely so called." Bad art is something else, equally nonart: the *attempt* to express that does not come off:

> What the artist is trying to do is to express a given emotion. To express it, and to express it well are the same thing. To express it badly is not one way of expressing it (not, for example, expressing it, but not *selon les règles*), it is failing to express it. A bad work of art is an activity in which the agent tries to express a given emotion, but fails. This is the difference between bad art and art falsely so called. . . . In art falsely so called there is no failure to express, because there is no attempt at expression: there is only an attempt (whether successful or unsuccessful) to do something else.[18]

And since art is language, language art, this is all true, *pari passu*, of painting pictures, composing string quartets, writing poems, or just talking with your friend. One may talk with one's friend with no intention at all of expressing an emotion, or fail in the attempt; and in both cases one fails to make art, and fails to make "language," in Collingwood's special sense of that word. But when one succeeds in ex-

17 Ibid., p. 275.   18 Ibid., p. 282.

pressing, even if it is merely in talking with one's friend, one has made "language," has made "art." And it is in this sense that: "Every utterance and every gesture that each one of us makes is a work of art."[19]

I hold no brief for Collingwood's metaphysics of art, language, and expression; but nor do I intend to make a critique of it. That has been done often enough. What does intrigue me is the notion that ordinary speakers of the language are artists, and their utterances works of art. I would like to pursue that notion a bit further.

We might tend to think of the English language (say) as a preexisting means to the end of expression: a tool, there to be taken up as needed. But in Collingwood's view, "when we speak of 'using' language for certain purposes, what is so used cannot be language itself, for language is not a utilizable thing but a pure activity." Language, properly so called, cannot be made use of like a tool or prefabricated template: "what can be [so used] is the deposits, internal and external, left by the linguistic activity: the habit of uttering certain words and phrases; the habit of making certain kinds of gesture." This habit, or set of habits, which ordinary people fall into most of the time through their daily lives is, so to speak, the detritus left behind by the truly creative, imaginative activity of language which does, as the former cannot, achieve true expression:

> The artistic activity which creates these habits and constructs these external records of itself, supersedes and jettisons them as soon as they are formed. We commonly express this by saying that art does not tolerate *clichés*. Every genuine expression must be an original one. . . . The artistic activity does not "use" a "ready-made language," it "creates" language as it goes along.[20]

So we might say that "language" – language as it is described by ordinary people – falls into two parts: what Collingwood would think of as language proper, which is imaginative, creative, innovative, and achieves expression; and

19 Ibid., p. 285. 20 Ibid., p. 275.

the "ready-made 'language' " of dead clichés that true language, true expression has left in its wake. Who speaks (or writes or gestures) which? Clearly, in Collingwood's view, one does not have to be a Dr. Johnson or an Abraham Lincoln to achieve true expression in conversation. It is not a function of technique or learning but of sincerity, uncorrupted consciousness; and, presumably, plumbers as well as poets can achieve that rare human condition. In any event, I shall not pursue Collingwood's position here, but leave off rather abruptly at this point and go on to what might be described as an imaginative application of some of Collingwood's ideas to the world of the operatic work. However, what follows, I must make perfectly clear, is Kivy, not Collingwood; and it should not be judged as either an accurate or inaccurate interpretation of the latter. For it is not an interpretation at all, being obviously inspired by Collingwood but no longer an *explication de texte*.

3

What follows is not a theory of language, or of expression, or of art. Indeed, it is not a theory of anything. What I propose is an imaginative way of looking at our world, and at the world of opera, that makes some kind of sense out of the latter in relation to the former. I do not think it is the only way. And I do not know if it is the best way. It is just a way, that is all. I am issuing an invitation, not making an argument: "Try it this way; see if it makes sense."

Certainly, Collingwood had a nice insight into ordinary language when he realised that, even in everyday life, discourse can be creative, innovative: making itself anew for novel situations. But perhaps he didn't go far enough in this, for he assigned a creative, innovative role only to what he thought of as language proper, not to the supposedly dead language of habits and clichés. Yet, when you get right down to it, *all* instances of ordinary discourse, even among the most inept, inarticulate, untalented practitioners, are to some degree creative responses to novel situations. That is the magic and the mystery of the thing: that we acquire a language we must, in a sense, reinvent each time we use it to react to what confronts us. Language is not like a wrench, preformed to fit a certain nut or bolt. Each linguistic response that we make is to a situation at least to some degree new. And thus each linguistic act that each of us performs is to a certain degree creative, innovative, made anew for a novel situation. Of course the novelty that each situation presents will be great or little or somewhere in between, as will be the degree of innovation in the response. However, to the extent that every linguistic response, even of the most ordinary kind, must be to some little degree "creative," one might take Collingwood as far more comprehensive than he has a right to take himself when he says that: "Every utterance and every gesture that each one of us makes is a work of art." He can only be referring to that part of language that is language proper, not to the "habits and *clichés.*" I would ask you, however, to see every one of us in every linguistic act that he or she makes as being at least to a degree "creative;" and, therefore, each of us, to a degree, an "artist," each linguistic utterance and gesture at least a minimal "work of art."

Of course, as speakers of the language – and it is conversation that I am mainly interested in here – we are, in this view, very special kinds of artists, namely, *improvisatory artists:* artists who create and perform in a single act. And, of course, we vary greatly in our proficiency. One scarcely needs an argument, I would think, to construe Dr. Johnson's conversation, at least as reported by Boswell, as "art" in the full-blooded sense of the word. And I have always imagined, from the little anecdotal information that we have, that Lincoln's must also have been at that level, although, unfortunately, he had no Boswell to preserve it for us. But each of us, in conversation, must be inventive: must respond to the not entirely expected. For how, after all, can we know, in every respect, what others will say? Each of us, in his or her discourse, must be "creative" to the extent that each of us must respond, on the spot, to what always must be in part surprising. So we are all, in conversation, brothers and sisters in art. That is how I ask you, for a time, to imagine our world.

But now imagine something else. Imagine that, through some bizarre series of mutations and adaptations, we evolve into speakers who, although we speak the same colloquial English as now, somehow speak it without all the gaps and glitches. Imagine also that we have become, to a far greater degree than heretofore, capable of self-knowledge and self-expression, as well as far deeper in our insights into the natures of those with whom we interact. Such a world would be very much like the world of naturalistic drama: a more Collingwoodian world than our own because far more often true expression would occur in it.

A further set of mutations and adaptations might bring us to speakers in blank verse, or rhymed couplets, in which case we would be in Shakespeare's world, or in Dryden's. But the point is that we are not, when we go from our world to these others, passing from a world where speech is not art to worlds in which it is, or from a world in which speakers are not artists to worlds in which they are. That particular discontinuity does not obtain in this way of looking at things. In the world of naturalistic drama, the inhabitants are improvisatory prose artists like us, although they are better, more proficient artists, perhaps by orders of magnitude. In the worlds of Shakespeare and Dryden, the inhabitants are improvisational poets. But, nevertheless, we share with them the discipline of art, though they are artists in poetry and we in prose.

It should now, I think, be obvious where this is leading: to a world, of course, in which the inhabitants are not improvisatory literary artists but improvisatory singer-composers. Another set of mutations and adaptations brings us into the strange world of opera. But having followed this route in getting there, we have avoided some of that sense of violent discontinuity between our world and the operatic world that Cone's route seems to me to suggest.

Cone first asks us to consider the world of opera as a world markedly different from our own, a world in which people sing rather than speak. Then, by perturbing the distinction internal to that world, between realistic and operatic song, he reaches the conclusion that the singers are composers as well. And the conclusion comes as something of a dual shock to common sense. The first shock comes when we learn that, in contrast to our own world, where we almost always sing songs that someone else has composed, in the world of opera the realistic singer always composes his or her own songs. And what seems like a second shock comes when we arrive at the further realisation that, since the line between realistic and operatic song will not hold, *all* operatic characters are composers, not merely those who on occasion sing a drinking song or a serenade. In the real world, very few of us are composers; in the world of opera *everyone* is.

But when one, instead, sees our own world and the world of opera in the revised Collingwoodian way that I am suggesting, the discontinuity, along with the shock, is greatly reduced. The sharp contrast between a world of many speakers and few composers, and a world entirely of singer-composers appears to be, as Cone makes it out, a contrast between a world where few are artists and a world where *everyone* is. Looked at from the revised Collingwoodian viewpoint, there are two worlds in which everyone, as speaker or "speaker," is an artist, the difference being that in one of them everyone is an improvisational literary artist, in the other everyone an improvisational musician. In our world each of us, and no one else, "composes" his or her expression in words. In opera each person, and no one else, "composes" his or her expression in musical notes. But we are all artists under the skin. I find that something of a comfort.

I have, then, discharged the first of my self-imposed obligations. I have presented a way of looking at our world and at the world of opera that decreases, it seems to me, rather than increases the gap between them, while preserving Cone's intriguing characterisation of opera's people as composer-singers. But to a certain extent, in so doing, I have discharged my second obligation as well: that of preserving the distinction between realistic and operatic song. For *if* the main motivation for blurring the distinction is to reach the conclusion that *all* operatic characters are singer-composers, then that motivation is removed by reaching the conclusion by a different route. This is not to say that there may not be independent grounds for claiming that the distinction is soft. But I am inclined to think this must be decided opera by opera, case by case. It seems to me to be a mistake to think that we can generalise in this regard for opera *tout court*. This point requires some amplification.

What I have in mind is this. It may very well be true that for one operatic work the line between realistic and operatic song might be blurred, but not for another where, on the contrary, it might be firm. Thus, I think, for example, that Cone is correct in characterising *Carmen* as a work in which it is next to impossible to draw the fine distinction between realistic and operatic song, whereas, although I think Cone might disagree, the world of *The Marriage of Figaro* is a world in which the line is finely drawn and the boundary scrupulously observed.

Three importantly different kinds of examples are to be recognised here. There are those cases which are clearly and unambiguously examples of realistic song: examples that cannot reasonably be taken in any other way. Then there are those that can be taken either way: that is to say, they seem, in themselves, to be consistent with either a "realistic" or "operatic" interpretation. And, finally, there are those – the truly problematic cases – which defy exclusive classification. In such cases, there is at least one feature inconsistent with its possessor being realistic song, and at least one feature inconsistent with its possessor being operatic song. Only an opera in which the last-named kind predominates is an operatic world in which the line between realistic and operatic song cannot be sharply drawn. And what I want to emphasise here is, quite simply, that operas in which the line cannot be sharply drawn do not constitute the whole world of opera.

4

Let me return now, in conclusion, to that most important feature of operatic worlds: that their inhabitants are improvisational singer-composers. For we have failed to take notice of one absolutely crucial thing. Denizens of the operatic world, oddly enough, find themselves almost never without the accompaniment of musical instruments, ranging from keyboard alone (in *secco* recitative) to a full Wagnerian orchestra. What are we to make of this?

The role of the orchestra in opera is complex and variegated: there is not just one single thing that the orchestra is or does. One thing that it does is to make common cause with the singing voice in expressing the thoughts and feelings of the characters. Let us call this its *expressive* function. It is this expressive function that will concern me exclusively here.

One imagines three questions arising with regard to the expressive music of the orchestra. Who (in the world of the work) composed it? Who (in the world of the work) hears it? What (if anything) is its counterpart in our world, the real world? The answer to the first question must be that the characters themselves compose the expressive instrumental accompaniment to their expressive utterances. With this Cone emphatically concurs. I will quote Cone's answer to the second question. It merits some discussion. Cone writes, "while the singers hear the orchestra in the pit, what the characters they enact hear is not that orchestra but the music it plays, which reproduces the music of the imaginary orchestra that they, as composers, perpetually carry around with them."[21]

There seem to me to be two problems here. To begin with, in none of his examples does Cone explicitly commit himself to saying that any character hears the expressive accompaniment except the character who is doing the expressing and who carries the orchestral accompaniment around in his or her head. But that is a serious omission. Is it merely an acci-

21 Cone "The World of Opera," pp. 136-7.

dental, unintended one? I doubt it. For I think it directly follows from what Cone has said above that in the world of the work only the character whose singing is being expressively accompanied can hear that accompaniment. Cone says that the characters do not hear the music in the pit. They hear the music "in the head" that the orchestra makes public for the audience. But no one can "hear" the music in someone else's head (unless operatic characters have a special dispensation in that regard, which Cone gives no indication of believing). Therefore, each character hears his or her own expressive accompaniment, not anyone else's. Surely, however, if the expressive accompaniment is not perceived by the other characters present, it is serving no expressive purpose *within the world of the operatic work.* Are we then to assume that it is meant only for the audience: a running expressive commentary by the omniscient author or implied narrator?

Second, if the "speaker" is the only character in the operatic world to hear the expressive orchestra, we will have to answer in response to our third question – What (if anything) is its counterpart in our world, the real world? – that there seems to be no counterpart at all, unless we believe that there is some kind of "secret" expression, which only the expressor is privy to, that always accompanies the occurrence of public expression in speech and gesture. I suppose that is not an altogether implausible conjecture. At least some people have held something like that position. There is a certain vague model of expression which has it that "it's all in the head" and that spoken utterance or written word makes it public to others, but never quite adequately ("Mere words just can't adequately describe or express exactly what I feel, think, etc."). On that model, the expressive orchestra might seem as a window onto the operatic character's private, subjective world that the audience has access to but the other characters have not – they having to rely merely on the always somewhat inadequate instrument of "speech." The "speaking" character "hears" the expressive orchestra in his or her "mind's ear," as it were, for it is his or her consciousness. And the audience is privileged to perceive this stream of consciousness as well through its realisation in the pit. But it is closed to the other characters in the world of the opera, as direct access to your stream of consciousness is closed to me.

We can forget about whether or not this model of expression will fit the facts of the world as we know it. For it certainly will not fit the facts of the operatic world since the premise on which it is based, that none of what the expressive orchestra puts out can be heard by the characters who listen but only by the character who "speaks," simply will not stand up. Here is why. If, when one character "speaks" to another in opera, all that the listening character hears is the melodic line, he or she will frequently miss what is being expressed, since the emotive character of the melodic line is not just a function of *it*, but of its harmonic underpinning, contrapuntal adornment, and instrumental colouration. Frequently it will be obvious that character A hears that character B is in emotional state ϕ, but that A could only know this if he or she had not only heard what B sang but also what the orchestra played. And if that is the case, which it clearly seems to be, it cannot be the case that the music of the expressive orchestra is always heard only by the character singing, not by the character or characters listening (although it might sometimes be the case, as, for example, where a character sings an accompanied "aside").

We are obliged to assume, then, that all the characters in opera hear some – I am inclined to say most – of the expressive orchestra's music, and that this music is the result of compositional acts on the part of whatever character is at present "speaking" and being so accompanied. And this leaves us still with the puzzling question of what in ordinary life might be the counterpart of this orchestral presence.

Well at this point perhaps one simply wants to throw in the towel. After all, there is no guarantee that every aesthetic feature of a representational work need be representational; and it may well be that the expressive function of the orchestra has no counterpart at all in "real life:" It may well be that it is a nonrepresentational feature, with other, nonrepresentational parts to play in opera.

This is not an impossible position to take. But I find it unpalatable. For in leaving the expressive function of the orchestra without a representational object, the gap is widened between opera and "reality" that it has been the whole purpose of this exercise to close. I operate here with a kind of Occam's Razor to the effect that, in representational works, one should not multiply nonrepresentational features beyond necessity. And a little ingenuity, coupled with a little tolerant imagination will, it seems to me, come up with a fairly plausible counterpart in reality for the expressive orchestra. It is, quite simply, *expressive gesture and bodily movement*.

But surely, it will immediately be objected, this suggestion, if it were taken up, would make the expressive function of the orchestra both redundant and absurd: redundant because, after all, opera singers have arms and torsos with which to gesture, just as do the rest of us, and do not require a substitute; absurd because gestures are seen and orchestras heard.

As to redundancy, let me remind you of some well-known advice that was once given to an actor: "Nor do not saw the air too much with your hand, thus, but use all gently."[22] This may be good advice to an actor. *It is absolutely essential doctrine for an opera singer.* We all know that singers are seldom good actors and actresses; that is just a statistical fact. But even in the rare instance, it is a mistake to indulge the talent except sparingly. And this for two obvious reasons. In the first place, because it impossible to sing well if you are "saw[ing] the air too much with your hand" and transacting too much stage business. In the second, and more important, because opera is in its most essential aspects a heard art, not a seen one, and too much acting distracts from its essentially musical nature. A wise Providence has substi-

22 *Hamlet*, Act III, scene 2.

tuted musical "gesture" for physical gesture in the world of opera in the form of the expressive opera orchestra. And since it is the gesture of the "speaker," of course he or she has "composed" it, and of course it can be heard by all in its presence, just as the gestures of the speakers in our world are seen (under the proper conditions) by all.

But is it absurd to talk about bodily gesture being represented by sound? Is it absurd to talk about the seen being represented by the heard? No more absurd, I would imagine, than talking about any other example of objects of one sense modality being represented by those of another, a fairly common thing, after all, in the representational arts and elsewhere. In the visual arts particularly such examples are so ubiquitous as to scarcely require citation here.

With these prima facie objections out of the way, what further can be said in support of this gestural interpretation of the opera orchestra in its expressive function? A great deal, I would venture to say, and that of a very particular nature. I would suggest, in closing, that the true test of this hypothesis lies in the examination of particular cases. And I would fully expect that such critical examination would reveal all sorts of instances in which both the details and the general outlines of specific orchestral accompaniments could be most felicitously described in gestural terms. Indeed, I suspect an examination of the critical literature would reveal that many writers have been operating all along under the very assumption I am defending here, as a good many of their descriptions are in gestural terms.

Let me, by way of illustration, instance but one case in point out of many. How are we to hear the seventeen-bar instrumental introduction to the Countess's cavatina that raises the curtain on the second act of *The Marriage of Figaro?* One might, I suppose, take it as a kind of musical setting of the scene. "Here is the Countess sitting at her dressing table. This is the way things are with her. In a moment she will express her thoughts and feelings." What I am suggesting as an alternative is that this instrumental introduction not be taken as prelude to the Countess's expressive act but, rather, as its beginning. It is what her body is expressively doing before she begins to "speak."

Apropos of this, I would like to draw the reader's attention to a puzzling point that has some bearing on the question. There are three editions of the full score of *Figaro*, familiar to me, with some claim to authority. The nineteenth-century Breitkopf and Härtel edition (in the complete works) has only the spare instruction for the first scene of the second act: "La Contessa." The Peters edition of 1941 has: "La Contessa (sola)." And the Bärenreiter *Neue Ausgabe sämtlicher Werke*, which, one would assume, has the latest word on authenticity, at least up to 1973, has only the slightly more loquacious: "La Contessa sola; poi Susanna e poi Figaro." But we find the following, far more elaborate stage directions, in Edward J. Dent's edition of the vocal score: "Susanna discovered with the Countess. She appears to have told the Countess something painful; the Countess makes a gesture of disgust and resignation, and Susanna goes to her room."

Where did Dent get all this? In particular, where did he get the "gesture of disgust and resignation?" Well, it is always possible that Dent had some authoritative document in hand unavailable to the editors of the aforementioned scores. But that seems highly unlikely. Rather, I strongly suspect that the gesture of "resignation," at least, came directly from listening to Mozart's seventeen-bar prelude. No one can fail to perceive the resignation there.[23] And that, in my opinion, is just where the "gesture of resignation" should remain: right where Mozart put it. Part of the Countess *is* that prelude: *it* is her "gesture of resignation."

CODETTA

Strange creatures these operatic people, worthy of the wildest of science fiction imaginations. What bizarre transformations they have undergone to have become able to speak in song and move as disembodied orchestral sound. O brave

---

23 I fail to hear the gesture of disgust.

new world that has such people in it. How remote they are from us and our prosaic and bodily lives. And what is the Countess to me that I should weep for her? Is it enough to say that we have both acquired the art of expression, but that she has got a little ahead of me? "Little" is hardly the word for it. She has Mozart's powers, and I only my own. Yet there must be common ground. Or so at least I assure myself, somewhat dubiously, each time I go to the opera to believe the impossible.

Chapter VIII

How did Mozart do it?: Living conditions in the world of opera

It used to be the case that the London Postal Service received a substantial quantity of mail annually, addressed to Mr. Sherlock Holmes, No. 221B, Baker Street. Perhaps this is a tribute to human credulity. But I see it, rather, as a tribute to the literary gifts of Sir Arthur Conan Doyle and instance Holmes himself as a paradigm of a fictional character whose creator has made almost to "come alive."

There are many such living fictional characters in world literature, and in the world of opera as well. I dare say that if Don Giovanni had a believable address in this world rather than the next, his post office too would have received letters in abundance, most of them, I like to imagine, proposals of marriage.

The way Conan Doyle put life into his creation is, I think, unproblematical. He did not, in one sweep of the brush, paint an unforgettable portrait in prose that, in itself, brought his detective to life for all time. That too is possible, and Dickens, among others, comes to mind as one capable of that literary feat. But Conan Doyle, rather, with innumerable details, throughout nearly two thousand pages of novellas and short stories, limned in the character, the personality we know so intimately, dot by dot, like a literary Seurat. And because of this intricate, pointillistic style, the Sherlock Holmes *oeuvre* has become, for some, a kind of Talmud, to be pondered over and scrutinized for yet further undiscovered information about its protagonist.

What a Conan Doyle can do with the piling up of detail,

or what a Dickens can do with the broad and bold sweep of
the brush, however different they may be in technique, and
perhaps in degree of genius required for their accomplishment, both depend, it is more than obvious, on one very
important resource of the English language, and language in
general: the potential to express conceptual thought in all its
complexity. To give a character life one must be able to express a broad and detailed and deep array of propositions
fictionally true of that character. That resource of natural languages is not available, as all sensible people know, to the
composer. In an instant Conan Doyle can, with the resources
of language, tell us that Mr. Sherlock Holmes is both physically strong and clever to a high degree, and in an unusual
way.

> "Dr. Watson, Mr. Sherlock Holmes," said Stanford, intro-
> ducing us.
> "How are you?" he said cordially, gripping my hand with
> a strength for which I should hardly have given him credit.
> "You have been in Afghanistan, I perceive."
> "How on earth did you know that?" I asked in astonish-
> ment. "Never mind," said he, chuckling to himself.[1]

How many bars of music would it require to convey this
small but important amount of information about the great
detective? If you answered "A thousand" you would be just
as mistaken as if you had answered "Three." Music just can't
do that sort of thing at all.

Now at this point it is important, I think, to make a distinction, after which we can go on to pursue the matter further. The distinction is between what I shall call "characterizing" and what I shall call "animating" a fictional persona
in a musical or literary work. Almost any mediocre literary
talent can *characterize* his or her dramatis personae so that
each is distinctive enough to have an individuality, to be told
apart from the others. Harlequin novels and soap operas have
stock characters, and no doubt you can't tell the heroine in

---

1 Sir Arthur Conan Doyle, "A Study in Scarlet," *The Complete Sherlock Holmes* (New
York: Doubleday, 1930), p. 6.

one apart from the heroine in another. But you can tell the heroine from the cheap blonde in whichever work you are currently consuming. These fictional personages have at least minimal *characterizations*. What they don't have is *animation*. They don't have life. The difference between Sherlock Holmes and the stock detective is that you will mistake Holmes for no one else: He has been animated; he is alive.

Now the point here is that music can, in very obvious ways, *characterize*. I have no problem with that. Mozart had at his disposal, for that purpose, the whole arsenal of operatic conventions, and musical materials by which one could make it immediately apparent to an audience the kind of personage presently holding forth. In a recent article called "The buffa aria in Mozart's Vienna," John Platoff writes that "Opera buffa of the classical period uses various types of aria, sung in particular situations and by particular kinds of characters." And because of this one can know instantly, merely from the aria type, many things about the character type, including, for example, "the social class of the character."[2]

These operatic conventions no doubt helped eighteenth-century audiences to immediately recognize what sort of character they were confronted with as soon as the first bars of music were out of his or her mouth. And to the extent that these conventions have been passed on to twentieth-century audiences through such well-known works as the Gilbert and Sullivan operettas, they may serve the same function to a certain degree today.

But even if these conventions as such are for the most part lost on us, unless we read musicological treatises, the expressive features of tonal music endure as part of our blood and bones. And so we know, as listeners, without being aware of eighteenth-century conventions of the musical stage, that Papageno is a simple soul, Tamino a heroic character, the Queen of the Night slightly hysterical, Zarastro divine, because their music is immediately read as expressive of these

2 John Platoff, "The buffa aria in Mozart's Vienna," *Cambridge Opera Journal* 2 (1990), p. 99.

qualities of character. (I do not, by the way, say that Papageno's music *is* simple but that it is *expressive of* simplicity. For there can be complex music expressive of simplicity, as well as simple music expressive of complexity.)

Thus, both by operatic conventions and by expressiveness of music, or, to be more direct, by operatic conventions and by just plain music, Mozart, like any other composer of his time, could characterize. But there's the rub. For the means of *characterizing* the personages of an opera were available to any of Mozart's less talented contemporaries. The operatic conventions were mastered by all, as Platoff amply demonstrates in comparing a buffa aria of Salieri's with one in the same style by Mozart. And as for the language of musical expressiveness, that too was a matter of craft, not genius. It is open to any operatic hack to write music expressive of simplicity or heroism, divinity or hysteria, and, as we all know, this was so clearly recognized by seventeenth- and eighteenth-century practitioners of the art that many of them compiled veritable dictionaries of expressive figures, not unlike the cue sheets and compendia provided in our own century for organists and pianists who accompanied silent films.[3]

A great deal of the recent analytic and critical literature on how Mozart delineated the characters in his great musical works for the theatre seems to me to be entirely concerned with what I have characterized as "characterization." There is nothing inherently wrongheaded about this as a subject of inquiry, but there are inherent dangers. And one of these dangers is obsessively pursuing such an inquiry in the belief that if you are obsessive enough in your pursuit you will reveal the magic secret of what it is that lifts Mozart's operatic characters qua fictional characters above those of his contemporaries: what makes Mozart's Figaro a living being for us and Paisiello's merely a character.

---

3 You can verify this for yourselves and see what I am getting at here by taking a look at a book by Erno Rapée whose title is self-explanatory: *Motion Picture Moods for Pianists and Organists: a Rapid-Reference Collection of Selected Pieces Adapted to Fifty-Two Moods and Situations* (New York: Schirmer, 1924; reprinted, New York: Arno Press and The New York Times, 1970).

An antidote to this potential confusion of characterization with animation can be found in the recent growth of interest in the musico-dramatic techniques of Mozart's contemporaries, of which the article by Platoff previously quoted is but one example. For the more we know about how ubiquitous the techniques of operatic characterization were in Mozart's time, the less eager we should be to try to understand what separates Mozart's characters from those of Cimarosa or Paisiello, Salieri or Martín y Soler, by searching out, ever more minutely and reductively, those techniques of mere characterization that his music possesses in common with the music of any eighteenth-century composer who had mastered the craft of musical composition for the stage.

There is a well-known danger, too, in learning more about the lesser: the danger of leveling – losing the sense of what separates Mozart's characters from those of his contemporaries, by obsessive concentration on and growing knowledge of what makes them the same. This danger of historical leveling is so eloquently cried down by Theodor Adorno, in a similar musico-historical context, that I can do no better than to quote him.

> Bach's music is separated from the general level of his age by an astronomical distance. Its eloquence returns only when it is liberated from the sphere of resentment and obscurantism. . . . They say Bach, [but] mean Telemann.[4]

We are here, I presume, to celebrate the astronomical distance between Mozart and the general level of *his* age. And part of that distance is measured, not by the characters he gave the inhabitants of his operas but by the life he was miraculously able to breathe into them. I have before me a book from which I shall quote in a moment. But we can learn something in this regard merely from its title: *Who's Who in Mozart's Operas: From Alfonso to Zerlina*. Unlike Sherlock Holmes, the characters in Mozart's operas do not receive letters. But that they should elicit a book with such a title sug-

---

4 Theodor W. Adorno, *Prisms*, trans. Samuel and Sherry Weber (Neville Spearman, 1967), p. 145.

gests very much the same thing about them that Holmes's one-sided correspondence does: Like Holmes, they have taken on a life in our imaginations so vivid as to seem almost to partake of reality. A "Dramatis Personae" suggests the obvious. A "Who's Who" suggests *life*. Nor need we rely only on an inference from the title to conclude that Joachim Kaiser, the author of the book in question, feels this way about his subject. For he writes in his Preface: "Mozart tempts us to assume that his are living characters, each different, who can therefore be described as if they were real, though not solely in terms of realistic psychology."[5]

If Kaiser recognizes the living quality in Mozart's dramatic personages, perhaps he possesses the secret of their life – their *modus vivandi*, if you will. After all, he has followed his observation with two hundred pages of particulars. In a way he does possess the secret and doesn't realize it; but in this he is no different from many of the others who have written about Mozart. And, in a more important sense, no one can possess this secret, for it is the secret, really, of beauty itself, or at least I shall so argue.

To begin to spell out what I have just said, I quote a phrase from Kaiser's *Who's Who*. But I hasten to add that I could have done equally well by quoting almost any other commentator on Mozart's operatic characters. I choose Kaiser for no better reason than that the title of his book blazons forth my subject and corroborates my intuition. Donna Anna's "marvelous resolution," Kaiser remarks, is musically expressed by "the wonderfully soaring sixths in her D major aria."[6]

I have a very simple point to make here. Suppose Kaiser had merely said that the marvelous resolution of Donna Anna's character was expressed by rising sixths in her D major aria? What would have been missing from his description? What does "wonderfully soaring" convey that "rising" does not?

---

5 Joachim Kaiser, *Who's Who in Mozart's Operas: From Alfonso to Zerlina*, trans, Charles Kessler (New York: Schirmer, 1987), p. 3.

6 Ibid., p. 23.

The answer, it seems clear, is that "wonderfully" functions evaluatively; and, although it may not be quite so obvious, so also does "soaring." To rise is merely to go up. Cakes rise. Eagles soar. And it must be a very special eagle indeed that soars wonderfully.

But notice: *any* composer can write rising sixths to represent resoluteness of character. And if one were merely trying to show how Mozart had *characterized* Donna Anna as resolute, "rising sixths" would have been an entirely sufficient description of how he did it, if indeed you *can* do it with rising sixths. Only a great musical artist can, however, compose "wonderfully soaring sixths." In a word, to call them "wonderfully soaring sixths" is to call them not just music but *beautiful music.* Now *if* Kaiser was groping here for the difference between musically *characterizing* a fictional personage as resolute, and *animating* such a personage, then I think he stumbled onto the right road, even though there is no sign in his book, so far as I can see, that he realized it. In the case of Donna Anna's resoluteness, I would urge, it is the difference between rising sixths and "wonderfully soaring sixths." This needs to be elaborated.

Kaiser must have been at least dimly aware of the problem that is puzzling me, for he warns us, you will recall, that although Mozart's personages are "living characters . . . who can therefore be described as if they are real," they cannot be described "solely in terms of realistic psychology." He does not tell us why they cannot be so described or what exactly he means by "realistic psychology." But I would venture to guess that what he is troubled by is the obvious inability of music to impart much in the way of fictional truths about the psychology of operatic characters, the way the language of a Euripides or a Dostoyevski can. By "realistic psychology" I think he must mean psychology in terms of intelligible psychological principles and motives, whether their source be common sense psychology, a theory-based one like Freud's, Descartes', or the doctrine of the humors, or the intellectual background of the work in question.

But if the characters in Mozart's opera are "living charac-

ters . . . who can therefore be described as if they are real,"
and if life cannot be given to them by the deep psychological
insights of their creators as expressed in discursive language,
how does Mozart impart it? Kaiser does not say, and, I would
think, does not know. But his instincts are true for they lead
him, when talking about how Mozart can *characterize*, to describe the musical techniques not just in value-neutral terms,
as resoluteness expressed by rising sixths, but in distinctively evaluative language: resoluteness expressed by "wonderfully soaring sixths." And I think one can find such evaluatively charged language throughout the critical literature.

My own misgivings about the power of music to express
fictional truths led me to the conclusion, in my recent book
on what I called the philosophy of opera, that, quite simply,
the life of operatic characters is imparted by the sheer beauty
of music. Here, briefly, is my argument and its conclusion. I
take the liberty, if it is a liberty, of quoting myself with regard to what I called in my book "a pervasive operatic illusion: what might be called the 'illusion of psychological
depth.'"

> The depth is an illusion, brought about by the fact that the
> music is surpassingly beautiful and makes these otherwise
> dead characters live, *just as if* they were products of literary
> genius and lived – like Dostoyevsky's characters, for example
> – because of the depth and complexity that literary language
> can impart. . . . [G]reat operatic characters do indeed have
> that kind of life. But it is not in the words, and cannot be in
> the music . . . No doubt, the beauty of the music makes these
> characters live, I do not pretend to know how – it is a brute
> aesthetic fact. However, their "depth" and "complexity" are
> illusion merely: the product of musical beauty, not psycho-
> logical insight, which can only be expressed in the requisite
> way, by discursive language.[7]

I was not at all surprised that my conclusion in this regard
should have been greeted with angry denials from at least
one reviewer of my book; for I have learned over many years

7 Peter Kivy, *Osmin's Rage: Philosophical Reflections on Opera, Drama and Text* (Princeton: Princeton University Press, 1988), pp. 268–9.

that whenever I deny *any* power to music, no matter how preposterous that power may seem in the light of common sense and careful analysis, it will inevitably be met with hostility, as if I were somehow a traitor to a cause, or deserting the faith. Anyway, here is what Michael Tanner says, of what he calls my "astonishing claim that music can vouchsafe no revelations of character, and that the idea that it can impart psychological depth is mere illusion":

> If Mozart doesn't, because one's argument has led one to claim that he cannot, give Donna Elvira a greater complexity and depth than Da Ponte's libretto has done, then what is the point of his enterprise. Kivy takes refuge, helplessly, in "surpassing musical beauty." However difficult it may be to provide an alternative and more satisfying account, it must be done if music drama is not ultimately to be written off as a vast confidence trick.[8]

Before I try to go further with the discussion of what I have been calling the "animation" of operatic characters, it would be well to point out straightaway and deny outright one implication of what Tanner is saying for the aesthetics of opera. He seems to suggest that if one denies an opera composer can give characters depth and complexity, one has denuded opera of its only possible *raison d'être*. What else, he asks, can be the point of the operatic enterprise? Well, clearly, depth and complexity, even if you believe operatic characters can have them as some literary characters do, are neither the whole point of any opera, nor any point at all of many operas. (I take it that no one would claim to find depth or insight in Rossini's *Barber of Seville* or his other comic masterpieces.) And this is true, *mutatis mutandis*, for plays, novels, and poems as well, where it is agreed, on all hands, that depth, complexity, and insight are possible.

Another point that ought to be directly responded to in Tanner's remarks, before I continue, is his rather puzzling, as well as alarmist conclusion concerning my views on character depth and complexity, to wit, that although it may be

8 *Cambridge Opera Journal* 1 (1989), p. 306.

difficult to "provide an alternative and more satisfactory account, it must be done if music drama is not ultimately to be written off as a vast confidence trick."

I say it is an alarmist conclusion because even if character depth and complexity were written off as "a vast confidence trick," which is to say, I guess, on Tanner's view, written off altogether, it would hardly follow that music drama in its entirety had been written off as "a vast confidence trick," written off altogether. Again, Tanner is operating here with the premise that the only interesting or valuable aesthetic feature of opera or music drama is character depth and psychological insight. Whereas it seems obvious to me that that is not the case. Thus, whatever there is in *The Barber of Seville* that makes it a great and enjoyable work for the musical stage is still there to admire and enjoy on my view, even if character depth and psychological insight are completely written off as "a vast confidence trick," since no one ever thought they were there in that work in the first place. And further, although many would think it a great loss to have character depth and psychological insight written off as "a vast confidence trick" in (say) *The Marriage of Figaro* or *Otello*, they would still, I dare say, find those works so abundant in other musical and dramatic riches as to hardly seem written off altogether.

But let us take a closer look at what I find *puzzling* about Tanner's conclusion: this notion that if one has reduced character depth and complexity to "a vast confidence trick" one has done something really bad, totally destructive of these things, from the point of view of the opera as an art form. Tanner introduces the phrase "confidence trick" as a synonym for my term "illusion," the point obviously being that since "confidence trick" is an expression of opprobrium, it will reveal in its true light the opprobriousness of my reduction of character depth and complexity to mere "illusion." I have turned Mozart, *horribile dictu,* into a "confidence man" – in other words, a charlatan and a fraud. Shame on me!

Some examples may help in my defense against this terrible charge. I long ago realized that stage magicians don't do it with magic but with legerdemain. It's all an illusion – a confidence trick. The impression of depth in Renaissance painting is an illusion achieved by careful application of the principles of linear perspective, which must make Leonardo, on Tanner's view, a confidence man. Plato, I suppose, would agree. And a few years ago I read an extremely clever time-travel novel, which was all decked out in the language of relativity theory – world lines and all that. It gave a convincing fictional illusion of the scientific respectability of traveling in time – an illusion vital to that particular literary genre. But if you read the "scientific" passages closely, they fell apart under critical scrutiny and all the familiar paradoxes of time travel emerged. It wasn't science but pseudoscience, the illusion of science – which is hardly surprising, since the book was "science fiction," not science, and its author a scientific "charlatan," if you want to put it that way.

So it's all done with mirrors. So what else is new? That I have reduced an aesthetic feature to an illusion – a confidence trick, if you like – hardly seems to me to be, of itself, a reductio ad absurdum of my view.

Now "illusion," perhaps, was a bad choice of words for what I was talking about, although it is in common use for that sort of thing. For "illusion" suggests trompe l'oeil, deception, whereas, in the examples cited above, I do not labor under false beliefs that the conjurer uses magic, that the painting is a real space, or that the "scientific" account of how time travel is possible, in the science fiction novel, really makes scientific sense. And indeed it has been emphasized often enough to qualify as received opinion that deception, far from being necessary for the proper appreciation of such aesthetic features is, indeed, destructive of it. My enjoyment in part is *in* my knowing that it seems like magic but isn't, *in* my knowing that it looks like space but is a two-dimensional surface, *in* my knowing the impression of scientific plausibility is really achieved by cleverly fashioned pseudoscientific gibberish.

A better and safer way, perhaps, to describe what I was talking about when I called character depth and complexity in opera an "illusion" is to call it simply an "aesthetic" or "artistic effect." But there was some method to my original madness in using the term "illusion," for I wanted in my book on opera to distinguish sharply between how the aesthetic effect of character depth and complexity is achieved (say) Dostoyevski's *Notes from Underground* and how it is achieved in *Don Giovanni*, in such a way as to bring out a certain, admittedly attenuated, sense in which the Underground Man or Hamlet has depth and complexity and the characters of Mozart's opera do not.

Of course neither the Underground Man nor Don Giovanni is real: They are both fictional, and whatever character traits either of them possesses are possessed fictionally. Their personalities are aesthetic effects. But the aesthetic effect of character depth and complexity, in the case of the Underground Man, is achieved in a way that might properly be contrasted with the way it is achieved in the case of Don Giovanni, as between the "real" and the "illusory" in the following sense. Dostoyevski's prose generates numerous fictional truths about the Underground Man which, if they were true of a real man, would mark him out as of deep and complex character. Mozart's music can generate no such fictional truths: No such real man of deep and complex character can be derived from it except by feats of imaginative construction that have little to do with the music itself and much to do with the mind of the imaginer. It directly follows from this contrast that one can gain some deep insights into the human psyche from a close reading of *Notes from Underground* – and I believe Freud did. But no such insights, in my opinion, are recoverable from *Don Giovanni*.

Now one can pronounce the incantation day and night until doomsday is here, that Mozart had deep insights into human nature, and that the expression of these insights, in the form of the musical characterization of the personages in his operas, makes them the great works that they are. But incantations won't make it true, and it is fair to ask of anyone who claims to have gained deep insights into human nature from experiencing Mozart's operas to tell us what those insights are and, perhaps even more important, to show us how the music has conveyed them. One would require no less from someone who claimed to have acquired psychological insights from reading Dostoyevski or the Greek playwrights. Everyone knows how an appeal to the text of a literary work might corroborate such a claim. To those who make a similar claim for the music of Mozart, or anyone else's music, for that matter, the means of corroboration are anything but clear or uncontroversial. I do not say the thing is impossible. It is notoriously difficult to prove the negative. But until the unicorn is produced, I think I have the right – indeed the duty – to remain skeptical.

Of course anyone who still retains his common sense intact with regard to this question does have one very powerful empirical argument, independent of any philosophical position as to the informative powers of music, that Mozart's does not convey deep insights into human nature. For we have, in my opinion, plenty of hard evidence, in his voluminous correspondence, that Mozart had little insight at all into the deeper psychology of the people he encountered in his adult life, although he had a good eye for the surface behavior and manners at the tip of the human iceberg. I agree with little else in Wolfgang Hildesheimer's book on Mozart, but I do agree with his assessment of Mozart's letters: "they are less evidence of an understanding of human nature than of a superior stage instinct, with exact descriptions of scenes and their possible effect on an audience."[9] Mozart but slenderly knew human nature, either other people's or, I suspect, his own. But if Mozart demonstrably had no deep insights into human nature to convey, then his music does not (by consequence) convey them.

Now the question still remains – and an imposing question it is – of how, in the light of these skeptical conclusions, Mozart did manage to achieve for his fictional characters the life that Dostoyevski and others achieved for theirs, without

9 Wolfgang Hildesheimer, *Mozart*, trans. Marion Faber (New York: Farrar, Straus & Giroux, 1982), p. 127.

being able to generate fictional truths with the power to impart the aesthetic effect of depth and complexity. I said in my book that the effect was achieved by the sheer beauty of the music. Tanner sounds as if that conclusion strikes him as an empty one, and in a sense it is. It is true but empty – empty, however, not because it cannot be fleshed out but merely because it came at the end of a book that had concerned itself for the most part with other matters. It was in the nature of a promissory note; and I will conclude by at least beginning to give it some cash value, although I certainly cannot complete the transaction here and now.

If I were to say of anything that it is beautiful, a perfectly reasonable response might be a request for further particulars: "In what respect is it beautiful?" or perhaps "What is beautiful about it?" There are kinds of beauty, and there are various ways in which something or someone may be beautiful. And it is so with music, as with other things. Can we then perhaps say in what way the music that characterizes operatic personages is beautiful, what kind or kinds of beauty it exhibits? And might this not at least help to tell us *how* the beauty of operatic music gives life to the characters? I hope to convince you of affirmative answers to both questions.

Don Giovanni, Papageno, Osmin – all sing beautiful music. It needs no ghost come from the grave to tell us this. But what kind of beautiful music do they sing? In what ways is it beautiful? Well one very obvious and useful answer to those questions emerges from the trivial observation that each of the three named is a fictional persona and music his mode of expression. And so it follows directly that each of these characters, in singing and being accompanied by beautiful music, expresses himself beautifully. And further, we can say that each of them expresses beautifully – as beautifully as we can imagine anyone expressing anything – his thoughts, his feelings, his personality traits. Don Giovanni expresses love and lust, passion and anger, amusement and arrogance in the most beautiful music imaginable. He expresses these things beautifully. The music is beautifully expressive of them. We can say the same things, *mutatis mutandis*, for Papageno's

earthiness and simplicity, or Osmin's lechery and irascibil-
ity. Not all these traits are admirable. But each is expressed
admirably.[10]

We have a name for this: it is *eloquence*. Whatever else Mozart's operatic characters are, they are always *eloquent*. My
suggestion, then, is that the aesthetic effect of character depth
and complexity is achieved by Mozart, not, *per impossibile* for
a composer, by generating fictional truths of detail and complexity, like a Dostoyevski or Shakespeare, but by making
his characters express themselves *eloquently*, no matter how
little of real substance they may have to express. And thus it
is that they live in our imaginations. It may perhaps sound
like a council of despair to say that the aesthetic effect of
character depth and complexity is achieved in Mozart's operas by the sheer beauty of the music. But once one begins
to spell out what *kind* of beauty we are talking about, namely,
beauty of expression, or, in other words, *eloquence*, the hypothesis, I think, begins to take on explanatory plausibility
and power.

Nevertheless, I imagine the following objection may be
thrown up straightaway: "You have demonstrated," it may
be argued, "no real *connection* between eloquence and the
aesthetic effect of complexity or depth. Certainly it is true
that the characters in all of Mozart's great works for the stage
express themselves *eloquently*. And it is certainly true that
they have produced in us the very strong aesthetic effect of
depth and complexity. But how do we know there is any
operative relation between the one and the other? Why should
eloquence of expression, in the absence of depth and complexity, convey the impression of them?"

But here I think we can appeal to a very real phenomenon,
familiar to us in our own experience, that makes that connection both comfortable and plausible. It is the phenomenon of the confidence trick which Tanner adduced as a supposed reductio ad absurdum of my view; for the more I think

10 For further remarks on operatic expression, see Peter Kivy, "Opera Talk: A
Philosophical 'Phantasie,' " *Cambridge Opera Journal* 3 (1991). Reprinted in this
volume, Chapter VII.

about it the more it seems to me to be the absolute truth of the matter, and I thank him for the unintended suggestion. A confidence trick is performed by that well-known and much admired figure, the confidence man, or flim-flam artist. And the way the confidence man, or flim-flam artist commonly works is with his powers of expression: glib talk. By giving us the linguistic trappings of substance, he makes us believe the substance is there. With an Oxford lisp, or a Viennese accent, he passes himself off as a savant. Speak nonsense with enough linguistic panache and you can take in multitudes, as has often enough been proven. To revert to some once popular cant, the confidence man makes use of the illusion that the medium is the message. His eloquence is empty; but it is a well-known human foible to take eloquence for substance. And whatever the root causes of the phenomenon, the con man uses it to his advantage.

The operatic character, then, is a kind of musical con man. He or she taps into a very deep-seated tendency of us all to take the medium for a message. It is not merely a unique phenomenon of the operatic stage; if it were, it would indeed make my claim both puzzling and highly suspect. But the operatic phenomenon in which musical eloquence produces the aesthetic effect of character depth and complexity is just another example of the familiar and ubiquitous human tendency to be gulled by eloquence.

And what of the operatic composer? What of Mozart? Well, is he not a confidence man too – a flim-flam artist? Indeed he is, for he is the mastermind behind the whole sordid scheme. He shamelessly plays on our insatiable appetites for being duped, and we love him for it, just as the victim so frequently loves the flim-flam man, even after the scam is exposed. Indeed the con man, far from being a despised enemy of society is, on the contrary, a folk hero. Nor, by the way, is the identification of artist with con man my own conceit. It is, indeed, a persistent cultural metaphor perhaps most memorably invoked in our own century by Thomas Mann's character, Felix Krull, who first emerged in a short story of the same name in 1918, later expanded into a novel with the

more revealing title: *Confessions of Felix Krull, Confidence Man*.
Of the earlier version, Mann wrote: *"Felix Krull* . . . is in essence the story of an artist; in it the element of the unreal
and illusional passes frankly into the criminal."[11] And in another of Mann's well-known literary evocations of this image
of the artist, he has Tonio Kröger writing of the literary man
as "this vain and frigid charlatan."[12]

We have all been conned, then, by Mozart, the ultimate
musical flim-flam man; teased into seeing complexity and
depth where there is *only* eloquence. What a damning word
that "only" – but *only* if you go to the opera with the Platonic
obsession that the point of the exercise must be the acquisition of knowledge: insight into human nature, as if *Lucia di
Lammermoor* might be a pleasant substitute for a treatise on
insanity.

I believe people who go to the opera under the impression
that they must look there for insight into human nature or
character are somehow missing the point – or, rather, the
points; for surely opera is rich with allurements, and, I confess, although it may sound patronizing, I rather feel sorry
for someone who goes to a performance of *Don Giovanni* to
learn something about the psychology of the seducer, or
whatever else. Opera is magic, not psychology. Above all, it
is drama-made-music. But that is a theme I have spoken to
elsewhere, and cannot speak to here and now.

But perhaps the altogether appropriate ending to make here
and now is by way of quotation from arguably the greatest
composer of opera that has ever lived, and the subject of this
gathering. I think, if one reads the lines, and between the
lines of passages like this one can learn more about what
opera really is than from all the philosophers in the world,
including the one who addresses you now.

Mozart to his father, 26 September, 1781:

> Now for the trio at the close of Act I. Pedrillo has passed
> off his master as an architect – to give him an opportunity of

11 Thomas Mann, *Stories of Three Decades*, trans. H. T. Lowe-Porter (New York:
   Alfred A. Knopf, 1955), Preface, p.vii.
12 Ibid,. "Tonio Kröger," p. 107.

meeting Constanze in the garden. Bassa Selim has taken him into his service. Osmin, the steward, knows nothing of this, and being a rude churl and a sworn foe to all strangers, is impertinent and refuses to let them into the garden. It opens quite abruptly – and because the words lend themselves to it, I have made it a fairly respectable piece of real three-part writing. Then the major key begins at once pianissimo – it must go very quickly – and wind up with a great deal of noise, which is always appropriate at the end of an act. The more noise the better, and the shorter the better, so that the audience may not have time to cool down with their applause.[13]

Sly rogue! Confidence man indeed. He has us in the palm of his hand; and we love him for it.

13 *Letters of Mozart and His Family*, trans. Emily Anderson (London: Macmillan, 1938), vol. 3, pp. 1145–6.

Chapter IX

How did Mozart do it?:
Replies to some critics

Two of my commentators, Paul Robinson and Wye Allan-brook, have homed in on my choice of Dostoyevski's *Notes from Underground* as an example of how character depth is achieved in literature and cannot be achieved in music. Perhaps I am to blame, I don't know; but both of them have completely missed my point, and in similar ways. Professor Allanbrook says that: "Prof. Kivy has removed music from the arena of characterization because he expects all characterization to be achieved by this Dostoevskian introspection or *self*-explanation."[1] But that was not the point at all. The point was simply that it is achieved by *language*. I could have chosen *any* example from world literature from Homer to James Joyce to illustrate my point.

Some literary characters, Professor Allanbrook quite rightly points out, have their characters revealed to us by their interaction with one another. And she quotes Aristotle's famous precept that character is revealed through action. Both of these claims seem to be advanced as counterexamples to my argument. But they are counterexamples only to the claim I did *not* make, that all character depth is achieved through the genre of introspective literature, not the claim that I *did* make, which is simply that character depth in literature cannot be achieved without the resources of *language*.

---

1 Wye Jamison Allanbrook, unpublished comments delivered at a symposium on characterization in Mozart's operas, Hofstra University.

Perhaps it may seem as if Allanbrook has produced counterexamples to my language thesis as well. After all, action and character interaction are neither of them "language": they are nonlinguistic "doings"; and if character depth can be achieved in literature (and opera as well) by nonlinguistic "doings," then my thesis is defeated. But this is not the case, as a brief consideration of "action" and "interaction" will immediately make clear.

An action is not merely the physical motion of a human body. Oedipus' character is revealed by what he does, and Hamlet's by what he does not do (also an "action"). True enough; so far so good. But how do I know *what* Oedipus did, or Hamlet delayed in doing? Surely not by the physical motions alone that the actors go through on the stage in playing their parts, not by dumb show or choreography. I know what *actions* Oedipus performed, and Hamlet did not through what they and the other characters *say*. Character depth may indeed be achieved in literature sometimes through action and interaction, not introspective autobiography (as in the case of the underground man). However, it is through the resources of a conceptually rich language that these actions, interactions, and inactions are constituted. And since my point was merely about the indispensability of language to the enterprise, not how language was used – as dialogue, narrative description, soliloquy, stream of consciousness, action, interaction, whatever – the fact that character, as Aristotle so profoundly observed, can be revealed in action is no counterexample to my argument.

Mary Hunter makes a nice observation on how she thinks Mozart, in one place, deepens Figaro's character with *music*. And I gather that this is offered as a counterexample to my thesis that character depth cannot be musically imparted.

In denying that he is the author of the letter that the Count knows full well he has written, Figaro sings the not very inspiring line: "My face lies but not I." But he sings it, Professor Hunter points out, to "a little hymn"; and she argues: "We should have expected Figaro to be able to introduce a convincing diversion at an otherwise awkward moment, but the use of a hymn for that purpose, I think, suggests 'heart' as well as 'strategy' – perhaps depth as well as complexity."[2]

Now here I think I must invoke the distinction I made in my essay between *characterizing* and *animating* an operatic persona. For what Hunter has pointed out in her example is, I think, a case of the latter. Figaro is a buffa character. Mozart has made him more serious here, as in other places, than a buffa character might be expected to be, by giving him music of an expressively "serious" quality, thus helping to characterize him as something other than merely buffa. Such techniques, I pointed out, were the common property of opera composers in Mozart's day. But only Mozart's characters "live"; so that cannot be what does the trick.

But suppose Professor Hunter wishes to go further. Suppose she wishes to push hard on the *hymn*-like quality of the tune that Mozart gives Figaro and to suggest that the composer is not merely imparting to him a serious but a specifically *religious* dimension as well. This might perhaps be seen as a way in which music can indeed deepen a character in the way the resources of literary language can. I am sure there are such cases, whether or not this is one, and I have no wish to stonewall on the matter. Let me suggest, however, that the multiplying of such cases will not do the job, *my* job, anyway.

My question is: How did Mozart make his characters "live"? They began to live for audiences, not, of course, from the very beginning. Mozart, like many other artists, was difficult for his contemporaries. "Too many notes, my dear Mozart" (except in Prague).

But when Mozart's great operatic works did begin to be appreciated, and his great operatic characters did begin to "live" for opera audiences, it must have been some quality or cluster of qualities that the ordinary opera lover heard, that made them live, not such minutiae, interesting though

---

2 Mary Hunter, unpublished comments delivered at a symposium on characterization in Mozart's operas, Hofstra University.

they are, that critics and musicologists like Professor Hunter have managed, with admirable ingenuity, to find. And I think we can lay that down as a kind of condition for *any* successful account of what has made Mozart's operatic characters "live" for the general opera public. If what is proposed as the animating quality is something that only the "experts" and "connoisseurs" have heard, then it simply does not answer *my* question, which is: What makes Mozart's characters live for opera lovers? Although perhaps it does answer the question: What makes Mozart's characters "live" for experts and connoisseurs?

The answer I have given to my question is: musical beauty, eloquence of musical expression. That, we can assume, all lovers of Mozart hear; and so my account does fulfill that necessary condition for a true explanation. It does not, of course, guarantee its truth. But I think Hunter's discovery, and those like it, are bound to fail from the start, in answering *my* question, although I am far from denying that they may help deepen my own appreciation of Mozart, when my ear tells me they are valid musical interpretations.

Paul Robinson says that he

> can see no meaningful correlation between musical beauty and characterological depth – whether real or imaginary. Surely the music that Don Ottavio sings is extraordinarily beautiful, but it does very little to create a vivid character. On the other hand, Elvira's music is no more beautiful than Ottavio's, yet she is both vivid and complex precisely to the extent that he is pale and flat.[3]

In his reference to Don Ottavio as a counterexample to my view, Robinson, I think, raises three separate issues which are all worthy of discussion. The first turns on a matter of terminology; I did not say "merely" a matter of terminology because this happens to be a rather important terminological matter, and I am at fault for not foreseeing the possible confusion that lack of clarity on this point might produce.

3 Paul Robinson, unpublished comments delivered at a symposium on characterization in Mozart's operas, Hofstra University.

When I referred in my essay to depth of character, I meant what is sometimes referred to as a character's having "three dimensions," as opposed to being "two-dimensional," "merely pasteboard," "flat," or something of that kind. It is a property of *representations*. The characters in Shakespeare's more important plays, or in the plays of Euripides are, in this sense, deep, whereas the characters in Oscar Wilde's *The Importance of Being Earnest* are "two-dimensional," "shallow," "flat."

But there is another sense of "deep" versus "shallow" in which, for example, Hamlet is a deep character, but Polonius a shallow one: Hamlet is a very complicated, profound human being, and Polonius a rather pedantic, pompous purveyor of clichés, a quite ordinary, shallow human being in fact. In this sense, "depth" and "shallowness" are not properties of *representation* but of the *characters represented, psychological properties*, if you will. But both Hamlet and Polonius are "deep" in the *representational* sense; both are therefore given "life" (for real human beings are, of course, always three-dimensional, even when psychologically shallow).

Let us, then, for purposes of clarity, distinguish between being *representationally* deep or three-dimensional and being *psychologically* deep or three-dimensional. With this distinction in hand, we can now turn to the particular case of Don Ottavio.

To begin with, I think Robinson may be confusing, in his discussion of Don Ottavio, representational depth with psychological depth. Don Ottavio is psychologically shallow; of that there is no doubt. He sings exquisitely beautiful, eloquent music; of *that* there is no doubt. I said in my essay that it is the singing of beautiful music that gives the impression of depth. Isn't Don Ottavio, then, a clear counterexample? No! Not if one remembers that a psychologically shallow character can be representationally deep. What I was arguing is that the sheer beauty of music is what gives operatic characters the impression of representational depth; and the impression of representational depth makes them "live." It is perfectly compatible with my view – indeed, if it weren't my view would be defective – for a character to be psychologically shallow and representationally deep. I think Don Ottavio might well be such a character.

But perhaps Robinson is claiming that Don Ottavio clearly is a character that does not "live," that cannot, therefore, possess even the impression of representational depth, yet sings beautiful, eloquent music, which should, on my view, not be possible. He now emerges again as a counterexample, this time in a more powerful form.

This brings me to the second issue, which is not a philosophical one but, rather, one of substantive interpretation. What *is* Don Ottavio? This is very much a judgment call. But I happen to think that Don Ottavio does "live." God knows, for a shallow pate, he has been talked about often enough in the literature to suggest that he has a powerful hold on our interest and attention. So Don Ottavio does not seem to me a genuine counterexample. He is a Polonius: psychologically shallow, but, because of the extraordinary eloquence and beauty of his musical expression, given by Mozart the impression of representational depth. However, if Don Ottavio is not in fact the kind of candidate for counterexample that Robinson is looking for, there are, I am sure, others that do fit the description. So I will propose some myself.

It is sometimes said that Osmin, the cantankerous harem keeper in *Die Entführung,* is Mozart's first great comic character; and I take him to be, in my terms, a character whom Mozart has made to "come alive." The rest of the characters in the work, particularly the "serious" ones, remain sticks: representationally two-dimensional. Yet they all sing music as beautiful as Osmin's; Constanze, as a matter of fact, sings two of the most eloquent arias that Mozart ever composed. So all the characters in *Die Entführung,* with the single exception of Osmin, seem to be palpable counterexamples to my thesis, for they express themselves eloquently yet fail to give the aesthetic impression of representational character depth.

However, these are only counterexamples to the thesis that singing beautiful music is a *sufficient* condition for representational three-dimensionality and "life." And that is not my thesis, although I was certainly at fault in not making it entirely clear in my essay. My thesis is that eloquent musical expression is a *necessary* condition for the impression of representational depth, and, indeed, far and away the most important one. But something else is also needed. The character does have to have, to start with, some intriguing quality or qualities, prior to being treated musically; and that all but Osmin, in *Die Entführung*, absolutely lack.

Where do these prior intriguing qualities come from? Sometimes, of course, from a superior librettist – a Da Ponte, a Boito, a Metastasio – who through his literary gifts gives the composer interesting characters to work with in the first place. Sometimes they come from a preexistent folk tradition or mythology, which has already imbued them with human interest, so that even in the hands of a poor librettist they exude a built-in fascination. I am thinking here of a Faust or a Don Juan, or any number of figures from various ancient and medieval mythic traditions. Sometimes they may come from preexistent literary works of a high quality, retaining some of their interest from associations with these works, even though they fall into the hands of distinctly inferior librettists. (Shakespeare's characters immediately come to mind here.) Osmin is, roughly speaking, a folk character: the lecherous harem keeper, although he may also gain some of his initial interest from the fact that Stephanie, although no Da Ponte, managed to do more with him than with the rest of the crew.

Of course much more needs to be said about the literary and broadly cultural factors that contribute to the initial interest that an operatic character may have, prior to the "life" that the great composer, with its help, may impart. But it cannot be said here.

Finally, I should like to address briefly Robinson's claim that: "To use somewhat old-fashioned language, music has more direct access to the soul than does language, and in the hands of a great artist like Mozart, it stands not in a disadvantaged, but in a privileged, relation to the creation of character."[4]

What am I to make of Robinson's notion that music, in contrast to language, has direct access to the soul? It has been said often enough to have infiltrated what is commonly called "common sense," and become part of that much abused faculty. It is a beautiful thought, and many people like to think it. But what does it mean, and, common sense notwithstanding, is it true?

Well, it has meant a lot of things to a lot of people since the time when Orpheus tamed the wild beasts and the furies. All I can do here is venture a guess as to what it might mean for Robinson. I dare say a lot of people do believe, and perhaps Robinson is one of them, that there is some kind of concept-emotion dichotomy, with discursive language on the one side, music on the other. The most influential source for this doctrine, in modern times, is Rousseau's *Origin of Language* (1764). But it goes further back than that. Be that as it may, it is seriously mistaken in two major respects, although I am interested in discussing only one of them here. It is seriously mistaken, to begin with, as contemporary philosophical analysis has amply demonstrated, in seeing a concept-emotion dichotomy in the first place; and it is mistaken, as well (and this is my present concern) in thinking that music, not language, is somehow the more emotively potent instrument. Indeed, "common sense" (perhaps) to the contrary, it is the other way around: *Language* is the far more potent emotive weapon.

Or perhaps I had better say, if one *really* applies "common sense" and forgets the "orphic mysteries" – if one *really* thinks for a moment about the profound penetration of language into our lives, and our very nature as human beings – it will readily be seen how mistaken it must be to think that music can possibly have a more direct access to our emotions than our own native language, whatever it may be. Every school

4 Ibid.

185

of philosophy that has flourished in the twentieth century, in Britain, America, or on the Continent, has emphasized the role of language in forming our world and ourselves; and, indeed, it has been insisted by many that language is a necessary condition for thinking, having beliefs, having a conscious life at all. The twentieth-century definition of "human" might well be: "linguistic animal."

That music speaks directly to the emotions is a saying commonly maintained, and a charming belief. But what is much more obvious is that *language* does. You can find that out easily enough by saying loudly the single word "fire" in a crowded theatre or "nigger" in an assembly of black Americans. *That* is going direct to the emotions and music can't come within a mile of matching it, except where it is music with extra-musical, particularly *verbal* associations (for example, playing "Dixie" in an assembly of black Americans).

I am not, by the way, denying that music has expressive (which is to say emotive) qualities, or that listening to music can be a deeply moving experience. I have written on both these aspects of it at some length. But I fail to see how either could be particularly germane to the present question; and appealing yet again, at this latter day, to the mysterious powers of music that give it direct access to the soul or to the emotions or to the heart, as somehow an answer to the question of how composers either characterize or animate or deepen their operatic personages seems to me just whistling past the graveyard.

It remains for me now to conclude by thanking Wye Allanbrook, Mary Hunter, and Paul Robinson for their contributions to this discussion and for their critical comments on my essay. I am sure I have not quelled all of their doubts – probably not any of them. But I do feel that the four of us together have advanced the subject. That seems to me accomplishment enough.

Music and the history of ideas

Chapter X

Mozart and monotheism: An essay in spurious aesthetics

In the *Allgemeine Musikalische Zeitung* for 23 August, 1815, J. F. Rochlitz printed a "letter," purported to be by Mozart, and now agreed on all hands to be spurious.[1] Since the time of its publication, this "letter" has had no little influence on psychologists and philosophers, beginning with William James,[2] owing among other things, to a rather bizarre, but nonetheless intriguing, account of how the composer was supposed to have mentally perceived his finished works. It is my purpose, in what follows, finally, both with historical and philosophical arguments, to lay this strange idea to rest.

The idea in question is contained in the following, frequently excerpted passage from the spurious "letter." The "pseudo-Mozart" (as I shall henceforth call him) says:

> my subject enlarges itself, becomes methodized and defined, and the whole, though it be long, stands almost complete and finished in my mind, so that I can survey it, like a fine picture or a beautiful statue, at a glance. Nor do I hear in my imagination the parts *successively*, but I hear them, as it were, all at once.[3]

---

1 *Allgemeine Musikalische Zeitung*, Siebzehnten Jahrgang vom 4. Januar 1815 bis 27. December 1815, No. 34, Der 23sten August, pp. 563–6.

2 William James, *Principles of Psychology* (New York, 1890), Vol. I, p. 255 n.

3 From the English translation reprinted in Edward Holmes, *The Life of Mozart* (New York, 1868), p. 329. The German reads: "da wird es immer weiter und heller aus; und das Ding wird im Kopfe wahrlich fast fertig, wenn es auch lang ist, so dass ichs hernach mit einem Blick, gleichsam wie ein schönes Bild oder einen hübschen Menschen, im Geiste übersehe, und es auch gar nicht nach einander, wie es hernach kommen muss, in der Einbildung höre, sondern, wie gleich alles zusammen" (pp. 563–4).

What has intrigued psychologists and aestheticians, of course, and confounded common sense, is the suggestion that Mozart – or anyone else, for that matter – could contemplate mentally a temporal event *atemporally*, as it were. For that indeed is what the passage seems to imply about Mozart's way of conceptualizing his works. To "hear" a work of music "in the head," one supposes, would be to "hear" it mentally just the way one would hear it at a performance. When a tune "runs through my head," what happens is that I "hear" it from beginning to end in my imagination, from incipit to cadence, just as I would if I heard it played on an oboe or flute. A tune, after all, is a temporal event. And, one has a right to presume, to "hear" a symphony (say) "in the head" would just be to multiply, horizontally and vertically, the "tune in the head" phenomenon. Now I "hear" not only tunes but their harmonic and contrapuntal accompaniment; and I "hear" them, their harmony and their counterpoint, not just abstractly, so to speak, but fully orchestrated: in other words, I "hear" timbre as well as pitch. But just as in the case of the tune "running through the head," I am having a temporal experience of a temporal event, as I would at a concert, I "hear" the symphony "in the head" from first to last, from *premier coup d'archet* to coda. This, we feel obliged to believe, was the kind of experience Brahms was alluding to when he was invited out to hear a performance of *Don Giovanni* (I think it was), and replied, pointing to his score of the work: "Why should I go out when I can hear a better performance at home?" And this, I am certain, is what common sense tells us the mental experience of music is for the gifted, even though we ourselves cannot duplicate it. For we all have had the "tune in the head" experience, and can imagine what it would be like to be able to "hear" a whole symphony that way, just as we all can add small numbers mentally, and so can imagine what it would be like to be able to add enormously large and long columns of figures, like the "calculating boy."

But try as hard as you can to imagine what it would be like to "hear" the whole Linz Symphony "in your head," yet not hear it from beginning to end: rather, to hear it as the pseudo-Mozart implies he might, not *"successively,* but . . . as it were, all at once." How would it be done? What would it be like? How can I "hear" the slow introduction to the first movement while, in the same timeless instant of mental legerdemain I am *also* "hearing" the episode in E minor, the trio of the minuet, and so on. Whatever I would be hearing (more like Ives than Mozart, no doubt), it would not be the Thirty-Sixth Symphony. I cannot imagine even what it would be like to hear "Yankee Doodle" that way, let alone the Linz.

It might perhaps be suggested at this point that a false interpretation is being put on the pseudo-Mozart's claim because the word "parts" is being misconstrued. Could it be that what is intended is "obbligato parts" or "voices" rather than the successive "parts" – that is to say, "sections" – of a work? If that were the case, then the pseudo-Mozart would be saying nothing bizarre or absurd at all: merely that he can "hear" (say) the four voices of a string quartet sounding all together, "in his head," the very way they would sound if he were actually hearing the work. That is to say, he would be claiming that his musical imagination can reproduce a mental "performance" of music in which he hears vertically as well as horizontally – something which we all agree many are capable of.

But appearances cannot, alas, be saved in this simple way. For later on in the "letter," where the pseudo-Mozart is clearly speaking of obbligato parts rather than successive sections of a musical work, he expresses himself in quite different language, using, as one would expect, the German word "Stimme,"[4] a word that does not occur at all in the passage in question. Thus we must conclude, I think, that the pseudo-Mozart was indeed saying what he has been taken to say: that he mentally "heard" temporal musical events, of even long duration, atemporally. That is the extraordinary claim we must deal with; it cannot be avoided by interpretational stratagems of the more obvious kind.

4 Rochlitz. *Allgemeine*, p. 566.

The first, and most effective step, I am sure, in coming to the conclusion that what the pseudo-Mozart has described is a palpable absurdity, is to try to do it, if not with the Linz Symphony, then with "Yankee Doodle" or "Smoke Gets in Your Eyes." Add 5 + 7 in your head and you will have *some* idea of what it would be like for the calculating boy to add in his head one hundred seven-digit figures. Hear in your head "Smoke Gets in Your Eyes" and you will have *some* idea of what it was like for Brahms to "hear in his head" a complete performance of *Don Giovanni* from overture to final sextet. (I presume Brahms would not have approved of ending with the penultimate scene.) But I have no advice to give you about how to imagine what it would be like to "hear in your head" a piece of music atemporally, at a glance. The problem is not one of finding something simple enough. You can, Humpty Dumpty-like, try 2 + 2 if 7 + 5 is too much for you. You can try "How Dry I Am" instead of "Smoke Gets in Your Eyes" if those little chromatic alterations bother you. There is nothing, however, no matter how simple, that I have ever found, that can help me to imagine what it would be like to hear a tune, let alone a symphony, all at once, at a glance. A tune takes time to get from incipit to cadence; and it takes the same time to hear it, whether mentally, or played on a penny whistle.

But wait a bit, the true believer will doubtless respond. The reason *you* or *I* cannot imagine what it would be like to "hear music in your head" atemporally is that we are not genuises. How do you presume to say what *genius* cannot do, especially if the genius is of the magnitude of a Mozart, whom Goethe called a "divine mystery"? He could memorize the *Miserere* of Allegri on first hearing, couldn't he? He could "read" *Singet dem Herrn* merely from a set of parts and compose a concert aria of imposing dimensions, on demand, while locked in a summer house. What *couldn't* the divine Mozart do? If he said that he "heard" music "in his head" *atemporally, believe* him, or you will be like a blind man who denies there are colors.

That, of course, brings us to the second step in dislodging this musical myth. For, as the scholars now agree, the letter is spurious.[5] No need therefore to acquiesce in the face of an "eye-witness" report of a genius. The report is a fraud. Mozart never told us how he "heard" music "in his head," and there is no reason to believe it was any different from the way we do: orders of magnitude more vivid and complete, no doubt; but like the rest of us mortals, after all, in kind. He had a most wonderful brain; but the same chemical structure to it. His wig, like my hat, rested on protoplasm. So much, then, for divine mysteries.

But there can still, I imagine, be a lingering doubt to this effect. Surely the idea expressed in the spurious letter is a remarkable one. And, one might insist, such a remarkable idea must either be the product of a remarkably fertile and original philosophical imagination, or else, whatever the *echtheit* (or lack thereof) of the document in which it is conveyed, the first-hand report of a genuine human experience. But Rochlitz was no genius, and that he had some unknown genius scribbling down his inspirations in the backroom of the *Allgemeine Musikalische Zeitung* seems highly improbable. So, the argument continues, the only reasonable conclusion to reach is that the letter does indeed, for all its lack of his-

---

5 It is no part of my purpose here to go into the quite convincing external and internal evidence for the inauthenticity of this letter. For me it is pretty much clinched by the following consideration. In an undoubtedly genuine letter to his wife, from Dresden, dated 16 April, 1789. Mozart describes a mass he has just heard, by Johann Gottlieb Naumann (1741–1801), as "poor stuff" (*The Letters of Mozart and His Family*, trans. Emily Anderson [New York, 1938], Vol. 3, p. 1372). The other "Mozart," however, describes what one presumes to be the same mass as "beautiful and well harmonized" (Holmes, p. 330). In any event, the *echtheit* of the letter had already been called into question by Otto Jahn in 1858. And Maynard Solomon has performed a similar service for a passage about Beethoven based on the spurious but always appealing Mozart letter which, doubtless, was woven out of whole cloth. Jahn says of the letter that it "is incontestably a fabrication" (Otto Jahn, *The Life of Mozart*, trans. Pauline D. Townsend [New York, n.d.] Vol. 2, p. 415 n). And Solomon says of Rochlitz: "There is an extensive pattern of fabrication in Rochlitz's contributions to the Mozart literature that would lead a prudent observer to reject the whole" ("On Beethoven's Creative Process: A Two-Part Invention," *Music and Letters* 61 [1980], p. 279).

torical credentials, report *some* composer's account of how he "heard" music "in his head," although the composer may not have been Mozart.

This brings us to the third, and final step in the long overdue debunking of a fascinating but fraudulent piece of "psychology of genius." For if it can be shown that the idea in question – namely, the atemporal imagining of music "in the head" – really has an obvious and readily available philosophical source, there will be no need to assume that its creation was beyond the mental powers of Rochlitz and his minions. Once, I think, the source of this idea is uncovered, it becomes very plain that it is the product not of a composer's introspective report, but, rather, of the busy Romantic imagination, working with materials ready to hand, far below the level of genius. I will turn now to the task of revealing that source.

In an address called "From Addison to Kant: Origins of the Modern Theory of Art," M. H. Abrams has called attention to the significance, for aesthetic theory, of the notion of the work of art as a "self-contained world."[6] This notion, which began developing in earnest in the Renaissance, had, by the end of the eighteenth century, become received opinion in many circles. Closely related to the idea of the work of art as a "world" was the idea of the artist as a "creator" in a very theological sense of that word. The artist's relation to the world of his work was seen as a direct analogue to the Deity's relation to the world at large; the artist's creative act, then, a direct analogue to the goings on in Genesis. I strongly suspect that this idea has its roots in Plato's notion of the poet as, in his creative frenzy, possessed of the god and, therefore, temporarily a god himself. But wherever it begins, it is already fairly well formed, with its Platonic origins quite out in the open, in Sir Philip Sidney's *An Apology for Poetry* (c. 1583), a work of no little influence. Sidney says:

6 M. H. Abrams, "From Addison to Kant: Origins of the Modern Theory of Art," lecture delivered on the occasion of the annual meeting of the American Society for Aesthetics, October, 1981.

Onely the poet . . . , lifted up with the vigor of his owne in-
uention, dooth growe in effect another nature, in making things
either better than Nature bringeth forth, or, quite a newe . . .
so as hee goeth hand in hand with Nature, not inclosed within
the narrow warrant of her guifts, but freely ranging onely
within the Zodiack of his owne wit.

And again: "Neyther let it be deemed too sawcie a comparison to ballance the highest poynt of mans wit with the effi-
cacie of Nature."[7] The poet, then, can create his own world,
with laws and relations of its own, as Nature, with the ac-
quiescence – indeed the direct cooperation – of God, her
Creator, grinds out the world that we know according to the
laws that we discover. Without further comment, I think the
analogy between work and world, artist and God, stands out
in full clarity.

I cannot relate the development of this idea any better than
Abrams has done, or with any greater erudition. So I shall
not try. All that is necessary, anyway, for present purposes,
is to be aware of the ubiquitousness of this analogy between
God and His world, and the artist and his work, in the eighteenth century, and beyond. For this is, I shall argue, the
source of the pseudo-Mozart's notion that the composer sur-
veys his work "in his head" at a glance, atemporally. The
step is an obvious one, once you think of it, for anyone who
has even a passing acquaintance with theology.

To illustrate how that step was taken, let me remind the
reader of a venerable question in theology: How does God,
who is eternal and unchanging, conceive of the course of
history? That He *must* be able to conceive of it follows from
His omnipotence. But if God conceives of the course of the
battle of Waterloo (say), then He must, it would seem, like
any of the rest of us, *first* perceive Wellington's departure for
the field, *then* the fight at Quatre Bras, *then* Blücher's arrival,

---

7 *Elizabethan Critical Essays*, ed. G. Gregory Smith (Oxford, 1904), Vol. I, pp. 156–
7. On the Platonic "frenzy" and its influence, see Peter Kivy, "Socrates' Discovery: Some Historical Refections," *Journal of Aesthetics and Art Criticism* 39 (1981).

and so on. For the battle of Waterloo was, after all, an *event*, with things occurring in a particular temporal order.

But now a familiar theological problem arises. For if God thinks *first* of Wellington's taking the field, and *then* the fight at Quatre Bras, and *then* Blücher's arrival . . . , the content of His mind *changes* as the course of His thoughts progresses. That, however, implies that God is *not* changeless, which is contrary to hypothesis. Thus, one asserts that God can conceive of the course of temporal events at the cost of denying His changelessness (and, by consequence, such other divine attributes as eternality, perfection, and necessary existence, for reasons it is unnecessary to go into here); or one denies it to save changelessness and the rest at the equally unacceptable cost of denying His omnipotence – a familiar theological pickle.

The traditional resolution of this dilemma, the medievalists tell us, has its source in Book 5 of *The Consolation of Philosophy*, where Boethius writes, with regard to God's foreknowledge and predestination,

> Since then all judgment apprehends the subject of its thought according to its own nature, and God has a condition of ever-present eternity, His knowledge, which passes over every change of time, embracing infinite lengths of past and future, views in its own direct comprehension everything as though it were taking place in the present. If you would weight the foreknowledge by which God distinguishes all things, you will more rightly hold it to be a knowledge of never-failing constancy in the present, than foreknowledge of the future. Whence Providence is more rightly to be understood as looking forward, because it is set far from low matters and looks forth upon all things as from a lofty mountain-top above all. . . . If one may not unworthily compare this present time with the divine, just as you can see things in this your temporal present, so God sees all things in His eternal present.[8]

8 Boethius, *The Consolation of Philosophy*, trans. W. V. Cooper (New York, n.d.), p. 117 (Book 5). I am indebted to my colleague, Seymour Feldman, for calling this passage to my attention.

This is echoed in, among other places, Book 1 of St. Thomas Aquinas' *Summa contra Gentiles*. Thomas says:

> Moreover, God's understanding has no succession, as neither does His being. He is therefore an ever-abiding simultaneous whole – which belongs to the nature of eternity. On the other hand, the duration of time is stretched out through the succession of the before and after. . . . Hence, whatever is found in any part of time coexists with what is eternal as being present to it, although with respect to some other time it be past or future. Something can be present to what is eternal only by being present to the whole of it, since the eternal does not have the duration of succession. The divine intellect, therefore, sees in the whole of its eternity, as being present to it, whatever takes place through the whole course of time.[9]

To put it simply, for present purposes, without picking apart these convoluted passages in detail, what Boethius and the Angelic Doctor are saying is that God does not perceive or conceive of temporal succession in time, but atemporally: as the pseudo-Mozart would say, "at a glance." We must think of the battle of Waterloo successively, one event after another; but for the divine intellect it is present at once, thus saving God's unchangeable wholeness, and the rest. And, to put the matter closer to home, so must the divine intellect perceive or conceive of the Linz Symphony: not introduction first, finale last, but all in a timeless instant, at a glance, present at once to God's mind.

But we need proceed no further to see directly what the source of the pseudo-Mozart's notion is: all we need do is put together the analogy, already widespread at the end of the eighteenth century, between God, as creator of the world, and artist-god as the creator of the world of his work, with

9 St. Thomas Aquinas, *On the Truth of the Catholic Faith: Summa contra Gentiles, Book I: God*, trans. Anton C. Pegis (Garden City, 1955), pp. 218–19 (Book 1, Chapter 66, Section 7).

the theological precept, common to protestants and catholics alike, that God perceives the temporal atemporally, to get the implication that since the composer-artist is "god," and his work, his created world, a temporal event, *he* must conceive of it, as God does the history of the world He has created, atemporally, all at once, at a glance, or as Spinoza would say, *sub specie eternitatis*, "under a certain species of eternity." This, I suggest, is the source of the pseudo-Mozart's bizarre and intriguing idea. Neither the result of a composer's introspective report, nor a genius' philosophical insight – it is a matter simply of adorning what had become almost an aesthetic cliché, with a crown of Sunday school theology.

It seems to me that finally seeing how obvious and ready to hand the pseudo-Mozart's literary and philosophical sources were should lay to rest forever even the sneaking suspicion that Mozart, or anyone else, could, or can conceive of music in the way the pseudo-Mozart describes. Indeed, it is much disputed whether God Himself, if He exists, can conceive of temporal events the way Boethius and Thomas, and a host of other theologians have testified that He must: whether, in fact, it is even logically possible, essentially, for God to perceive temporal events but not "be in time." And what God cannot do I imagine even the most unregenerate Mozart worshipper will be forced to agree Wolfgang Amadeus couldn't do either.

On external grounds we know that the Mozart "letter" is spurious. On common sense grounds we ought to know that what its author suggests about musical thought is impossible. And now I hope I have shown, by tracing the lineage of the pseudo-Mozart's idea, that there is no mystery in where it came from: that we need assume neither the genius of a philosopher unknown, nor, failing that, the introspective report of a composer unsung, as its source. But, I fear, the desire to believe the impossible, if it is bizarre or interesting enough, will overpower all attempts to dislodge this myth of the psychology of music. Like the poisoning of Mozart, the canals of Mars, astrology, and flying saucers, it will survive all rational argument. Well, as the *real* Mozart was fond of saying: *Basta!*[10]

10 An earlier version of this essay was presented to the Greater New York Chapter of the American Musicological Society, 11 December, 1982. I am most grateful to the audience on that occasion for many helpful criticisms and suggestions, and, particularly, to Maynard Solomon, my respondent, for his insightful and well informed remarks.

Chapter XI

Child Mozart as an aesthetic symbol

Not very long ago the late Alfred Einstein expressed the view that "Mozart's effect on musical history" was still but little understood.[1] I would extend this judgment to include not only the history of music but the history of ideas as well; I would include too not only the effect of Mozart's music but the effect of his personality and his life as they are embodied in the legend of the child-man and man-child so familiar to us all. I do not claim that the legend is wholly true, although legends of course have an element of historical truth. For the truth or falsity of the Mozart legend has no relevance to my argument. What *is* relevant is the fact of the legend's existence. This fact must itself be acknowledged and scrutinized by the historian.

My theme is the relation of the Mozart legend to one branch of intellectual history: the history of aesthetics. But I cannot represent what I have done as, in any sense, a systematic study. I offer only reflections on some very well-known passages, both literary and philosophical, that seem to suggest a rather strange and fortuitous connection between the life and character of a musical prodigy and the philosophy of art.

Goethe carried into his old age an image of the child Mozart: "I saw him . . . when he was seven and gave a concert while travelling our way," the poet told Eckermann in 1830;

This is a slightly revised version of a paper read before the Greater New York Chapter of the American Musicological Society, 12 February, 1966.
1 *Mozart, His Character, His Work*, trans. Arthur Mendel and Nathan Broder (New York, 1945), pp. 469–70.

"I myself was about fourteen, and remember perfectly the little man with his frisure and sword."[2]

What Goethe's memory provided him, one could also cull from the early biographies, with all the details that have made Mozart the very symbol of the musical *Wunderkind*. I need hardly rehearse these well-worn stories here; but a small reminder of what Mozart was up to at Cub Scout age may not be out of place. I quote from his sister Nannerl's reminiscences of 1792:

> The son was three years old when the father began to instruct his seven-year-old daughter in the clavier.
>
> The boy at once showed his God-given [and] extraordinary talent. He often spent much time at the clavier, picking out thirds, which he was always striking, and his pleasure showed that it sounded good.
>
> In the fourth year of his age his father, for a game as it were, began to teach him a few minuets and pieces at the clavier. It was so easy for this child and for his father that he learned a piece in an hour and a minuet in half an hour, so that he could play it faultlessly and with the greatest delicacy, and keeping exactly in time. He made such progress that at the age of five he was already composing little pieces, which he played to his father who wrote them down.[3]

However, Mozart the child prodigy is but one aspect of the Mozart legend. Another, perhaps more significant, is Mozart, *the man who remained a child*. "Among his friends he was confiding as a child, full of fun," wrote Niemetschek in his biography of 1798.[4] And according to a Suard, another of the early biographers, "Mozart was all his life a sort of child."[5]

In what sense was Mozart the man childlike? Many of his early biographers portray him as, to use the modern jargon,

2 *Conversations of Goethe with Eckermann,* trans. John Oxenford (London and New York, 1930), p. 347 (Wednesday, Feb. 3, 1830). Mozart gave three concerts in Frankfort in the summer of 1763.

3 O. E. Deutsch, *Mozart: A Documentary Biography,* trans. Eric Blom, Peter Branscombe, and Jeremy Noble (Stanford, 1965), p. 455.

4 Franz Niemetschek, *Life of Mozart,* trans. Helen Mautner (London, 1956), p. 68.

5 Jean-Baptiste-Antoine Suard, "Anecdotes sur Mozart" (1804), Deutsch, op. cit., p. 498.

"emotionally immature." Thus Suard tells us that "All his sentiments had more violence than depth"; that he was "Light and inconsistent in his affections."[6] But there is another childlike quality which might be classified if you will, under the head: "musical fun and games." It is this side of Mozart's so-called childlike nature that I wish to explore briefly.

From his earliest years, Mozart mixed music with games, even to the extent of composing as a game. Perhaps making a game of music, as Nannerl seems to suggest, was the easiest teaching method the shrewd Leopold Mozart could devise for a five-year-old composition student. Johann Andreas Schachtner, a long-time friend of the Mozarts whose reminiscences formed the basis for many of the early biographical memoirs concerning Wolfgang's childhood, gives us a notable instance of this musical game phenomenon. "[Even] children's games," he writes, "had to have a musical accompaniment if they were to interest him; if we, he and I, were carrying his playthings from one room to another, the one of us who went empty-handed always had to sing or fiddle a march the while."[7] Nannerl contributes another account of a musical game that Wolfgang "continued until he was in his tenth year":

> [H]e composed a melody which he would sing out loud each day before going to sleep, to which end his father had to set him on a chair. Father always had to sing the second part, and when this ceremony, which might on no occasion be omitted, was over, he would kiss his father most tenderly and go to bed very peacefully and contentedly.[8]

The association of music and play endured to the very end of Mozart's life – so, at least, the Mozart legend would have it. From the many anecdotes which come to mind, I have chosen but a few, with no other principle of selection than my own preference; for their particular content, even their authenticity, are not at issue here. Their significance lies in

6 Ibid. 7 Deutsch, op. cit., p. 451.
8 Ibid., p. 493. Memoirs of Mozart's Sister, *Allgemeine Musikalische Zeitung* (Leipzig, 22 January, 1800).

the image they convey of the creative process and the creative personality.

On May 27, 1784, Mozart bought a starling bird for 34 kreuzers, dutifully entering the purchase in his expense book. Beneath the entry he jotted down the finale theme of the piano concerto in G (K. 453), and added, "That was fine" – approving, apparently, either the bird's performance or its powers of invention, since it is not clear whether the bird gave him the theme or he gave it to the bird. On June 4, 1787, the short-lived bird was buried by Mozart in his garden with elaborate ceremony. "When the bird died," Nissen wrote, "he arranged a funeral procession, in which everyone who could sing had to join in, heavily veiled – made a sort of requiem, epitaph in verse."[9]

I do not believe there is any record of what funeral music Mozart provided for this occasion. But we do possess extant works which seem to have had their origins in domestic tomfoolery every bit as trivial as the starling's funeral. One such is the comic terzet, "Liebes Mandl, wo ist's Bandl?" (K. 441), written in 1783 and dedicated to Gottfried von Jacquin. Here is the story as told by Otto Jahn:

> Mozart had made his wife a present of a new belt ribbon which she wished to wear one day when she was going for a walk with Jacquin. Not finding it she called to her husband: "Liebes Mandl, wo ist's Bandl?" (Where is the belt, my dear?) They both looked for it in vain till Jacquin joined them and found it. But he refused to give it up, held it high in the air, and being very tall, the Mozarts, both little, strove in vain to reach it. Entreaties, laughter, scolding, were all in vain, till at last the dog ran barking between Jacquin's legs. Then he gave up the ribbon, and declared that the scene would make a good comic terzet. Mozart took the hint, wrote the words in the Vienna dialect (which is essential for the comic effect), and sent the terzet to Jacquin.[10]

"Das Bandl" of course reflects the circumstances which occasioned it. Born of the trivial and humorous, it is itself a

9 Deutsch, op. cit., p. 225.
10 Otto Jahn, *Life of Mozart*, trans. P. D. Townsend (London, 1882), Vol. 2, p. 362.

trivial and humorous diversion – one of many such that Mozart let fall during his wonderfully prolific career. However, in the magnificent scena, "Bella mia fiamma" (K. 528), we have quite another musical phenomenon, occasioned indeed by the same kind of domestic play as the Bandl-Terzet, yet a serious and profound composition, not at all reflective of the trivial events which apparently surrounded its inception. And although these events came to light long after the Mozart legend wielded its influence, I cannot bring myself to omit them, for they seem to me to distill the very essence of that legend. I quote from a Berlin periodical of 1856:

> Petranka is well-known as the villa in which Mozart enjoyed staying with his musician friends, the Duscheks, during his visit to Prague, and where he composed several numbers for his "Don Juan." On the summit of a hill near the villa stands a pavilion. In it, one day, Frau Duschek slyly imprisoned the great Mozart, after having provided ink, pen, and notepaper, and told him that he would not regain his freedom until he had written an aria he had promised her to the words *bella mia fiamma addio*. Mozart submitted himself to the necessary; but to avenge himself for the trick Frau Duschek had played on him, he used various difficult-to-sing passages in the aria, and threatened his despotic friend that he would immediately destroy the aria if she could not succeed in performing it at sight without mistakes.[11]

Are such anecdotes but curiosities? Or do they tell us something about the nature of the creative intellect? Eduard Mörike, for one, saw a deep significance in Mozart's games and amusements: "in the mysterious ways in which genius pursues its unconscious ends," he wrote, "they did not fail to communicate the delicate, fleeting impressions by which it is sometimes fertilized."[12] And to at least some of the architects of nineteenth-century aesthetic philosophy who for

---

11 *Berliner Musik-Zeitung Echo*, 6 (1856), pp. 198–9. The anecdote is attributed to "Mozart's son"; the only surviving son at this time was Karl Thomas (1784–1858).

12 *Mozart on His Way to Prague*, trans. Mary Hottinger, *Nineteenth Century German Tales*, ed. Angel Flores (New York, 1959) p. 328.

reasons of their own were beginning to worship the child-like, Mozart became a symbol: an embodiment of their theories, a living example of what, a priori, had become the genuine creative nature.

One aesthetic concept which came to be seen as particularly related to the childlike was that of *aesthetic disinterestedness*. I am going to examine this concept at some length here and conclude my discussion with a few remarks on Schopenhauer; for it is in Schopenhauer's philosophy that aesthetic disinterestedness and the childlike become intertwined. And it is the spirit of Mozart, I will argue, that hovers over these philosophical proceedings as a kind of patron saint.

The concept of aesthetic disinterestedness is familiar to most modern aestheticians through the influential article by Edward Bullough entitled "Psychical Distance."[13] In the perception of an aesthetic object, Bullough claimed, we must psychologically distance ourselves from our own practical needs and the practical aspects of the object itself. "Distance . . . is obtained," he wrote, "by separating the object and its appeal from one's own self by putting it out of gear with practical needs and ends. Thereby the 'contemplation' of the object alone becomes possible."[14] Further, Bullough maintained that psychical distance was not only a prerequisite for aesthetic perception but for the creative act as well: "It marks one of the most important steps in the process of artistic creation and serves as a distinguishing feature of what is commonly so loosely described as the 'artistic temperament.' "[15]

I do not know to what extent Bullough was acquainted with the historical origins of the concept he called "psychical distance." Surely he must have been familiar with the contributions of both Kant and Schopenhauer. But in fact the concept was already fully formed when Kant came to write the *Critique of Judgment*. It was rife in the writings of the eighteenth-century British aestheticians and critics;[16] and Kant,

---

13 *British Journal of Psychology*, (1913), reprinted in *A Modern Book of Aesthetics*, ed. Melvin Radner (New York, 1935).
14 Rader, op. cit. p. 319.   15 Ibid.
16 The history of aesthetic disinterestedness has recently been explored by Jerome

as is well known, was a careful student of British philosophy. It will be useful, I think, to place the concept of aesthetic disinterestedness in historical perspective, so that we
can better understand what it means and how it became associated with the childlike in general, and Mozart in particular.

If I am *interested* in an object, it is often self-interest, in the
sense of practical advantage, that is involved. In such instances, the utility of the object – what the object can do for
me – is paramount. Such interest is, at least, irrelevant to
aesthetic perception; at most, it may well be destructive of it.
The "Pleasure of Beauty . . . is distinct from that *Joy* which
arises from Self-love upon prospect of Advantage," writes
Francis Hutcheson early in the eighteenth century.[17] Remove
interest in the utility of an object and you remove the necessity of controlling it or, in plain terms, of owning it. To *use*
an object, it must be in your possession. But to contemplate
it aesthetically, possession is irrelevant. So Edmund Burke
writes some years later,

> By beauty, I mean, that quality or those qualities in bodies by
> which they cause love, or some passion similar to it. . . . I
> likewise distinguish love, by which I mean that satisfaction
> which arises to the mind upon contemplating anything beau-
> tiful, or whatsoever nature it may be, from desire or lust; which
> is an energy of the mind, that hurries us on to the *possession*
> of certain objects that do not affect us as they are beautiful,
> but by means altogether different.[18]

It would seem, then, that the concept of aesthetic disinterestedness involves successive steps, as it were, away from
the physical reality of the object. If one disregards utility,
then the possession of the object loses all significance. Further, if the possession of the object is no longer relevant, its

Stolnitz in his excellent article, "On the Origins of 'Aesthetic Disinterestedness,' "
Journal of Aesthetics and Art Criticism, 20 (1961).

17 Francis Hutcheson, *An Inquiry into the Original of our Ideas of Beauty and Virtue* (2d
ed.; London, 1726), p. 12.

18 Edmund Burke, *A Philosophical Enquiry into the Origin of our Ideas of the Sublime
and Beautiful,* ed. J. T. Boulton (London and New York, 1958), p. 91. Italics mine.

actual existence can be disregarded. And we arrive here at the Kantian notion of aesthetic disinterestedness as expressed in the third *Critique*. Kant writes, for example,

> The delight which we connect with the representation of the real existence of an object is called interest. . . . Now, where the question is whether something is beautiful, we do not want to know, whether we, or any one else, are, or even could be, concerned in the real existence of the thing, but rather what estimate we form of it on mere contemplation (intuition or reflection).[19]

Or, again, "One must not be in the least prepossessed in favor of the real existence of the thing, but must preserve complete indifference in this respect, in order to play the part of judge in matters of taste."

At about this stage the concept of disinterestedness came into the hands of Schopenhauer, no doubt through his reading of Kant, and was woven into the complex metaphysical fabric of *The World as Will and Idea*. Schopenhauer made much of the claim that he had combined two major concepts of Western philosophy: the Platonic idea and the Kantian thing in itself. With this claim he inaugurated his philosophy of art. And for our purposes, therefore, it makes a good beginning although it presupposes a great deal that we shall be obliged to pass over in silence.

Kant maintained that all objects of possible experience are limited by the a priori conditions of space and time. Such objects are "mere appearances, and not given us as things in themselves which exist in this manner."[20] What then lies beyond the appearance? What is the nature of the thing in itself? Kant insisted, of course, that we cannot say; for it lies beyoud the possibility of our experience: "nothing whatever can be asserted of the thing in itself, which underlies these appearances." Schopenhauer, however, presumed to know the nature of the Kantian thing in itself: It is a metaphysical *will* manifesting itself at one level as the Platonic idea and at

---

19 *Critique of Aesthetic Judgement*, trans J. C. Meredith (Oxford, 1911), pp. 42–3.
20 *Critique of Pure Reason*, trans. Norman Kemp Smith (New York, 1950), 86–7.

another, lower, level as appearance or representation. Schopenhauer stated, "the idea is only the immediate and therefore adequate, objectivity of the thing-in-itself, which itself, however, is the *will* – the will in so far as it is not yet objectified, has not yet become representation."[21]

Now knowledge of representation, of appearance, is possible only in terms of what Schopenhauer calls (after Liebniz and the German rationalists) the *principle of sufficient reason*. This principle provides Schopenhauer with four categories of explanation: (1) cause and effect; (2) premise and conclusion; (3) space and time; (4) motivation and action. Encompassed here is the whole realm of positive science as well as what we would call practical common sense knowledge.

But what of the ideas, and even the will itself? Are there ways of knowing them? Certainly we can know them only if we can escape the principle of sufficient reason which leads us ever and again to the appearance and not beyond. The fine arts are the way to the ideas; and music, which in Schopenhauer achieves an epistemological significance it had not enjoyed since the middle ages, leads us directly to the will. "We can," Schopenhauer maintains, define art "as *the way of considering things independently of the principle of sufficient reason*, in contrast to the way of considering them which proceeds in exact accordance with this principle, and is the way of science and experience."[22] The work of art

> repeats the eternal Ideas apprehended through pure contemplation, the essential and abiding element in all the phenomena of the world. . . . Its only source is knowledge of the Ideas; its sole aim is communication of this knowledge.

There are, of course, two processes that must be considered in relation to the work of art: the act of *creation* and that of *perception*. Both, for Schopenhauer, are in principle

---

21 *The World as Will and Representation*, trans. E. F. J. Payne (Indian Hills, Colorado, 1958), Vol. 1, p. 174. Payne has translated *Vorstellung* as *Representation* rather than *Idea*. In the body of this essay, I have preferred the older and more familiar title, *The World as Will and Idea*, simply because that is the title by which most English-speaking people know Schopenhauer's work.
22 Ibid., Vol. 1, pp. 184–5.

the same. Whatever ability the artist must possess must be possessed too by his audience: "This ability must be inherent in all men in a lesser and different degree, as otherwise they would be just as incapable of enjoying works of art as producing them."[23] This ability, called *genius* in the great artist, is nothing more than the ability to achieve aesthetic disinterestedness. And aesthetic disinterestedness, as we have seen, is the ability to contemplate an object without regard to its practical value or even its existence. To express this in Schopenhauer's terms, it is the ability to contemplate an object independently of the principle of sufficient reason. For it is through this principle that all the practical aspects of an object are expressed. Cause and effect, premise and conclusion, space and time, motivation and action – which make up the fourfold root of the principle of sufficient reason – exhaust the practical aspects of the object. To contemplate an object without reference to them is at the same time to achieve what Kant and the British aestheticians were claiming was the sine qua non of aesthetic perception.

In the first edition of *The World as Will and Idea* (1818), Schopenhauer was particularly interested in relating this doctrine to the old Platonic theory of divine madness – the artist "possessed." Madness is a falling away from reality; that is, from the world of practical affairs and objects. The madman is disoriented in time and space, unable to reason rationally from premise to conclusion, cause to effect, or motive to action. In other words, he is, like the genius, free of the principle of sufficient reason. Thus, Schopenhauer concluded,

> the madman correctly knows the individual present as well as many particulars of the past, but . . . he fails to recognize the connexion, the relations, and therefore goes astray and talks nonsense. Just this is his point of contact with the genius; for he too leaves out of sight knowledge of the connexion of things, as he neglects that knowledge of relations, which is knowledge according to the principle of sufficient reason, in order to see in things only their Ideas, and try to grasp their real inner nature which expresses itself in perception.[24]

23 Ibid., Vol. 1, pp. 194.   24 Ibid., Vol. 1, pp. 193–4.

But there are others besides madmen and geniuses who are relatively unencumbered by the principle of sufficient reason: I mean *children*. For it is experience of the empirical world, after all, which forces us to think in the practical way, the way of the principle of sufficient reason. And children, innocent of experience, are still free of its domination. When Schopenhauer published the second edition of *The World as Will and Idea* in 1844, he added to it a volume of supplementary discussions, including one concerning the relation between genius and the childlike. It is here, naturally enough, that the figure of Child Mozart appears – not, however, before both Hegel and Goethe had made some relevant observations.

Hegel was not, by any means, one to underestimate the role of experience in the process of artistic creation. Yet he was forced to admit that music appeared as a form of art for which experience was not at all necessary. Music, he wrote,

> which has exclusively to deal with the soul within, with the musical tones of that which is, relatively, feeling denuded of positive thought, has little or no need to bring to consciousness the substance of intellectual conception. For this very reason musical talent declares itself as a rule in very early youth, when the head is still empty and the emotions have barely had a flutter; it has, in fact, attained real distinction at a time in the artist's life when both intelligence and life are practically without experience.[25]

Surely Mozart was Hegel's exemplar here as he was Goethe's, when the poet expressed a similar sentiment, to wit, "The musical talent . . . may well show itself earliest of any; for music is something innate and internal, which needs little nourishment from without, and no experience drawn from life," adding apologetically, as if to excuse the blasphemy of providing rational explanations for divine mysteries, "Really,

---

25 G. W. F. Hegel, *The Philosophy of Fine Art*, trans. F. P. B. Osmaston (London, 1920), Vol. 1, p. 37. The translator adds in a footnote to this passage that Hegel perhaps had both Mozart and Schubert in mind.

however, a phenomenon like that of Mozart remains an inexplicable prodigy."[26]

It is noteworthy that Hegel and Goethe should have made the connection between musical prodigies, lack of experience, and the nature of music itself. But it is important to notice also what they are *not* saying. They were not saying that lack of experience is either necessary or desirable for the composer. Their point was a negative one: that music can do without experience, witness the early musical maturity of a Mozart. The composer *can* function "when the head is still empty and the emotions have barely had a flutter"; his talent does not *require* "nourishment from without" or "experience drawn from life." It is not to say that he cannot function when he has become intellectually and emotionally mature.

Schopenhauer, however, took the bigger step and proclaimed that, to a certain extent, lack of experience – or, rather, the naive attitude of objective wonder which characterizes those who are not rich in experience – is a *necessary* condition of artistic genius. It is this attitude of the child, or the childlike attitude in those who can preserve it, that constitutes aesthetic disinterestedness or genius. "In fact," says Schopenhauer,

> every child is to a certain extent a genius, and every genius
> to a certain extent a child. A relationship between the two
> shows itself primarily in the naivety and sublime ingenuousness that are a fundamental characteristic of true genius.
> Moreover it comes to light in several features, so that a certain
> childlike nature does indeed form a part of the character of
> genius. In Riemer's *Mittheilungen über Goethe* (Vol. I, p. 184) it
> is related that Herder and others found fault with Goethe,
> saying that he was always like a big child; they were certainly
> right in what they said, only they were not right in finding
> fault. It was also said of Mozart that he remained a child all
> his life (Nissen's Biography of Mozart, pp. 2 and 529).
> Schlichtegroll's Necrology (for 1791, Vol. II, p. 109) says of
> him: "In his art he early became a man, but in all other respects he invariably remained a child." Therefore every ge-

26 *Conversations of Goethe with Eckermann*, p. 382 (Monday , Feb. 14, 1831).

nius is already a big child, since he looks out into the world as into something strange and foreign, a drama, and thus with purely objective interest. Accordingly, just like the child, he does not have the dull gravity and earnestness of ordinary men, who, being capable of nothing but subjective interests, always see in things merely motives for their actions. He who throughout his life does not, to a certain extent, remain a big child, but becomes an earnest, sober, thoroughly composed and rational man, can be a very useful capable citizen of this world; but he will never be a genius.[27]

As *music* became, for Schopenhauer, the highest form of art, so innocence, which Hegel and Goethe had already associated with *musical* genius, became for him the highest form of the aesthetic attitude.

With Schopenhauer, then, the image of Child Mozart merges into the concept of aesthetic disinterestedness in a way which suggests that the Mozart legend wielded a not inconsiderable influence on the aesthetic thought of the period. Conversely, the legend of Child Mozart was, no doubt, magnified and exaggerated by the aesthetic theories which demanded a child genius and a childlike man. Aesthetic disinterestedness was *one* of those theories; the play theory of art was another which must have found the figure of Child Mozart a congenial one. The theory of aesthetic play is far too broad a subject for detailed analysis here. Suffice it to say, it is another example of the growing interest in childlikeness as an aesthetic concept. Nietzsche wrote, "Man's maturity: to have regained the seriousness that he had as a child at play."[28] He wrote too that the pathos of musical tragedy was "but a sublime esthetic play."[29] It seems entirely predictable therefore that Nietzsche should have eulogized,

---

27 Schopenhauer, op. cit., Vol. 2, p. 395. For Schopenhauer's references, here, see: Friedrich Wilhelm Riemer, *Mittheilungen über Goethe* (Berlin, 1841); Georg Nikolaus von Nissen, *Biographie W. A. Mozart's* (Leipzig, 1828); Friedrich Schlichtegroll, *Nekrolog auf das Jahr 1791* (Gotha, 1792–1793).

28 Nietzsche, *Beyond Good and Evil*, trans Marianne Cowan (Chicago, 1955), p. 78 (#94).

29 Neitzsche, *The Birth of Tragedy*, trans. F. Golffing (New York, 1956), p. 134 (22).

among other things, the "child-like" aspects of Mozart's music.[30]

Paul Henry Lang has observed that Mozart was "enthroned as the symbol of genius" by the early nineteenth century. "It was inevitable," Lang adds, "that his untimely death would arouse interest in the child prodigy, and it was the precocious youngster whom they saw in everything."[31] Why was he "enthroned"? Why was interest in the child prodigy and untimely death "inevitable"? Handel was a child prodigy; and Mainwaring, his first biographer, did not neglect to record the fact.[32] Purcell was Mozart's age when he died. Yet England hardly saw fit to idolize a Handel in diapers; nor, so far as I know, did the English think Purcell's precocity evidence for the childlike nature of musical genius. The answer is that the Enlightenment was (with some notable exceptions) "for adults only." It was the nineteenth century that chose as its text "become as little children." This, it seems to me, goes a long way toward explaining the inevitable enthronement of Child Mozart as an aesthetic symbol.

30 *Beyond Good and Evil*, p. 180 (#245).
31 Paul Henry Lang, "Mozart After 200 Years," *Journal of the American Musicological Society*, 13 (1960), p. 197.
32 [John Mainwaring], *Memoirs of the Life of the Late George Frederic Handel* (London, 1760), pp. 2–42, passim. Daines Barrington, who interviewed Mozart in 1769, compared his accomplishments as a child to Handel's, referring specifically to Mainwaring's biography, which indicates that Handel's precocity did not go completely unnoticed in the eighteenth century. See *Philosophical Transactions*, 60 (1771), in Deutsch, op. cit., pp. 95–100.

Chapter XII

Charles Darwin on music

The year 1959 marks the one-hundreth anniversary of the publication of Charles Darwin's *The Origin of Species*, probably the most important book of the nineteenth century. As the biological sciences attempt to reevaluate this work from their vantage point of a century, many other disciplines will join the in acknowledging their debt to Darwin and the theory of evolution. It is fitting that the musical world too should take note of this centennial, for music had its place in Darwin's account of evolution. Darwin's notions of the origin and effects of music, his criticism of Herbert Spencer's speech theory, and Spencer's subsequent reply represent a fascinating era in the history of English music aesthetics.[1]

THE ORIGIN OF MUSIC

Two major principles operate in Darwin's theory of evolution: *natural selection* and *sexual selection*. The characteristics of any species vary within certain limits. Those variations that prove favorable to the survival of the individual will tend to be preserved since the individuals who possess them will be best fitted to survive and most likely, therefore, to repro-

1 An account of English music aesthetics in this period, including Darwin and Spencer, is given by one of their German contemporaries, Carl Stumpf, in his article, "Musikpsychologie in England," *Vierteljahrsschrift fur Musikwissenschaft* 1 (1885). A brief account of Darwin and Spencer can also be found in H. Ehrlich's *Die Musik-Aesthetik in ihrer Entwickelung von Kant bis auf die Gegenwart* (Leipzig, 1881).

duce. Conversely, those variations that prove unfavorable will not tend to be preserved since the individuals who possess them will be less likely to reproduce. "This preservation of favourable individual differences and variations, and the destruction of those which are injurious," says Darwin, "I have called Natural Selection, or the Survival of the Fittest,"[2] But with regard to species in which male and female individuals exist, another process of selection takes place – the selection of mates during the elaborate activity of courtship. In this process of *sexual selection*, Darwin maintains, the origin of music lies.

Early in his career, Darwin stated clearly the theory of sexual selection in the so-called *Essay of 1844*, published posthumously by his son, Sir Francis Darwin, in 1909.[3] Here Darwin planted the seed of his music theory which was not to flower until the publication of *The Descent of Man* (1871) and *The Expression of the Emotions in Man and Animals* (1872). In the essay, Darwin states,

> Besides this natural means of selection, by which those individuals are preserved, . . . which are best adapted to the place they fill in nature, there is a second agency at work in most bisexual animals tending to produce the same effect, namely the struggle of the males for the females. These struggles are generally decided by the law of battle; but in the case of birds, apparently, *by the charms of their song*, by their beauty or their power of courtship."[4]

This, then, is the basis for Darwin's theory of the origin of music. The songs of birds, which had fascinated so many

2 Darwin, *The Origin of Species* (New York, 1900), Vol. 1, p. 98.
3 Darwin, *The Foundations of the Origin of Species*, ed. Sir. Francis Darwin (Cambridge, 1909).
4 Ibid., pp. 92–3. The italics are mine. There seems to be a certain ambiguity here with regard to the term "bisexual." Darwin is clearly using the term here to refer to species in which the male element is present in one individual and the female element in another. However, modern scientific dictionaries give "hermaphroditic" as the synonym for "bisexual." In this sense, a bisexual animal is one with both male and female sex elements. Darwin must have seen this problem for, when this passage appeared in print in 1858, the term "bisexual" was replaced by the term "unisexual."

writers on music in the seventeenth and eighteenth centuries and excited so much idle speculation, became through the machinery of sexual selection, reasonable phenomena on which to build an evolutionary theory of music.

In the year 1858, Darwin's theory of natural selection first saw the light of day along with the theory of Alfred Russel Wallace. Papers by Darwin and Wallace were presented before the Linnean Society of London on July 1, 1858, and published on August 20 of the same year.[5] Interestingly enough, one of Darwin's two brief papers contained the excerpt from the *Essay of 1844*, quoted previously, indicating that Darwin considered bird songs to be of more than passing interest with regard to sexual selection.[6] Again in *The Origin of Species*, the songs of birds are discussed, but Darwin goes no further in his speculation on this subject than the point at which he had arrived in 1844.

It was the consideration of the evolution of man and his mental faculties that led Darwin to extrapolate from the music of birds to the music of men. According to the principle of sexual selection the strongest, most active, or *most attractive* male will be the one most likely to gain a mate and reproduce. With respect to birds, the production of pleasing sounds, that is, singing, is a primary means of attraction. In *The Descent of Man*, Darwin took pains to point out that in addition to birds, animals much closer to man on the evolutionary scale seem to demonstrate similar patterns of behavior, a conclusion with which Spencer, as we shall see, took issue in his criticism of Darwin. "In the class of Mammals, with which we are here more particularly concerned, the males of almost all the species use their voices during the breeding season much more than at any other time; and some are absolutely mute excepting at this season."[7] The ultimate con-

---

5 Darwin and Wallace, "On the Tendency of Species to Form Varieties: and on the Perpetuation of Varieties and Species by Natural Means of Selection," *Journal of the Linnean Society, Zoology* 3 (1858).

6 Ibid., p. 50.

7 Darwin, *The Descent of Man* (2d ed. rev., New York, 1897), p. 567. All references to *The Descent of Man* are to the second edition except where otherwise stated.

clusion to be drawn is, of course, that primitive man himself depended partly on the beauty of his voice to attract a mate. Through the process of sexual selection those characteristics of voice that were attractive to the opposite sex would have been passed on to succeeding generations, resulting finally in vocal music. "The impassioned orator, bard, or musician, when with his varied tones and cadences he excites the strongest emotions in his hearers, little suspects that he uses the same means by which his half-human ancestors long ago aroused each other's ardent passions, during their courtship and rivalry."[8]

THE EFFECTS OF MUSIC

In the aesthetics of music, the question of origin has always been bound up with more pressing problems, both normative and descriptive. Time and again theories of music's origin have formed a basis for theories of its effect, nature, and proper function. More often than not, a theory of the origin of music comes into being for the sake of these other considerations rather than for its own sake as a theoretical inquiry. Darwin, however, along with many scientifically oriented aestheticians of the late nineteenth century, seemed motivated to consider the origin of music only by its intrinsic interest. In this regard Darwin seems to embody the spirit of Charles Burney's statement made almost a century before: "The feeble beginnings of whatever afterwards become great or eminent, are interesting to mankind."[9]

But although Darwin had no specific aesthetic program to support, he nevertheless had certain vague notions of music's effect, notions that he felt could be justified and explained through his evolutionary theory of music's origin. Darwin believed that music could arouse specific emotions. He states in *The Descent of Man*, "Music arouses in us various emotions, but not the more terrible ones of horror, fear, rage,

8 Ibid., p. 573.
9 Burney, *A General History of Music* (New york, 1957), Vol. 1, p. 11.

&c. It awakens the gentler feelings of tenderness and love, which readily pass into devotion."[10] In maintaining that music could arouse emotions, Darwin placed himself in a tradition of musical speculation which can be traced as far back as Plato. In attributing to music the "gentler feelings," Darwin was following a trend in the aesthetics of music that had made itself felt a century before, especially in England.[11]

To what extent can Darwin's theory of music's origin account for this emotive power of music, so universally accepted by Darwin's predecessors? Clearly the emphasis on "love and tenderness" as the primary musical emotions dovetails nicely with the theory of origin. For if music's origin lies in the activity of courtship, would it not be expected that its basic effect should be the arousal of these emotions commonly associated with that activity, namely, "love and tenderness"? "Love is still the commonest theme of our songs," says Darwin.[12] He concludes, "The sensations and ideas thus excited in us by music, or expressed by the cadences of oratory, appear from their vagueness, yet depth, like mental reversions to the emotions and thoughts of a long-past age."[13] In *The Expression of the Emotions in Man and Animals*, this idea is articulated still more clearly. "Music has a wonderful power, . . . of recalling in a vague and indefinite manner, those strong emotions which were felt during long-past ages, when, as is probable, our early progenitors courted each other by the aid of vocal tones."[14] The emotions in music, then, are to be explained by a sort of primeval memory in man which is awakened by music through its connection with primitive courtship behavior.

10 *The Descent of Man*, p. 571.
11 See, for example, Charles Avison, *An Essay on Musical Expression* (London, 1752), pp. 5ff.
12 *The Descent of Man*, p. 571.   13 Ibid., p. 572.
14 Darwin, *The Expression of the Emotions in Man and Animals* (New York, 1955), p. 217.

DARWIN AND SPENCER

In the eighteenth century, theories of music's origin usually involved the origin of language as well. Priority in time has been a question of particular importance. Such eighteenth-century theorists as Jean Jacques Rousseau in France, Johann Adam Hiller in Germany, and John Brown in England maintained the priority of language, not, however, an articulate language of ideas and concepts but, rather, a primitive language of emotions. Darwin, in placing music so far down on the scale of evolution, was obliged to maintain that it preceded articulate language. But rather than postulate an emotional language as the source of music, Darwin maintained that music itself was the source of language, a belief that he shared with his German contemporary, Richard Wagner. "As we have every reason to suppose that articulate speech is one of the latest, as it certainly is the highest, of the arts acquired by man, and as the instinctive power of producing musical notes and rhythms is developed low down in the animal series, it would be altogether opposed to the principle of evolution, if we were to admit that man's musical capacity has been developed from the tones used in impassioned speech. We must suppose that the rhythms and cadences of oratory are derived from previously developed musical powers."[15]

In taking such a position, Darwin placed himself in direct opposition to Herbert Spencer who in 1857 had published "The Origin and Function of Music," an essay that rigorously set forth the theory that music's origin lay in speech.[16] Spencer's account of music takes its departure from a broad physiological generalization. He states, "We may set it down as a general law, that alike in man and animals, there is a direct connexion between feeling and movement; the last growing more vehement as the first grows more intense."[17] The relevance of this principle to music follows directly from

15 *The Descent of Man,* p. 572. This statement was added in 1874 in the second edition. The reference to "impassioned speech" seems to be aimed at Spencer.
16 *Fraser's Magazine* 56 (1857).   17 Ibid., p. 397.

the belief that music was originally a vocal phenomenon. "All music is originally vocal. All vocal sounds are produced by the agency of certain muscles. These muscles, in common with those of the body at large, are excited to contraction by pleasurable and painful feelings. And therefore it is that feelings demonstrate themselves in sounds as well as in movements."[18] Here then is the kernel of Spencer's position. Emotional states result in muscular activity of one kind or another. Music is such a muscular activity, and its origin is of a physiological character, intimately connected with emotional states.

Spencer distinguishes five characteristics of vocal utterances: *loudness, quality* or *timbre, pitch, intervals,* and *rate of variation*. In emotional speech the increased emotional energy tends to increase loudness, increase sonority, raise pitch, widen intervals, and produce a greater variety of sounds. In short, excited speech begins to resemble music. "These vocal peculiarities which indicate excited feelings, *are those which especially distinguish song from ordinary speech.*"[19] For Spencer, therefore, music is an extension of natural physiological phenomena. It arises through exaggeration of vocal characteristics inherent in the physiology of the human species. So Spencer concludes, "Song employs and exaggerates the natural language of the emotions – it arises from a systematic combination of those vocal peculiarities which are the physiological effects of acute pleasure and pain."[20]

Darwin had little specific criticism to make of Spencer's position. His criticism was implicit in his theory. There was in fact a great deal in Spencer's analysis of emotional speech which Darwin admired. On more than one occasion, Darwin remarked on the excellence of Spencer's observations. So, for example, Darwin made the following comment in *The Expression of the Emotions in Man and Animals:* "No one can listen to an eloquent orator or preacher, or to a man calling angrily to another, or to one expressing astonishment, without being struck with the truth of Mr. Spencer's remarks."[21]

18 Ibid.   19 Ibid., p. 400.
20 Ibid., p. 401.
21 *The Expression of the Emotions in Man and Animals,* p. 86.

However, on the point of musical expression, Darwin had requested his son-in-law, R. B. Litchfield, to insert a comment in *The Expression of the Emotions in Man and Animals* in which Spencer received some direct criticism. Litchfield felt that Spencer's analysis failed to account for the real effect of music, "an effect indefinable in language. . . . For it is certain that the *melodic* effect of a series of sounds does not depend in the least on their loudness or softness, or on their *absolute* pitch."[22] Loudness and pitch were, of course, two of the terms Spencer used in his characterization of music and emotional speech.

In a letter to Darwin dated "*Nov. 16th, 1872,*" Spencer acknowledges receipt of a copy of *The Expression of the Emotions in Man and Animals*.[23] In the course of this letter, as an answer to Litchfield, he reiterates his belief in music's origin in emotional speech and his belief that this origin accounts satisfactorily for the nature of musical expression. It would seem that Litchfield's comments did not make much of an impression on Spencer. They drew no very extensive reply and were completely ignored by Spencer in 1890 when he published his thorough criticism of Darwin's position.

Despite Darwin's approval of many of Spencer's observations, he recognized the wide gulf that separated the two positions.

> Mr. Spencer comes to an exactly opposite conclusion to that at which I have arrived. He concludes, as did Diderot formerly, that the cadences used in emotional speech afford the foundation from which music has been developed; whilst I conclude that musical notes and rhythm were first acquired by the male or female progenitors of mankind for the sake of charming the opposite sex.[24]

Their disagreement on music's origin was symptomatic of their widely divergent approaches to intellectual problems. Darwin's one significant criticism of Spencer's music theory,

22 Ibid., pp. 89–90.
23 This letter was published by Spencer in his *Autobiography* (London, 1904), Vol. 2, pp. 238–9.
24 *The Descent of Man*, p. 572, fn. 39.

indicative of this divergence, is directed against the over-generality of Spencer's basic premise, stated by Darwin as "the general law that a feeling is a stimulus to muscular action." "It may be admitted that the voice is affected through this law; but the explanation appears to me too general and vague to throw much light on the various differences, with the exception of that of loudness, between ordinary speech and emotional speech, or singing."[25] What Darwin criticizes here is Spencer's reliance on a single premise of great generality, from which he evolves a basically deductive argument. This method was common to all of Spencer's writings, and for a thinker as empirically oriented as Darwin, it was anathema. He makes this quite clear in his *Autobiography* where he says of Spencer, "His deductive manner of treating every subject is wholly opposed to my frame of mind. . . . His fundamental generalizations (which have been compared in importance by some persons with Newton's laws!) – which I daresay may be very valuable under a philosophical point of view, are of such a nature that they do not seem to me to be of any strictly scientific use."[26] William Irvine, in his book *Apes, Angels, and Victorians*, characterizes Darwin in this manner: "No man ever enjoyed a fact more. . . . Facts were his pleasure and his amusement."[27] Conversely, T. H. Huxley had said of his friend Spencer, "Oh! you know, Spencer's idea of a tragedy is a deduction killed by a fact."[28] Herein, I think, lies Darwin's opposition to Herbert Spencer.

Although Darwin was content to refrain almost entirely from any direct criticism of Spencer's position, Spencer was not of such a mind. In 1890, eight years after Darwin's death, Spencer published a detailed criticism of Darwin's theory as well as that of Edmund Gurney.[29] Gurney holds an interesting position in this dispute. On the one hand, he was an

---

25 *The Expression of the Emotions in Man and Animals*, pp. 86–7.
26 *Autobiography of Charles Darwin* (New York, 1958), p. 109.
27 William Irvine, *Apes, Angels, and Victorians* (New York, 1955), p. 43.
28 Spencer, *Autobiography*, Vol. 1. p. 403.
29 This criticism first appeared as an article in *Mind* 15 (1890). Spencer appended this "postscript," as he called it, to later editions of the essay on music.

outspoken critic of Spencer's theory. Gurney maintained a purist music aesthetic that excluded any attempt to describe music in extramusical terms. Spencer's emphasis on the emotive element in music made his position antagonistic to Gurney. Yet Gurney was inclined, on the other hand, to favor Darwin's account, which was no less emotive than was Spencer's. What had attracted Gurney to Darwin's position was its emphasis on the vagueness of musical emotions. For Gurney did not wish to divest music entirely of its emotive content. He wished only to point out that emotions in music were purely musical in character, not describable in the usual emotive terms. The indefiniteness of musical emotions, which was implied in Darwin's notion of primeval memory traces, made his theory acceptable to Gurney. So Gurney stated of Darwin's theory, "When we realize the extraordinary depth and indescribability of the emotions of music, the very remoteness and far-reachingness of the explanation is in favour of its validity."[30]

Darwin had thought Spencer over-general and deductive in his method. As if to give Darwin the lie, Spencer presented a basically empirical argument against his theory. Spencer begins by stating the real nature of the dispute as he sees it. "The interpretation of music which Mr. Darwin gives, agrees with my own in supposing music to be developed from vocal noises; but differs in supposing a particular class of vocal noises to have originated it – the amatory class."[31] From this point onward, Spencer presents empirical evidence to support his own position – evidence ranging from his observation of birds to the behavior of the Sandwich Islanders.

Spencer's evidence is aimed at two points in Darwin's position. To begin with, Darwin had based his argument on the assumption that vocal sounds manifest themselves primarily in the expression of sentiments connected with courting behavior. But Spencer maintains that Darwin "does not bear in

---

30 Edmund Gurney, *The Power of Sound* (London, 1880), p. 119.
31 *Mind* 15 (1890), p. 450.

mind how large a proportion of vocal noises are caused by other excitements."[32] Second, Spencer maintained that evolutionary evidence did not support Darwin's position. "To give appreciable support to Mr. Darwin's view, we ought to find vocal manifestations of the amatory feeling becoming more pronounced as we ascend along that particular line of inferior *Vertebrata* out of which man has arisen."[33] Spencer felt that no such tendency was present and pointed out that Darwin had all but admitted it. "Indeed in his *Descent of Man,* vol. II, p. 332, Mr. Darwin himself says: – 'It is a surprising fact that we have not as yet any good evidence that these organs [*i.e.,* the vocal organs] are used by the male mammals to charm the females': an admission which amounts to something like a surrender."[34]

It must be conceded that music did not hold an important position in Darwin's thought. He was, by his own admission, largely ignorant of musical matters.[35] If his theory struck a responsive chord at the time of its promulgation, this was not due to the force of what Darwin was saying but rather to the overall success of his evolutionary theory and to the fact that he approached music as a scientist at a time when scientific aesthetics was very much in vogue. In anthropological research this scientific impulse produced such works as Richard Wallaschek's *Primitive Music* (1893); in physiology and acoustics, Helmholtz's *On the Sensations of Tone as a Physiological Basis for the Theory of Music* (1863), and Carl Stumpf's *Psychology of Tone* (1883–1890). Today Darwin's theory of music remains merely a curiosity – an interesting but rather insignificant appendage to the theory of sexual selection.

32 Ibid., p. 451. 33 Ibid., p. 454.
34 Ibid., pp. 454–5. Spencer's reference is to the first edition of *The Descent of Man* (London, 1871). The reference may be found on p. 567 of the edition used in this essay.
35 See Henrietta Litchfield, ed., *Emma Darwin, A Century of Family Letters, 1792–1896* (London, 1915), Vol. 2, p. 208. In a letter to his daughter Henrietta, requesting the use of her husband's comments on music for *The Expression of the Emotions in Man and Animals*, Darwin states: "Litchfield's remarks strike me (ignorant as I am) as very good; and I should much like to insert them."

More might be made of Herbert Spencer's musical speculations. He was certainly more interested in music than was
Darwin, and aesthetics undoubtedly played a more important role in his thought. Spencer had concluded his essay
with a statement of high purpose for music. He stated, "Music must take rank as the highest of the fine arts – as the one
which, more than any other ministers to human welfare."[36]
Alfred Einstein has remarked on the importance of this statement, calling it, in fact, a triumph for music.[37] But, I think,
the musical world must look beyond its own boundaries to
discover the real significance in the musical speculations of
Darwin and Spencer. What they said about music is of small
importance. But that they did concern themselves with music and a multitude of other peripheral subjects leads one to
the realization that herein lies a magnificent synthesis of human knowledge. Few generations have had the confidence
to attempt such a synthesis.

36 Spencer, "On the Origin and Function of Music," p. 408.
37 Einstein, *Music in the Romantic Era* (New York, 1947), p. 342.

Music and emotion

Chapter XIII

Mattheson as philosopher of art

I

Philosophical distinctions are hard won, long in the making, and often difficult to sustain in the face of an obstinate determination to blur distinctions and be lazy over language. No distinction that I know of in the philosophical lexicon more fully illustrates this than that among the various ways in which the word "express" has been used by critics, philosophers of art, critical theorists, art historians, and musicologists, in characterizing the objects of their study. Anyone who thinks that music can "express" at all will agree, I am sure, that the second Kyrie of Bach's Mass in B Minor "expresses" grief and anguish. But what that exactly *means* will vary greatly with the person who utters it, and, indeed, will often seem to mean one thing to Mr. X when he says it on page 25, and quite another on page 52.

It is my intention, now with the benefit of Ernest C. Harriss' complete translation of *Der vollkommene Capellmeister*, to try to tease out of Johann Mattheson's magnum opus a consistent account of his views on musical "expression." I will be concerned, needless to say, with making use of the hard-won distinctions, alluded to above, among the various ways the term "expression," and its cognates, have been used in the philosophical and critical literature. This to the end of first saying with greater clarity and accuracy than heretofore exactly what Mattheson's views on the important question of musical "expression" were, and second to reassess, on the

229

basis of this (it is to be hoped) more satisfactory interpretation, Mattheson's historical place in the "philosophy of music," which is largely unknown to philosophers and musicologists and, where known, both misunderstood and grossly
underestimated.[1] But before I settle into this twofold task, a
preliminary remark with regard to strategy will be necessary.

In an article called "What Mattheson said," I outlined, some
years ago, an interpretation of Mattheson on musical expression which ran counter to received opinion and, it seemed to
me, indicated that Mattheson was a far more subtle and forward-looking "philosopher of music" than he had ever been
given credit for being.[2] This interpretation was, as I frankly
stated at the time, based for the most part on a translation
by Hans Lenneberg of excerpts from *Der vollkommene Capellmeister* that amount to only a small fraction of that compen-
dious work,[3] and was advanced, tentatively, as a hypothesis
to be tested by further encounters with Mattheson's text. Such
an encounter is now made possible for me by Harriss' splen-
did new translation of the *complete Complete Capellmeister*. It
is, then, the testing of this hypothesis that is my major concern. So, after making some necessary distinctions of a philosophical kind in Section II, I will devote the remaining sections to, first, stating as briefly as possible what that hypothesis
is, and, second, defending it in the light of Harriss' translation.

So much, then, for preliminaries. I go on now to the business at first hand. First. *distinctions*.

II

In ordinary usage, the verb "express" and noun "expression" describe the following kind of case. Jones is angry, and

---

1 I do not, of course, mean to suggest that Mattheson's place in *music history* is
  either unknown or misunderstood in musicological circles.
2 "What Mattheson said," *The Music Review* 34 (1973); reprinted and somewhat
  revised as Chap. 5 of *The Corded Shell: Reflections on Musical Expression* (Princeton,
  1980).
3 "Johann Mattheson on Affect and Rhetoric in Music," *Journal of Music Theory* 2
  (1958).

he *expresses* his anger by tightening his lips and narrowing his eyes. His face now wears an angry *expression*. Used in this literal sense, Jones could not be truly said to *express* his anger with his tight lips and narrowed eyes unless he were truly angry; and, likewise, unless he were truly in that emotional state, his face could not be said to wear any angry *expression*, even though it might exhibit tight lips and narrowed eyes. In other words, a necessary condition for correctly describing X's appearance or behavior as expressing ϕ, is X's actually being ϕ (where ϕ is an emotion or mood); and, likewise, X's being ϕ is a necessary condition for correctly ascribing an expression of ϕ to X's appearance or behavior.

If, then, I were to say that the second Kyrie of the Mass in B Minor "expresses" sadness and anguish, and claimed to be using "express" in the ordinary way, the music would have to stand in the same relation to *someone*'s emotions as the angry expression of Jones's face stands to Jones's anger. The only likely candidate, needless to say, is J. S. Bach, who, one might suppose, *expressed* his sadness and anguish through the fashioning of the Kyrie, as Jones *expresses* his anger by "pulling a face." And, as Jones's face cannot be correctly described as expressing anger, in the ordinary sense of "express," unless Jones were in fact angry, so, if one were using "express" in the ordinary way in claiming that the second Kyrie of the Mass in B Minor expresses anguished grief, one would not correctly describe it so unless Bach were in a sad and anguished state during (or at least shortly prior to) the composition of the chorus. For this reason, I shall, in what follows, describe the view that "The music is sad" means "The music *expresses* sadness" (in the ordinary sense of "express") as the "self-expression" theory.

But the fact is people do not always seem to be claiming that music *expresses* sadness when they describe it as sad; and even when they do, they do not always seem to be using "express" in the ordinary sense. What *else* might they be claiming? And how else might they be using "express" than in the canonical way?

One common construal of "The music is ϕ" (where "ϕ" names an emotion or mood) has been something to the effect that the music *arouses* ϕ in the listener. And this was, of course, a particularly common view of the matter in Mattheson's day. According to it, Bach was not expressing *his* emotion of anguished sadness in writing the second Kyrie of the Mass in B Minor but, rather, fashioning a musical composition that, in the proper circumstances, would make its *auditors* sad and anguished. I shall henceforth, for obvious reasons, refer to this theory as the "arousal" theory of musical expression.

In recent years another notion has become prevalent, especially in philosophical circles, to the effect that music neither "expresses" (in the ordinary sense of the word) nor "arouses" in listeners the emotions which are customarily ascribed to it. Rather, music *possesses* such emotions as "phenomenological" properties, much in the way that a weeping willow or the jowly face of the bloodhound are seen to be sad, in spite of the obvious act that the weeping willow cannot be *feeling* sad, and the bloodhound need not be (for the epithet to apply properly). I shall call this the "possession" theory of musical expression, meaning the theory according to which "The music is ϕ" (where ϕ is an emotion or mood) means more or less exactly what it says: namely, neither that the emotion belongs to the composer (as the "self-expression" theory would have it) nor to the listener (as the "arousal" theory would) but to the music itself, as a property or feature of *it*.

Which of these three theories (and they by no means exhaust the possibilities) is the more plausible? For various reasons, which there is no time to elaborate on fully here, my own preference is for the "possession" theory.[4] The "self-expression" account, clearly, founders on the fairly commonsensical observation that Bach hardly needed to wait for sadness and anguish to overcome him in order to write a sad and anguished Kyrie – particularly not in a century in which music was made to order, on schedule, rather than at the

4 This is the view I defend in detail in *The Corded Shell*.

command of the muse. (The contractor does not wait for inspiration if he wants to stay in business.) Nor does the "arousal" theory fare any better in the face of a healthy common sense. To begin with, there is no reason to suppose people would seek out or enjoy "anguished" music if it truly caused that emotion to be aroused in them; for anguish is a very unpleasant emotion indeed, which we assiduously avoid if we can. Second, there is no evidence at all – in fact there is evidence to the contrary – that "anguished" music makes anguished listeners; for a brief, unbiased look at one's concert companions will reveal none of the telltale behavioral signs of anguish in them: neither tears nor sighs, nor groans nor the wringing of hands. Third, where music *does* acquire power over the emotions, by association with events in one's personal history, they are private, aesthetically irrelevant, and only by sheer accident the ones that the music might be described as having. (The second Kyrie of the Mass in B Minor might perhaps cause me anguish when I listen to it, because it calls to my mind, with all attendant feelings, an anguished period in my life which just happens to be the time I first heard it; but, on the other hand, it might just as well arouse cheer and good feelings if, by chance, it reminds me of the happy period of my life when I played second oboe in a college performance.)

If, then, the "possession" theory of musical expression is both the more recent, and the more plausible of the three, it would be paying Mattheson a double compliment – ahead of his time as well as closer to the truth – if we could make out a case for his at least having adumbrated the "possession" theory, and avoided the other two, in his most extensive study in the aesthetics and practice of music: *Der vollkommene Capellmeister*. That essentially is the interpretation I attempted to put on Mattheson – and the compliment I wished to pay him – in my earlier article, "What Mattheson said." It is the interpretation I intend to take a second look at here, now in the light of Harriss' complete translation. But before I get to that second look, I must outline briefly my hypothesis, as it stood in the previous essay.

III

The bloodhound's face is expressive of sadness in virtue of its likeness to human faces, whose expressions of sadness we have all experienced, and whose images we all can read in their canine incarnations. The weeping willow, more distantly perhaps, but no less recognizably, bears a likeness to the human posture in dejection. In general, expressiveness in nonhuman "objects," animal, vegetable, or mineral, is parasitic on the expression-behavior of human beings (including, of course, vocal utterance) which their visual appearance or emitted sounds may more or less resemble.[5] And such is the case also, I am persuaded, of the expressiveness of music.[6] It wears that expressiveness, be it sadness or anguish, jollity or jauntiness, in virtue of resembling the appropriate expressions of human voice, gesture, countenance, posture, and gait. I believe Mattheson, prisoner though he was of his own time and its conceptual frame, was at least partially persuaded of this as well.

The nuts and bolts of Mattheson's expression theory were the Cartesian *esprits animaux*. These refined corpuscles were imagined by Descartes, in his highly influential *Passions of the Soul* (1649), to be diffused throughout the body and, by their particular motions, to be the efficient cause of the emotions: that is to say, of the "passions of the soul." They were not, of course, observable entities but "theoretical constructs," if you will, whose operation and character could be inferred from what *was* observable: the "feel" that the affections were experienced as having, in introspection, and the behavioral outcome of these subjective states in the form of observable human expression. Thus, one could deduce that an emotion expansive in feeling and expression must be caused by a violent expansion of the vital spirits, an emotion constricting and oppressive in nature by a contraction of these elastic bodies.

In the hands of musical theorists, the vital spirits became

---

5 See *The Corded Shell* for an elaboration of this point.   6 *The Corded Shell.*

the object of musical representation. Music, like the vital spirits, was thought basically to be a medium in "motion." Could it not, then, be made to ape the motion of the vital spirits, thus becoming a kind of emotive "icon"? And perhaps, indeed, this is what musicians may have been doing all along, without knowing it. So Mattheson and his contemporaries of the same persuasion could finally bring together these three seemingly disparate equations: music as "expression," art as "imitation," and music as a "art." For music could be expression and imitation and (therefore) art all at once: expressive in its similarity to the "forms" of the emotions as vital spirits; imitation at least when it was intentionally so; and art at least whenever imitation.

At this point, in my view, the theory tended to diverge into two not altogether clearly differentiated versions. For *most*, the musical representation of the vital spirits was not an end in itself but a means to the more familiar end of arousing the appropriate emotions in the listener. For if the expansion or contraction of the vital spirits caused the arousal of expansive or oppressive emotions, music, it was thought, by either expansive (large) intervals or constrictive (small) ones might do the same, by a kind of intervention in the natural process.[7] Thus, in this view, the expressiveness of music turned out, in the end, to lie in the arousal of emotions, with the "representation" of the emotions as vital spirits merely an intermediary step in the process. We have, then, for all of its sophistication and suggestiveness, a version of the "arousal" theory pure and simple, with all its implausibilities rehearsed above.

Mattheson took another path, as I suggested in my previous article, and will suggest again, in a more qualified way, in this one.[8] His *theoretical* account of musical expression – as

---

7 An example of this view can be found, for instance, in Daniel Webb's *Observations on the Correspondence between Poetry and Music* (London, 1769); and although the name of Descartes never appears in Webb's book, the thinking is clearly Cartesian throughout.

8 That I have at least *qualified* my previous interpretation of Mattheson would, I know, have been appreciated by the late Wilson Coker, who has remonstrated

distinct from the various passages in *Der volkommene Capell-meister* where practical advice is given, or casual observations are made concerning it – is contained *entirely*, and *only* in Part 1, Chapter 3: "On Sound in Itself, and the Natural Theory of Music" (as Harriss translates it). I emphasize the fact that this is not merely the principal, but the solitary and complete theoretical discussion for reasons which will become apparent later on, when I return to a consideration of its significance. For now I only record the fact and add that Lenneberg translated a very substantial part,[9] which served as a main source of my earlier interpretation. To that interpretation I briefly turn.

In Part 1, Chapter 3 of *Der vollkommene Capellmeister*, Mattheson made it clear that he subscribed, chapter and verse, to the Cartesian theory of *esprits animaux*, as outlined in *De passionibus animae*. (Descartes is mentioned by name, and recommended to Mattheson's readers.) And this theory provided the key to musical "expression." If one wished to write music expressive of this or that emotion, then, according to Mattheson, one was obliged to make it conform to the particular motion and disposition of the vital spirits as manifested in their arousal of this or that emotion in human beings. Thus, for example, "if one knows that sadness is a contraction of these subtle parts of our body, then it is easy to see that the small and smallest intervals are the most suitable for this passion." Or again, "If we consider further that love is in fact essentially a diffusion of the spirits, then we will rightly conform to this in composing, and use similar relationships of sounds."[10]

It is worthy of some note, in this regard, that the relationship of the vital spirits and the actual emotions they were supposed to cause was thought to be so close and intimate as to make it all one to Mattheson whether he was talking

with me concerning Mattheson on various occasions, and to whom I am extremely grateful for forcing me to reconsider and rethink my position.

9 Pp. 51–69.

10 *Der vollkommene Capellmeister*, trans. Ernest C. Harriss (Ann Arbor, 1981), p. 105 (I, iii, 57 and 58).

about the vital spirits, or just the emotions themselves (a fact that was not sufficiently appreciated or acknowledged in my previous article). And thus he often simply made it out that what is being represented or imitated is the emotions directly, as where he writes. "Next to love, one must represent [*vorstellen*] sadness more in music."[11] No suggestion here that it is some intermediary that is being portrayed by the composer: it is the thing itself; the passion naked, not merely its cause.

A second, and even more important point is that *nowhere* in Part 1, Chapter 3 – which, I emphasize again, is the *only* account in *Der vollkemmene Capellmeister* of the vital spirits – does Mattheson explicitly state, or even implicitly suggest, that the purpose of representing the motions and dispositions of the vital spirits in music is to the *further* end of *arousing* the emotions in the listener which those specific motions and dispositions would arouse. Rather, the impression we are left with is that music is expressive, say, of love and sadness merely in virtue of its representing the particular motions and dispositions of the vital spirits associated with those emotions; and, as we have just seen, *that* is sometimes thought tantamount to representing the emotions themselves. Thus, it would appear, Mattheson is maintaining here not that we *feel* the love and sadness that the music might somehow embody, but that we *recognize* the love and sadness that the music represents, much in the same way we *recognize* the Madonna and Child that Raphael depicts. No "arousal" theory here.

But Mattheson does write in one place in Part 1, Chapter 3, that sadness is "moving" (*beweglichten*), and this might seem to suggest, lone instance though it is, that the *arousal* of the particular emotions is really what he had in mind after all. That, however, would be a needless concession to the "arousal" theory. For one need not deny that music can be "moving" – that is to say, "exciting" – in denying that it is expressive of sadness in virtue of arousing sadness. Sad mu-

11 Ibid., p. 107 (I, iii, 68).

sic may very well be "moving" – that is to say, "exciting" – without moving to sadness. Indeed, one would of course expect that well written "sad" music would be "moving," that is,"exciting," music, whereas boring, badly written "sad" music would not be "moving" or "exciting" at all.

Further, however, Mattheson has told us in Part 1, Chapter 3, *exactly* what it means for music to be moving; and it has nothing to do with the arousal of sadness, love, or the like. He writes that "it is in the true nature of music that it is above all a teacher of propriety." To accomplish this musical morality, the composer must "present the virtues and vices in his music well, and . . . arouse skillfully in the feelings of the listener a love for the former and disgust for the latter."[12] Thus, music *does* arouse two kinds of "emotions" in listeners; but they are emotions only in a distant sense: the "emotions" of moral approbation and blame, what David Hume called "calm passions," "commonly . . . soft and gentle,"[13] which we, I think, would be more likely to refer to as "attitudes." Thus music may indeed *represent* sadness; and the musical representation of sadness may indeed be "moving." What it moves us to, however, is not sadness, but moral approbation or blame: approbation of virtue, disapprobation of vice, if the composer has done his work well.

I can now briefly summarize the main points of my provisional interpretation, based on Lenneberg's partial translation of Part 1, Chapter 3:

(1) Mattheson was giving neither an "arousal" theory of musical expression nor a "self-expression" theory: that is to say, he was neither claiming that music is expressive in virtue of stimulating the listener's emotions nor in virtue of expressing the composer's.

(2) Mattheson was, rather, giving a "possession" account: that is to say, claiming that music is expressive in virtue of representing the motions and dispositions of the vital spirits; or, what apparently comes to the same thing for him, representing the emotions, pure and simple.

12 Ibid., p. 104 (I, iii, 54).
13 *A Treatise of Human Nature*, ed. L. A. Selby-Bigge (Oxford, 1955), p. 470 (III, i, 2).

(3) Mattheson did, indeed, believe that music is moving; but he meant by that not that music arouses the emotions it represents – love, sadness, and the like – but rather that music, when properly brought off, is exciting, and, further, exciting in the sense that it awakens in the listener an attitude of approval toward virtue and disapproval toward vice.

(4) Music, in short, apart from its specific moral effect, is not an emotive stimulus at all, but an emotive "presentation" to the intellect.

It remains to determine whether this provisional interpretation will hold up in the face of some apparently recalcitrant material now available to me in Harriss' complete rendering of *Der vollkommene Capellmeister*. This determination will involve two separate tasks: answering the charge that Mattheson, in the remainder of his work, was guilty of backsliding into a "self-expression" theory; and, likewise, answering the charge that he fell back into an "arousal" account. To the first of these tasks I now turn.

IV

In my earlier interpretation, I gave very short shrift to the possibility that Mattheson might be venturing a "self-expression" kind of theory.[14] But with a complete translation of the *Capellmeister* now available, and considering the importance of the kind of theory in question, it is incumbent on me now to go into the matter with more thoroughness than heretofore.

The passages in Part 1, Chapter 3, that might seem to suggest a "self-expression" theory are, indeed, quite benign. For what they amount to, really, is not the claim that feeling an emotion is a logically necessary condition for "expressing" it in music, but, merely, that it is difficult to represent an emotion one has not, *at some time or other*, experienced; since if one does not know what the emotion is like, one can hardly

---

14 "What Mattheson said," p. 133.

239

know how to form one's music in such a way as to represent it. So, for example, Mattheson writes: "A composer of amorous pieces must certainly here consult his own experience, whether present or past, for he will find the best model in himself and in his own affect according to which he could compose his musical expressions."[15]

It cannot be too strongly urged that there is a world of difference between Mattheson's suggestion, in the above quotation, and a fullblown "self-expression" theory. To, as Mattheson says, "consult one's experience," is to recall an emotion once felt, and to cold-bloodedly examine its character, for the purpose of representing it in an artistic medium. It is not to feel it in its immediate urgency, which alone can lead to "expression" in the literal sense of that word. I can "express" an emotion I feel, not an emotion I recall having felt, whether five years ago or five minutes past. This is simply a matter of logic, not of practice, skill, or innate ability. I can no more "express" a remembered emotion than I can "cure" a remembered cold.

Bearing this simple, but vital fact of "logical grammar" in mind, and recalling that Mattheson suggests we consult our experience of past emotions to better represent them in music, a rather puzzling passage later in the *Capellmeister* becomes quite clear. Mattheson writes, in Part 2, Chapter 3: "It is not really necessary that a composer, if for example he wants to write down a dirge, a lamentation, or something of the sort, would begin to cry and weep: yet it is absolutely necessary that he open his mind and heart to the affection at hand to a certain measure, otherwise, he will fare badly."[16] What is puzzling, if one reads the passage in isolation is its apparent self-contradictory character. For if "cry and weep" is a literary synonym for "sad," and "open his mind and heart to the affection" is so as well, then when Mattheson says that the composer need *not* "cry and weep," and, on the other hand, insists that he must "open his mind and heart to the affection," he is essentially telling the composer *both*

15 Harriss, p. 105 (III, iii, 62). 16 Ibid., p. 262 (II, ii, 65).

that he need not feel sad, and that he must. But viewed in the light of our previous distinction between remembering what it is like to be in a certain emotional state, and actually (here and now) *being* in it, the contradiction dissolves. To "weep and cry" is to feel sadness in all its immediacy and have its "expression" forced from one's being; but merely to "open one's mind and heart to the affection" is to remember and contemplate. The composer need, and perhaps *ought* only do the latter, in Mattheson's view. The composer, to appropriate a phrase from Thomas Mann, serves emotions up ice cold, or, to appropriate another, more familiar evocation of the concept, the composer's emotion is not emotion *in vivo*, but only "recollected in tranquillity."

Why, it might be plausibly asked, did Mattheson, although not an adherent to the "self-expression" theory, so strongly urge the composer to consult, and scrutinize his own emotions? Clearly, to begin with, because, in Mattheson's view, one of the major tasks of the composer was to make music expressive, by somehow capturing the "form" or "structure" of the emotions in musical form and structure. And what better way to know the "form" or "structure" of an emotion than to "know thyself" – to come to understand the "form" and "structure" of one's own "passions" and "affections"? What one could *not* do, in the nature of the case, was to examine directly the vital spirits, whose own motions and dispositions were, by hypothesis, congruent with those of the emotions. Indeed, one only knew the nature of the vital spirits by inference from the emotions as experienced: first assuming that they were structurally similar to the emotions they caused and then inferring the "shape" of that structure by determining, through introspection, or the observation of expression-behavior, the "shape" of the emotions themselves. Had one been able, by turning some "microscope of the emotions" on the vital spirits, to observe their structure directly, Mattheson might not have been obliged to lay such heavy emphasis on introspection. But that was not possible. In lieu of directly observing the vital spirits, what was left to the seeker after knowledge of the emotions was an examination of his own and the observation of the expression-behavior of others. And in an age where "behaviorism" was yet to be heard of, expression must have seemed far more remote from what it expressed than it does to us now. What was left to Mattheson, and his age, was the familiar method of introspection. That, in effect, is what he urged, and what has, under the baleful influence of the "self-expression theory of art," been sometimes mistaken for that very thing.[17]

Mattheson may, at times, flirt with compositional self-expression; but he never marries the lady. It may be of some interest, however, in concluding with this topic, to remark that where Mattheson does seem to succumb to self-expression is (predictably, I shall argue) in regard to *performance:* "The singer and player," he says, "can help a great deal if they understand and feel [*empfinden*] what they perform"[18] – a sentiment echoed later by, among others, C. P. E. Bach.

Why should *performance*, rather than composition, seem to Mattheson a fertile field for "self expression"? The answer, I think, is fairly obvious, if performance and composition are viewed in their Baroque context. There is to "self-expression," in the ordinary sense, a kind of spontaneous element. When one is angry, one strikes out, unpremeditatedly, perhaps even involuntarily (which is why a crime committed in the heat of passion is reduced in degree). When sad, one cries; one does not *plan* to cry, or *try* to express one's grief – indeed one must try, on the contrary, to hold back the tears, as one "counts to ten" when angry, to censor one's expressive behavior: to prevent the guilty blow, or the regretted insult. But it is precisely in Baroque performance practice where spontaneity – in other words, *improvisation* – holds sway. The keyboard player must create, from figured bass, his or her own accompaniment, in the heat of the moment, as the soloist, whether singer or instrumentalist, must

17 As Susanne Langer does, for instance, in *Philosophy in a New Key*, and Eduard Hanslick in *Vom Musikalisch Schonen*.
18 Harriss, p. 367 (II, vii, 21).

create his or her own embellishments to the musical line (nor need the reader be reminded how intimately involved in "expression" these ornaments were thought to be in the period). Here is where spontaneity and (therefore) self-expression lie, not in the composition of a double fugue, invertible counterpoint, or a canon in augmentation. If the composer had to be, to a certain extent, cold-blooded to succeed in his craft, the performer had to be caught up in the heat of the moment. Where the composer had to plan, the performer had to "play it by ear," make it up along the way. Mattheson was *perhaps* drawn to the "self-expression" theory of musical *performance* – but musical *composition* never.

V

Having acquitted Mattheson of the charge of "self-expression," we must now turn to the more difficult case against him, of succumbing to the ubiquitous "arousal" theory of musical expression, so widespread particularly in his own time. It is a difficult case partly because of the sheer length of Mattheson's book – 484 pages in the original German edition, 871 in Harriss' translation – and the opportunity, therefore, of a proliferation of potential counter examples. Coupled with the fact that the "arousal" theory was received opinion in Mattheson's time, and the terms associated with it just the ones that would naturally come to one's mind in passing, rather than carefully considered references to musical expression, this prolixity did indeed produce, in Matthesons' text, a gaggle of passages that, at least on first reflection, appear to be lapses into the "arousal" idiom. That the appearance is far worse than the reality will, I trust, become clear in what follows, although I cannot claim to be able to dispatch all recalcitrant passages. Those that cannot be dispatched can, at least, be accounted for, if interpretation is combined with historical "sympathy."

What would be helpful, at the outset, and what I provide below, is a brief (and necessarily incomplete) catalogue of verbs most frequently used by Mattheson in describing musical "expression." They are *ausdrucken* (express); *beschrieben* (describe, depict, portray), *bewegen* (stir, move, agitate, excite, affect); *dringen* (penetrate, pierce); *empfinden* (perceive, be sensible of, experience); *erregen* (excite, stir up, agitate, provoke, promote, cause, inspire); *erwecken* (rouse, awaken, stir up); *rege machen* (stir up, excite); *rühren* (stir up); *vorstellen* (present, represent).[19]

A quick survey of these verbs reveals, to begin with, that the majority suggest "arousal," and that only three of the eleven unequivocally do *not*: *ausdrucken, beschrieben,* and *vorstellen*. (*Empfinden* is neutral, suggesting arousal if one *experiences* an emotion, but not if one merely *perceives* or *is sensible of* its presence in the music.) It might seem, then, that the sheer preponderance of arousal over nonarousal verbs clinches the case for Mattheson as an adherent to the "arousal" theory. However, these numbers themselves tell us very little; for *vorstellen,* and *ausdrucken,* and their noun, adjective and adverb derivatives, account for just as many *individual occurrences* as the rest put together, or more, *ausdrucken* being by far Matthesons' favorite emotion-word. We need more than arithmetic to draw a reasonable conclusion.

Another general consideration will be helpful, before we get down to an examination of some specific passages. It is this. The mere occurrence of an arousal verb does not, of itself, constitute a counterexample to the denial that Mattheson is holding an "arousal" theory. For in the altogether ambiguous contexts in which many of them occur, they are theory-neutral vis-à-vis the "possession" theory and the "arousal" one, since in either case Mattheson thought that music is supposed to arouse moral approbation and blame. Nor, in addition, as we have seen, need we deny on the "possession" account that music can be "moving" and "exciting," which, again, in many contexts may be all that the occurrence of an arousal verb signalizes.

It should, then, be clear that the occurrences of arousal

---

19 I have given, in parentheses, only those meanings relevant to the question at hand, based on *Cassell's New German Dictionary* (New York, 1939).

verbs divide into two distinct groups: (1) those that are compatible with the "possession" theory, in that they suggest either that music arouses the moral "emotions" of approbation and disgust, or (if it does not come to the same thing) that it is simply "moving" and "exciting"; and (2) those that are not compatible, in that they suggest unequivocally that music is expressive in virtue of arousing the basic emotions – fear, love, happiness, and the like. The latter, fortunately for the interpretation of Mattheson being proffered here, are few, arguable, and quite understandable as temporary lapses in philosophical vigilance of linguistic purity.

There is no need, at this point in the argument, to canvass the cases outside of Part 1, Chapter 3, that support the interpretation of Mattheson being urged here. That is to say, there is no need to quote passages in which Mattheson uses *beschrieben*, *vorstellen*, or *ausdrucken* to convey the sense of music "representing," "presenting," or "expressing" the emotions. For when he is arguing to the effect that music "represents" or "presents" the emotions, he is strongly suggesting a version of the "possession" theory; and when he is arguing that music "expresses" them, his statements are theory-neutral as between the "possession" and "arousal" accounts. Indeed, throughout *Der vollkommene Capellmeister* Mattheson uses *ausdrucken* much in the same, theoretically uncommitted way that "express" has been used in our own times to talk about the emotive in art. That is to say, neither *ausdrucken* nor "express" is being used in the *literal* sense, as "He expressed his anger with a clenched fist and the set of his jaw." Rather, in all of Mattheson's uses, and in much of current usage as well, one cannot tell what exactly is meant by "express": whether "arouse," or "embody," or what have you. The task of finding out what a critic or theorist may mean by "express," then, very often turns out just to be the task of determining whether or not the party in question is committed to the "arousal" theory. And such is certainly the case with Mattheson: Where *ausdrucken* is used, it is compatible with the "arousal" or the "possession" interpretation. So we need concern ourselves no further with multiplying occurrences of its use – which are numerous. They cannot tell us anything more than we already know, least of all whether Mattheson lapses into the "arousal" theory or remains steady to the text (as I have construed it) of Part 2, Chapter 3.

It appears, then, that the only crucial cases are those involving the out-and-out arousal verbs: *bewegen, dringen, erregen, erwecken, rege machen, rühren*. And there is certainly (and happily) no need to examine them all, but merely to go through a "best case" and "worst case" analysis. The occurrences fall about evenly into the two groups (with the "best case," I suspect, being the more populous).

Let us look at the best case first. Here are some fairly typical examples. Mattheson writes that a good melody "has the power to arouse [*erwecken*] a true affection or a real feeling in us."[20] Again: "Clarity emanating from the midst of art is the only means of moving [*rühren*] the heart and mind of the listeners, consequently stirring [*bewegen*] their very souls, which must be the true goal of all musical work"[21] Or, finally: "The goal of our musical work, next to honoring God, is pleasing and stirring [*Bewegung*] the listeners."[22]

We are told a good melody has the power to arouse real feelings in us. But what Mattheson means by *real feelings* here might very well be the moral sentiments that, in Part 1, Chapter 3, he takes to be the final goal of the musical art: that is, the point of the "moral lesson" the composer is meant to inculcate. Again, we are told that music is to move the heart and mind of the listener, to stir his or her very soul. Move the heart and mind to what? If we want to give an answer consistent with Part 1, Chapter 3 (and why shouldn't we?), then that answer is: Move the heart and mind of the listener to approval of virtue and disapproval of vice. The passage in question is quite consistent with that construal. Finally, the purpose of music, next to honoring God is to please and stir the listener. Perhaps Mattheson means by "stir"

20 Harriss, p. 364 (II, vii, 3). 21 Ibid., p. 685 (III, xix, 30).
22 Ibid., p. 295 (II, iv, 66).

to arouse sadness, and anger, and all those kinds of emotions in the listener. Why believe *that*, however, when Mattheson has already made clear in Part 1, Chapter 3 – clearer than in any other place in the *Capellmeister* – exactly what he means by music stirring or moving or arousing the listener, namely, stirring or moving or arousing moral attitudes? There is nothing, then, in these kinds of nonspecific uses of arousal verbs to suggest that Mattheson has fallen into the ordinary "arousal" theory. They are all consistent with a "possession" analysis of Part 1, Chapter 3.

So much, then, for the "best case" analysis. Let us turn to the "worst." Mattheson writes that "simple melody in certain circumstances actually can by itself effectively excite [*erregen*] all tender inclinations such as love, hope, fear, etc."[23] Again, it is more difficult for instrumental music to "move [*bewege*] the feelings of the hearers to this or that passion; because there are no words present, but merely musical discourse."[24] Or, finally,

> Printz speaks here of a sweet, pleasant, amorous and pious melancholy. Whoever wants to arouse [*erregen*] such must certainly use other artifices than those which derive from introduction or avoidance of unharmonious cross relationships.[25]

Here *are* instances, I think, in which only a perverse reading can possibly rescue a "nonarousal" interpretation. Mattheson, surely, and unmistakably, slipped into the familiar "arousal" idiom of his times; and that reference to the older writings of Wolfgang Caspar Printz should be one of the occasions for doing so is not without significance in pointing up the fact that anyone trying to forge a "possession" theory of musical expression in Mattheson's time would certainly be bucking the tide of recent traditions as well as received opinion. There can be no escape from the conclusion that in the passages just quoted Mattheson is construing musical expression in terms of excitation. Melody is said to

23 Ibid., p. 308 (II, v, 35).   24 Ibid., p. 420 (II, xii, 8).
25 Ibid., p. 575 (III, ix, 30).

arouse love, hope, and fear, not to represent or express them. The goal of vocal composition, that eludes pure instrumental music, is the *moving* of *this* or *that specific emotion*, it would seem. And it is the means of *arousing* melancholy, not representing or expressing it, about which Printz and Mattheson disagree. These implications cannot be avoided. They cannot be explained away; but they *can* be *explained*.

Even were Mattheson a *philosopher* by trade, with the systematic and rigorous gifts of a Spinoza or a Kant, the complete avoidance of contradictions and terminological inconsistencies in a work as long as *Der vollkommene Capellmeister* would be quite unlikely. It is hardly surprising, therefore, that they should not be avoided by someone who had no pretensions to the title of philosopher, or to the rigor and system that the title would have suggested to the eighteenth century (and to us). The question is: How significant are these inconsistencies, and how are they to be treated?

There are two choices for the interpreter here: to class Mattheson as an "arousal" theorist, who simply forgot to mention that rather important fact in the *only* place in his work where musical expression is given a theoretical exposition (that is, Part 1, Chapter 3); or to class him as an innovative thinker, breaking new ground in the aesthetics of music in propounding a version of the "possession" theory, who, quite understandably, lapsed into a language more consistent with the thought of his time, when he was making casual, nontheoretical observations, *en passant*, about the emotive character of music. In order to opt for the former interpretation, one would have to believe *both* that Mattheson thought music should represent the vital spirits for the purpose of arousing the emotions in listeners which the vital spirits themselves arouse *and* that in the *only* place where he discussed the vital spirits at all he omitted or forgot to inform the reader what the purpose of this representation was. This seems to me too fantastic for credence. So I opt for the latter interpretation, on the basis of what might be called a principle of "charity" or "optimalization." That principle simply tells us: All things being equal, choose the interpretation according to which the work you are interpreting is given the highest valuation. We have the choice of treating Mattheson as an absentminded follower of other mens' thoughts, or a forward-looking breaker of new ground who sometimes faltered because of the difficulty of the task. *Der vollkommene Capellmeister* is consistent with both. The principle of "charity" or "optimalization" dictates the latter choice, and this is the choice I quite cheerfully make on the occasion of Johann Mattheson's three hundredth birthday.

Chapter XIV

Kant and the *Affektenlehre:* What he said, and what I wish he had said

The influence of Kant on musical thought is out of all proportion to the space he devoted to the subject in the third *Critique,* or elsewhere. To be more specific, his notion of music as the beautiful play of sensations has been frequently alluded to by writers on music, and many think it to be the most philosophically interesting expression of what we now call musical formalism prior to Eduard Hanslick's monograph of 1854.

What Kant said about the vexed question of music and the emotions, however, has not been nearly so well received. Indeed, it is perhaps more accurate to say that Kant's discussion has been peremptorily dismissed as, in the words of a recent commentator, "historically accidental and systematically unnecessary."[1] In a word: irrelevant, a philosophical afterthought. That indeed is the view of the matter I have subscribed to myself in the past. And I will take the liberty of quoting myself to that effect, having written in 1988 that "The doctrine of the affections hangs on to most philosophical accounts of music [in the eighteenth century] like an extraneous barnacle; and this is as true of Kant at the end of the century as it is of Hutcheson at the beginning."[2]

Surely there could be no better occasion than the present

---

1 John Neubauer, *The Emancipation of music from Language: Departures from Mimesis in Eighteenth-Century Aesthetics* (New Haven: Yale University Press, 1986), p, 187. Neubauer ascribes this view to Carl Dahlhaus and acquiesces in it.

2 Peter Kivy, *Osmin's Rage: Philosophical Reflections on Opera, Drama and Text* (Princeton: Princeton University Press, 1988), p. 125.

one, the bicentennial of the third *Critique,* on which to reexamine this harsh judgment passed on Kant's philosophy of music; and that is what I propose to do here. My question is, quite simply: Did Kant say something original and distinctively "Kantian" about the emotive character of music, or did he merely, *de rigeur,* feel obliged to mention it, in the accepted banalities of his time?

Let me begin, somewhat abruptly, by quoting the passage in which Kant first introduces his version of the view that music arouses the affections. Here, as elsewhere, I will be using Pluhar's translation, compared always with the translations of Bernard and Meredith, as well as the German text (although the last named exercise may well be a case of the blind leading the sighted). Kant writes in §53 of the third *Critique:*

> Its [music's] charm, so generally communicable, seems to rest in this: Every linguistic expression has in its context a tone appropriate to its meaning. This tone indicates, more or less, an affect of the speaker and in turn induces the same affect in the listener too, where it then conversely arouses the idea which in language we express in that tone. And just as modulation is, as it were, a universal language of sensations that every human being can understand, so the art of music employs this language all by itself in its full force, namely, as a language of the affects; in this way it communicates to everyone, according to the law of association, the aesthetic ideas that we naturally connect with such affects. But since these aesthetic ideas are not concepts, not determinate thoughts, the form of the arrangement of these sensations (harmony and melody), which takes the place of the form of a language, only serves to express, by means of the proportioned attunement of the sensations, the aesthetic idea of a coherent whole of an unspeakable wealth of thought, and to express it in conformity with a certain theme that is the prevalent affect of the piece.[3]

3 Immanuel Kant, *Critique of Judgment,* trans. Werner S. Pluhar (Indianapolis: Hackett, 1987), pp. 198–9. It seems to me that "intonation" is a far better choice than "modulation" to render the German word *Modulation* in this passage, for it avoids the possible confusion of "modulation," as Kant uses the word here, with the

To be observed straightaway is that Kant buys into the notion, widespread among his contemporaries, of a universal language of the passions, inherent in the intonation of the human speaking voice.[4] "Every linguistic expression," Kant says, "has in its context a tone appropriate to its meaning"; and this tone is indicative of the speaker's emotional state, which it tends to arouse in the listener. Kant is not saying, of course, that every linguistic expression has a single emotion appropriate to it, which would clearly be absurd. It is "in its context" that an expression acquires one passionate tone rather than another, so that, for example, "I see a policeman" will be uttered in tones of fear and consternation by the potential mugger, and in tones of joy and relief by the potential muggee.

Music obviously cannot reproduce the meaning of an expression, but it can reproduce its tone, thereby, like speech, arousing the corresponding emotion. Therein, as Kant and many of his contemporaries believed, lies its charm. And because what music is reflecting is a universal language of passionate intonation beneath the surface of articulate speech, "the natural language of mankind," as Thomas Reid described it,[5] the charm is, in the distinctive Kantian terminology, "generally communicable."

Up to this point, what we have is far from new or original. Kant is presenting here a shopworn view of the musical experience. His exposition of it, as one would expect, possesses a philosophical clarity and depth far exceeding what most contemporary writers on the subject had achieved, but except for that, there are no surprises. The notion that the pleasure of music is derived from its arousing the emotions – either merely the pleasing ones, or the painful ones as well, some-

---

technical word in music, already current in Kant's time, meaning transition from one key to another. Meredith and Bernard also render *Modulation* as "modulation." Kant, of course, is referring here to the intonation of the speaking voice, which can also be described correctly as "modulation." But to introduce the word here may suggest to the unwary reader that Kant has started to talk about music before he has stopped talking about language.

4 Of particular relevance here is the use made of the notion by Thomas Reid in connection with the fine arts. On this see Peter Kivy, "Thomas Reid and the Expression Theory of Art," *The Monist* 61 (1978).

5 Thomas Reid, *Inquiry into the Human Mind, Works of Thomas Reid*, ed. Sir William Hamilton (8th ed.; Edinburgh: James Thin, 1895), Vol. 1, pp. 121–2.

how made pleasing by the composer's craft – was common coin throughout the eighteenth century and before. And were this as far as Kant had taken the subject, we would have good reason to conclude that he contributed nothing distinctively original to it.

But Kant does not let the matter rest here. For it becomes clear in the middle of the passage quoted above that the arousal of the emotions by music is not where the musical experience comes to an end. Rather, as Kant says, "in this way," that is, by the arousal of the emotions, music "communicates to everyone, according to the law of association, the aesthetic ideas that we naturally connect with such affects." And now it appears we are breaking new ground.

You may remember that I framed the question of my essay in the following way: Did Kant say something original and distinctively "Kantian" about the emotive character of music, or did he merely, *de rigeur,* feel obliged to mention it, in the accepted banalities of his time? Up until the introduction of the aesthetic ideas the answer to this question would seem to be that he did nothing but mouth, to be sure, somewhat more elegantly than his contemporaries, the familiar musical clichés of his time. As soon as the aesthetic ideas are worked into the equation, however, the answer is seen to be quite unequivocally the opposite, and my discussion at an abrupt end. For what could be more original and distinctively Kantian than the murky but intriguing notion of the aesthetic ideas that figures so prominently in Kant's discussion of the fine arts? And by the integration of that notion into the familiar doctrine of the musical affects surely Kant has transformed the *Affektenlehre* into something entirely novel, indelibly marked with the signature of the third *Critique.*

Alas, matters are not nearly so cut and dried as all that. And perhaps, "alas" is not the appropriate expletive here, for if they were, like Hamlet had he killed Claudius in the first act, I would have nothing more to say. Rather, the answer to the question of whether or not the injection of the aesthetic ideas into the doctrine of emotive arousal in music really does represent an advance over the old doctrine of the affections turns out, in the event, to be far less obvious and decisive than might appear at this stage in the argument. I shall get to this muddying of the waters in a moment. But before I do, I should like to pause here to dwell on the possible implications the introduction of the aesthetic ideas might have had for Kant's (and future) musical philosophies, had Kant not later in the *Critique of Judgment*, as we shall see, seemingly defused the notion altogether, rendering it philosophically inoperative.

Having introduced the evocation of the aesthetic ideas as the end result of music's emotive arousal, Kant goes on to say, you will remember:

> But since these aesthetic ideas are not concepts, not determinate thoughts, the form of the arrangements of these sensations (harmony and melody), which takes the place of the form of a language, only serves to express, by means of the proportioned attunement of the sensations, the aesthetic idea of a coherent whole of an unspeakable wealth of thought, and to express it in conformity with a certain theme that is the prevalent affect of the piece.

A very rich and suggestive passage, this, with all kinds of reverberations for a philosophy of music. But what strikes us most forcefully at first is the phrase *unnennbaren Gedankenfülle*, rendered "unspeakable wealth of thought" by Pluhar and Bernard, "unutterable wealth of thought" by Meredith (a better alternative, I think) and which it seems to me is most idiomatically understood as "inexpressible wealth of thought."[6] It has become something of a Romantic cliché, of course – and a dangerous one, in my opinion – to describe music as expressing thoughts inexpressible in words: dangerous because it suggests that music has a content when, it appears to me, it clearly does not, and dangerous because it suggests that our inability to paraphrase or gloss that content should be taken not for what it is, namely, evidence against content, but merely as a pedantic attempt to express the ineffable. When Kant was formulating this notion, however, it

6 See Immanuel Kant, *Kritik der Urteilskraft* (Hamburg: Felix Meiner Verlag, 1959), p. 186; *Critique of Judgment*, trans. J. H. Bernard (New York: Hafner, 1951), p. 173; *Critique of Aesthetic Judgement*, trans. James Creed Meredith (Oxford: Clarendon Press, 1911), p. 194; *Critique of Judgment*, trans. Pluhar, p. 199.

was hardly a cliché, breaking, as it did, new ground in musical thought. And second, it was not, I want to argue, a misguided attempt on Kant's part to give music a content, but rather an insightful if not entirely explicit attempt to reveal that music possesses a "logic," to uncover what many today would call its "syntax." Here is what I mean.

Kant's first and most familiar description of music, as the beautiful play of sensations, does full justice to the insight that music is a completely contentless art. But what it perhaps unfortunately suggests is a beautiful play of sensations such as one would get it in a kaleidoscope, which is to say, vertically symmetrical and lawlike, but horizontally, temporally, random or at least directionless, without inner coherence along the time dimension. And surely music is not that. What the notion of the aesthetic ideas might bring to Kant's description of music is that inner temporal coherence that the characterization, "beautiful play of sensations" lacks, while still preserving what is so felicitous about the expression, namely, its emphasis on music's pure aesthetic beauty, naked of conceptual content.

One of the characterizations of the aesthetic ideas in §49, where the notion is first laid out, is particularly illustrative of my point. Kant says there that "an aesthetic idea is a presentation of the imagination which is conjoined with a given concept and is connected, when we use imagination in its freedom, with such a multiplicity of partial presentations that no expression that stands for a determinate concept can be found for it."[7] What attracts me here is the notion of *connectedness* without a determinate concept under which to place it, perfectly captured, I think, in a gloss of the passage by Paul Guyer, which reads: "An aesthetic idea involves a manifold of the imagination the constituents of which are felt to belong together, and to illustrate a given concept, although as with aesthetic response in general, this coherence does not derive from a rule imposed by the concept being illustrated or by any other concept, although as with aesthetic

7 Kant, *Critique of Judgment*, trans. Pluhar, p. 185.

response in general, this coherence does not derive from a rule imposed by the concept being illustrated or by any other concept."[8] This notion is more apparent still – which is itself significant – in the passage, already quoted, where Kant applies the aesthetic ideas to music, speaking of "the aesthetic idea of a coherent whole . . . in conformity with a certain theme that is the prevalent affect of the piece." What Kant groped for here, and what the aesthetic ideas were supposed, I believe, to capture, is that feeling of logical coherence we have, but cannot state in conceptual terms, in a well wrought musical structure, a feeling of connected discourse, although it is, needless to say, a "discourse" without a content. It was the very thing that Hanslick was getting at, many years later, when he wrote in *Vom Musikalisch-Schönen:* "Music has sense and logic – but musical sense and logic. . . .[W]e recognize the rational coherence of a group of tones and call it a sentence, exactly as with every logical proposition we have a sense of where it comes to an end."[9]

Now Kant's idea of musical discourse – if I may so call it – is of a discourse of the passions: a connected, coherent progression of aesthetic ideas, brought to consciousness by the arousal of emotions. There are, of course, other descriptions under which to understand the logical progression of musical sound, but to understand it as a progression of expressive properties is certainly one valid way, and a very persuasive one at that. And having chosen the aesthetic ideas associated with emotional states, rather than the felt emotional states themselves, as the aesthetically significant emotive materials, one is forced to regret, with twentieth-century hindsight or course, that Kant employed such a cumbersome, problematic mechanism as emotive arousal to account for the production of emotive aesthetic ideas in music. It would have been so much more elegant and plausible for Kant to

8 Paul Guyer, *Kant and the Claims of Taste* (Cambridge, Mass.: Harvard University Press, 1979), p. 233.

9 Eduard Hanslick, *On the Musically Beautiful: A Contribution towards the Revision of the Aesthetics of Music,* trans. Geoffrey Payzant (Indianapolis: Hackett, 1986), p. 30.

have argued that we recognize emotions as properties of musical form and structure, with the aesthetic ideas following quite naturally and directly from that recognition. Why could Kant not have made this move? He surely had the philosophical genius to do so and his century was not far from discovering this alternative. (In fact I think one or two people had.)

The reason for this, as for other Kantian failures in musical discussion, was Kant's abysmal ignorance of music as an *art*. In particular, the third *Critique* – arguably the cradle of musical formalism – shows absolutely no evidence whatever that its author had the slightest acquaintance with anything that a musician or music lover would recognize as musical form: that is to say, sonata form, song form, rondo, theme-and-variations, and so forth, which would be, along with the elements that make them up, such as melodic structure and harmonic and contrapuntal syntax, the bearers of expressive properties as I conceive of them. In the absence of such expressive materials, all Kant had to work with was the intonation of the human voice, and music's analogy to it. And although more could be made even of that, along the lines I am suggesting, than Kant perceived, it is not sufficient for the purpose, as I have tried to show elsewhere.[10] It was natural, therefore, though regretable, that Kent should acquiesce in the old and familiar doctrine that music arouses the emotions through its representation of the passionate accents of the human speaking voice – a doctrine which, in its modern formulation, was already abroad in the sixteenth century, with roots as far back as Plato.

So far I have been telling you the good news about Kant and the doctrine of the affections. For, apart from the use of the arousal mechanism to bring the aesthetic ideas to consciousness, Kant's treatment of the role of the emotions in music appears to be both original and pointing very much in what I take to be at least the right direction. For if the ex-

---

10 See Peter Kivy, *The Corded Shell: Reflections on Musical Expression* (Princeton: Princeton University Press, 1980); reprinted in *Sound Sentiment: An Essay on the Musical Emotions* (Philadelphia: Temple University Press, 1989).

pressive properties of music are not to succumb to purist skepticism, or become a mere epiphenomenon, a strong case must be made for them as an essential part of the syntactic structure of music. And that case is at least suggested by Kant's introduction of the aesthetic ideas into what would have been, but for that, just another version of the arousal theory of musical expression: the theory that music possesses its expressive properties in virtue of arousing emotions in listeners.

Now for the bad news, which is that Kant apparently backslides into the very view that §53 saves him from when the subject of music and the emotions is pursued further in §54. The outstanding question would seem to be: What is the nature of our satisfaction in the train of aesthetic ideas that the arousal of emotions by music succeeds in initiating? The answer one wants, of course, and would expect from Kant in his critical period, is that it is that satisfaction issuing from the free play of the cognitive faculties. What we get instead, so far as I can see, is nothing more than the standard, pre-critical explanation in the British manner, in terms of physical or mental "physiology," which Kant had so decisively put behind him in the Analytic of the Beautiful. Kant writes in §54:

> But music and something to laugh about are two kinds of play with aesthetic ideas . . . by which in the end nothing is thought; it is merely the change they involve that still enables them to gratify us in a lively way. This shows rather clearly that in both of them the quickening is merely bodily, even though it is aroused by ideas of the mind, and shows that all the gratifications we find at a lively party extolled as being so refined and inspired, consists merely in the feeling of health that is produced by an intestinal agitation corresponding to such play. It is not our judging of the harmony we find in tones or in flashes of wit – this harmony, with its beauty, merely serves as a necessary vehicle – but the furtherance of the vital processes in the body, the affect that agitates the intestines and the diaphragm, in a word the feeling of health (which we cannot feel without such prompting), which constitutes the gratification we find in the fact that we can reach

the body through the soul as well, and use the soul as the physician of the body.[11]

I have quoted Kant at some length here because I hope to share with you the kind of horrible fascination with which someone deeply committed to music and to the philosophical understanding of its appeal to the human intellect, follows the descent of the argument in this passage, from the remarkable insights of §53 to the abysmal depths of a conclusion that makes no more of our enjoyment of the expressive in music than an aid to digestion: the sonic counterpart of Tums for the tummy. This in 1790: While audiences in Vienna, Mannheim, Prague, Paris, and London were sitting in rapt attention at performances of the mature instrumental works of Haydn and Mozart, with Beethoven on the verge of making his stormy entrance onto the Viennese musical scene!

It tells us a lot about Kant's conception of instrumental music that in the third *Critique* he still conceived of its institutional setting as the dining room rather than the concert hall. You may remember that in the *Observations on the Feeling of the Beautiful and Sublime* Kant describes a man of taste as, in part, someone who "Can devote part of his mealtime to listening to a piece of music."[12] Thirty-five years later his view of music had certainly deepened, and yet music still remained for him merely what the Baroque called *Tafelmusik*, thus not worthy of a person's full, undivided attention.

It is perfectly clear that the end result of Kant's argument from §53 to §54 is to make music, insofar as it is *expressive*, an agreeable rather than a fine art. The arousal of emotions, which has as its intermediate result the evocation of the aesthetic ideas, with all that might imply for a truly original, forward-looking account, resolves itself, in the event, into mere physiological exercise and relaxation, a way of treating the emotions in music which dates back at least to L'Abbé

11 Kant, *Critique of Judgment*, trans. Pluhar, pp. 202–3.
12 Immanuel Kant, *Observations on the Feeling of the Beautiful and Sublime*, trans. John T. Goldthwait (Berkeley, Los Angeles, London: University of California Press, 1960), p. 72n.

DuBos' influential work if 1719, the *Critical Reflections on Poetry, Painting and Music*, hardly a promising account, at this stage of the game, of what we enjoy in the perception of expressive musical form. "In music," Kant says, "this play proceeds from bodily sensations to aesthetic ideas (of the objects of affects), and from these back again to the body." In this music has as its direct analogue not the fine arts but "jest (which, just as much as music, deserves to be considered more an agreeable than a fine art)."[13]

It should not be inferred from this, I would like to add, that Kant opts unequivocally, in §54, for music as an agreeable art *tout court*. For he is speaking here specifically of music's expressive part, and any unqualified references to music can, I think, be understood in that context alone if one wishes to do so. What implications this has or does not have for his general account of music as the beautiful play of sensations is a question that must be postponed for another occasion. But this much can be said: What begins in §53 as an ingenious and original account of the expressive in music becomes, in §54, merely a more complicated version of the standard eighteenth-century notion that the expressive in music is the disposition to arouse emotions, and the arousal of emotions has, as its direct aesthetic purpose, bodily enjoyment of one kind or another. It is fair to say, in light of this, that the path Kant follows from §53 to §54 of the third *Critique* represents for the philosophy of music one of its greatest and most disappointing failures of nerve.

What went wrong? I have only the most speculative of answers.

To begin with, it would be useful to go back to the point where Kant first introduces the notion of the aesthetic ideas, in §49. He says there: "it is actually in the art of poetry that the power of the aesthetic ideas can manifest itself to full extent."[14] And he follows this assertion with some examples, the most elaborate of which, not surprisingly, being some lines from a poem. Kant glosses these lines – which are, you

---

13 Kant, *Critique of Judgment*, trans. Pluhar, p. 203.   14 Ibid., p. 183.

will remember, by Frederick the Great – in a quite ordinary way, showing how, in the brief compass of six lines, one idea follows logically from another: the idea of the setting sun from the idea of death. But these of course are not the aesthetic ideas. The latter follow *from* them. As Kant says:

> The king is here animating his rational idea of a cosmopolitan attitude, even at the end of life, by means of an attribute which the imagination (in remembering all the pleasures of a completed beautiful summer day, which a serene evening calls to mind) conjoins with that presentation, and which arouses a multitude of sensations and supplementary presentations for which no expression can be found.[15]

It is the "multitude of sensations and supplementary representations" that constitute the chain of aesthetic ideas. And unlike the "argument" of the poem, this chain can be given "no [cognitive] expression." It is, however, neither irrational nor merely productive of bodily enjoyment. "But the understanding employs this material not so much objectively, for cognition, as subjectively, namely, to quicken the cognitive powers, though indirectly this does serve cognition too."[16]

Let me now summarize some Kantian facts and then I will venture a conjecture. Here, then, are the facts. First, music arouses the emotions. Second, these emotions evoke aesthetic ideas. Third, these aesthetic ideas give us in their experiencing merely bodily pleasure. Fourth, poetry presents a kind of "argument" or connection of ideas that can be cognitively, rationally glossed. Fifth, this rational progression of ideas – the argument of the poem, whether it be a rational argument, or a narrative, fictional one – gives rise to a chain of aesthetic ideas. Sixth, this chain of aesthetic ideas, for which no cognitive expression is adequate, nevertheless engages the free play of the cognitive faculties, in which its enjoyment lies. Seventh, poetry is the only art in which "the power of aesthetic ideas can manifest itself to full extent." These are the facts; now for my conjecture.

There are three obvious differences between music and

15 Ibid., p. 184.   16 Ibid., p. 185.

poetry on Kant's view, two of them explicit, and one it can be reasonably assumed that Kant accepted as obvious enough not to require spelling out. Music, unlike poetry, cannot fully manifest the power of the aesthetic ideas, since poetry is the only art that can. The aesthetic ideas that music evokes, unlike those evoked by poetry, do not engage the free play of the cognitive faculties but merely stimulate bodily relaxation and well-being. And whereas we can give a cognitive gloss of a poem's "argument," we cannot provide any such thing for a musical composition because, of course, it has no cognitive content at all.

My conjecture, based on nothing more sophisticated than Mills' method of difference, is simply that Kant must have connected the ability of the aesthetic ideas in poetry to engage the free play of the cognitive faculties with the nature of their source, namely, a cognitive content; and, by parity of reasoning, he must have connected the inability of the aesthetic ideas in music to engage the free play of the cognitive faculties with the nature of their source, which was, by contrast, completely devoid of statable cognitive content: What was left for the aesthetic ideas in music to engage were merely the pleasurable sensations of the body, which did, after all, coincide with general opinion in the eighteenth century, as with Kant's rather low opinion of music's intellectual pretensions.

I confess that I do not have a shred of a notion as to what Kantian reason might be given for why, just because the aesthetic ideas in poetry are evoked by a cognitive "argument" or story, they can engage the free play of the cognitive faculties, whereas the aesthetic ideas in music, because they are evoked by what Kant must have thought of as a haphazard arousal of emotions, cannot. But that I suspect is behind it all. It cannot be a mere coincidence that a *cognitive* content leads to aesthetic ideas that can engage the *cognitive* faculties, and a contentless, noncognitive play of sensations cannot. Beyond that I cannot go.

Assuming, however, that my conjecture lies somewhere near the truth of the matter, we again come to the conclusion that Kant's failure to capitalize on the considerable musical insights of §53 must be laid to his almost complete ignorance of music as an art, and, in particular, his apparent lack of acquaintance with the larger elements of musical form. For if Kant, for example, had been conversant with the structural principles of sonata form – the most important musical form of the classical period – he would have seen that although such musical works as were cast in sonata form had no statable cognitive content, they were far from haphazard plays of emotion, but followed, rather, a statable sequence of musical elements with a palpable aesthetic logic and syntax. And their affective properties were part of that logical and syntactic progression. Thus, if rational connectedness of some kind in the source of aesthetic ideas is a necessary or sufficient condition for engaging the free play of the cognitive faculties, then the music of 1790 possessed such connectedness in the form of the structural and syntactical features of late classical style, of which sonata form is its ripest and fullest manifestation.

In conclusion, let me return once again to the question that I hoped to answer here: Did Kant say something original and distinctively "Kantian" about the emotive character of music, or did he merely, *de rigeur*, feel obliged to mention it, in the accepted banalities of his time? The answer, as we are now fully in a position to see, cannot be an unqualified one. He did, in the end, say nothing more than what a great many writers before him had said, that music arouses emotions, and that this arousal eventuates in bodily pleasure, or pleasure to the senses. But although he got the same result, he got it through a means – the aesthetic ideas – that is highly original and distinctively Kantian. It could have led to a realization, some two hundred years ahead of its time, of the role that expressive properties can play in a basically formalistic account of the purely musical experience. Instead, because of Kant's failure to follow through on his insights in §53, it led to the expressively barren formalism of Hanslick and his followers that we are only now extricating ourselves from. On this two-hundredth anniversary of the publication of Kant's great work on aesthetics, it is, of course, incumbent on us as scholars to recognize what was; but we should be perceptive enough, and generous enough as philosophers, to recognize what might have been. And somehow I cannot help thinking that what might have been in Kant's aesthetics of music was forestalled by none other than his well-known familial pietism. But for that perhaps he would have had music lessons.

Chapter XV

Something I've always wanted to know about Hanslick

The most obvious benefit of Geoffrey Payzant's new translation of Hanslick's *Vom Musikalisch-Schönen* is, needless to say, that it gives us an English text superior to the one we have been using heretofore. The second most obvious benefit, after that, is that Hanslick has once again been thrust into the forefront of musical thought, a place he has occupied in the past and deserves to occupy again. Many philosophers will, I think, be stimulated by Payzant's translation to consider and reconsider various aspects of Hanslick's argument. It has already had that effect on me; and the subject of the present essay is the result of my return to a specific point in Hanslick.

For many years I have been puzzled by a passage in Hanslick where he discusses the famous aria in Gluck's *Orfeo ed Euridice* – "Che farò senza Euridice!" – which Orfeo sings after he has lost Euridice for the second time by violating the stipulation not to look back at his wife while leading her from the underworld. The text is, of course, an expression of profound grief. Here is what Hanslick says about the aria (in Payzant's translation).

> When Orpheus' aria "Che farò senza Euridice!" . . . moved
> thousands (including J. J. Rousseau) to tears, Boyé, a contem-

This essay was presented as part of a symposium on Geoffrey Payzant's new translation of Hanslick, at the 45th Annual Meeting of the American Society for aesthetics, University of Missouri-Kansas City, 28-31 October 1987. I am grateful to my fellow symposiasts, Geoffrey Payzant and Gordon Epperson, as well as to the moderator, Jerrold Levinson, for helpful and stimulating discussion of my essay.

porary of Gluck, remarked that one could just as well or, indeed, much more faithfully, set the opposite words to the same tune. . . .

We are, indeed, not quite sure that the composer is entirely absolved in this case, insofar as music certainly possesses far more specific tones for the expression of passionate grief.[1]

Now the most obvious way of reading this passage – which, it seems to me, coincides both with sound philosophy and common musical sensibility – is as follows. Hanslick is claiming, quite rightly, that Gluck's music is, at least on first reflection, inappropriate to the text and to the situation of the character who enunciates it. For the situation requires and the text provides an expression of profound grief. Gluck, therefore, should have provided appropriate music, which would be music expressive of profound grief. But he has not done so. As Hanslick says, "Music possesses far more specific tones for the expression of passionate grief" than Gluck has provided. Thus, it would seem we have a right to conclude from this passage that Hanslick believes there is music expressive of grief, and music expressive of happiness, and that Gluck is at fault in choosing happy music rather than sad music for Orfeo's aria.

The problem, of course, as anyone familiar with Hanslick's text will immediately see, is that this interpretation seems to be in direct conflict with what Hanslick has been arguing for up to this point, which is, as I read him, that music, qua aesthetic object, has no expressive character at all; it cannot, that is to say, be described aesthetically as happy, mournful, and the like. And the oddity of the thing is that one of the three major arguments that Hanslick uses to debunk emotive characterizations of music is an argument about musical text-setting of which the passage about Gluck is an integral and (apparently) inconsistent part. For Hanslick is in the process of arguing that the continual re-use of their music, by great composers, to set widely divergent texts, proves that the music

1 Eduard Hanslick, *On the Musically Beautiful: A Contribution towards the Revision of the Aesthetics of Music,* trans. Geoffrey Payzant (Indianapolis, 1986), pp. 17–18.

has no expressive qualities at all, since if it did, discrepancies between the expressive character of the music and text would show up in the re-use – which, Hanslick avers, does not occur. And yet cheek-by-jowl with this argument is the charge that Gluck chose expressively inappropriate music to set "Che farò."

I have thought about this apparent contradiction, on and off, for years, and have always dismissed it simply as sloppy thinking on Hanslick's part. But I have never felt quite comfortable with that verdict since the first duty of an interpreter when faced with such an apparent inconsistency is to try to resolve it by a closer reading of the text. And that is what Payzant's new translation has finally spurred me on to do here. But I must say, straightaway, before I go into this any further, that I am in disagreement with Payzant, initially, as to how we should understand Hanslick's arguments against musical expression – what Hanslick calls the "negative thesis." For he describes it as the thesis not that music cannot "arouse, express, or portray human feelings," but merely the thesis that "to do so is not the defining purpose of music."[2] My own interpretation of the negative thesis, as has already become apparent, is much stronger. I think Hanslick is indeed saying that being expressive of the emotions is not the defining purpose of music. But I think part of Hanslick's argument for this thesis is that being expressive of such garden variety emotions as joy, grief, fear, and the like cannot be the defining purpose of music just because music *cannot* be expressive of them. I should add as a cautionary note that I am not denying that Hanslick may have believed music is expressive of some other "feeling" or "emotion" besides those which I have been calling the garden variety emotions. All I am claiming is that Hanslick denied that music an be expressive of the familiar emotions with the familiar names: fear, anger, joy, and so forth. And whenever I refer to Hanslick's denial that music has expressive qualities, it is only to those familiar, garden variety emotions that I have reference. I can-

2 Ibid., p. xvi.

not argue for this interpretation here. All I can do is warn you that it is assumed throughout. It is *my* interpretation of the negative thesis that, I am claiming, Hanslick's discussion of Gluck contradicts.

Well, clearly, the first place to look for the resolution of an apparent contradiction, when dealing with a translated text, is the translation itself. This is an altogether appropriate context, therefore, in which to ask whether, perhaps, we have here a case of *traduttore é traditore*. So let us compare Payzant's rendering of the offending passage with the earlier one of Cohen, and with Hanslick's original.

Payzant's translation, previously quoted, of what I take to be the crucial part of the crucial sentence, goes, you will recall, like this: "Music certainly possesses far more specific tones for the expression of passionate grief." Cohen renders these same words: "Music must assuredly possess accents which more truly express a feeling of profound sorrow."[3] And Hanslick's original German text goes like this: *"Die Musik für den Ausdruck schmerzlichster Traurigkeit gewiss weit bestimmtere Töne besitzi."*[4]

As usual, Cohen's translation is more literary, Payant's more literal, and, I think, more accurate; and for philosophical purposes generally I have no doubt that the latter is to be preferred. But does Payzant's rendering of the sentence in question give us any advantage over Cohen's in resolving our contradiction?

Well, one thing to notice is that Cohen renders *"Töne"* as "accents" while Payzant goes for the English cognate "tones." Both are correct according to my dictionary, but Cohen's choice just might blur a distinction in Hanslick's text that should be preserved. To say that music possesses accents appropriate to the expression of sorrow is simply a somewhat flowery way of saying that music can be expressive of sorrow. But

---

3 Eduard Hanslick, *The Beautiful in Music,* trans. Gustav Cohen (New York, 1957), p. 34.
4 Eduard Hanslick, *Von Musikalisch-Schönen: Ein Beitrag zur Revision der Ästhetik der Tonkunst* (Wiesbaden, 1980), p. 39.

although saying that music possesses specific tones for the expression of passionate grief might be saying much the same thing, it just might be, rather, that Hanslick is pressing a distinction here between music and the tones of which it is made up, those out of which it is contructed. If so, we might interpret Hanslick as saying here that *tones* can be expressive of grief and that Gluck should have used such tones to construct his aria. And this reading resolves our contradition. For what Hanslick is insisting in the negative thesis is that *music* lacks expressive qualities. It is no more a contradiction to say that tones are expressive of grief, but the music of which they are the material is not, than to say that bricks are small but the houses we build with them are large.

However, the cost of resolving our contradiction in this way is far too high; for the reading I have given is tortured at best, and, it seems to me, imputes to Hanslick a position that is just plain crazy. To begin with, it seems quite bizarre to entertain the view that individual tones are expressive, but that the complex musical objects of which they are the materials are not. If anything, it must be the other way around: expressiveness must be an emergent quality of tonal combinations. If one thinks, as Hanslick apparently did, that complex musical compositions such as Beethoven's do not possess expressive properties, the notion that the individual tones – the concert A's and middle C's – of which they are constructed do is hardly going to seem a *more* attractive alternative; rather, it must seem even a less likely one.

Further, even if it were true that tones are expressive while the musical compositions of which they are the parts are not, this would be completely irrelevant, so far as I can see; for it is the perceived inappropriateness of Glucks' *music*, not the parts thereof that is the issue. If Hanslick were really criticizing Gluck for not choosing "tones" expressive of grief in composing "Che farò," all the while insisting that the music is not expressively inappropriate (since music cannot be expressive at all), it would be like castigating the chef for putting a cup of paprika in the goulash, since a cup of paprika,

swallowed neat, tastes horrible, and in the same breath telling the chef how delicious the goulash is. The thing just
doesn't make any sense at all.

So we must look elsewhere than at the translations, I think,
for a resolution of this contradiction. For even the more accurate of the two does not help. One place to look is at Hanslicks' discussion of the emotions, and the argument that
comes out of it to the effect that music cannot supply the
materials necessary for either embodying them or arousing
them (depending on how you read him in this regard). On
Hanslick's view, emotions require objects, and judgments or
beliefs for their existence. In this he is quite up to date, and
presents, albeit in sketchy form, something like the so-called
"Cognitive" analysis of the emotions defended by, among
others, Anthony Kenny and, more recently, William Lyons.[5]
Hanslick writes, in this regard, that the emotions "depend
upon ideas, judgments, and (in brief) the whole range of
intelligible and rational thought, to which some people so
readily oppose feeling." And again:

> Only on the basis of a number of ideas and judgments . . .
> can our state of mind congeal into this or that specific feeling.
> The feeling of hope cannot be separated from the representa-
> tion of a future happy state which we compare with the pre-
> sent; melancholy compares past happiness with the present
> . . . without this cognitive apparatus we cannot call the actual
> feeling "hope" or "melancholy."[6]

Now music, Hanslick argues, can present this conceptual
apparatus neither for the arousal nor for the embodiment of
recognizable human emotions. It cannot give us the objects
for our emotions to fasten on, and it cannot give us representations of them, as painting can, for us to recognize. It cannot, therefore, be expressive of the emotions, either in the
sense of arousing them or in the sense of displaying them
forth. But – and here is the crucial point – it *can* possess what

5 See Anthony Kenny, *Action, Emotion and Will* (London, 1963); and William Lyons,
  Emotion (Cambridge University Press, 1980).
6 Hanslick, *On the Musically Beautiful*, p. 9.

Hanslick calls the "dynamic" of an emotion: the gentleness of the gentle emotions, the vigor of the vigorous ones, and so forth. As Hanslick puts his point:

> What, then, from the feelings, can music present if not their content? Only that same dynamic mentioned above. It can reproduce the motion of a physical process according to the prevailing momentum: fast, slow, strong, weak, rising, falling. Motion is just one attribute, however, one moment of feeling, not feeling itself. . . . Motion is the ingredient which music has in common with emotional states and which it is able to shape creatively in a thousand shades and contrasts.[7]

This suggests a rather tidy resolution of our contradiction. Perhaps it was precipitous of me to rush to the conclusion that Hanslick, in the offending passage, was talking about a disparity between the emotion expressed by the text and the expressive quality of Gluck's music. Perhaps, rather, he was saying that the *dynamic* of Gluck's music did not match the *dynamic* of the emotion expressed in the text. That claim is perfectly consistent with Hanslick's insistence that music can possess no expressive qualities at all. For, as he says in the passage quoted above, to possess the dynamic of an emotion is to possess only a part of it, not the emotion itself. Thus, if the text a composer is setting expresses violent anger and the music the composer provides is calm and tranquil, it is inappropriate, not because it is expressive of an emotion other than anger – for, *ex hypothesi*, it can be expressive of no emotion whatever – but because violent anger is characterized by a violent, active dynamic, and the music by a calm, tranquil one.

As attractive and initially plausible as this strategy might seem on first reflection, it presents some pretty sticky difficulties, the first and most obvious being that it really does not jibe with what Hanslick actually says, which is that there is music better suited to *express* grief than the music Gluck has composed ("express" is the word he uses). But even supposing that this is a *lapsus calami*, and what Hanslick really

---

7 Ibid., p. 11.

meant is that Gluck chose music with the wrong dynamic for grief, we are not much better off. For, as a matter of fact, the dynamic of Gluck's aria is quite consistent with the dynamic of grief, something it is hard to believe a musician and critic of Hanslick's sensibilities would have missed. If Gluck's music is inappropriate to Calzabigi's text, then, it cannot be because of a mismatch between the dynamic of the music and the dynamic of the text's emotion – and Hanslick would have know that.

Anyway, the position is implausible, even if, contrary to some pretty obvious evidence, Hanslick held it. For it will not do the job which it is invoked to do, namely, tell us what it is we are bothered by, in cases like the one under discussion, where we seem at least to perceive an emotive incongruity between music and text. Suppose I were to argue that the music of an aria is unsuited to the text because the dynamic of the text's dominant emotion is vigorous and the dynamic of the music tranquil. Surely, the ordinary person would take it as implied by my remark that the disparity of dynamics makes the music *expressively* inappropriate; that the dynamic of the music gives it an expressive quality different from the text's. And if I denied that implication, why should my argument carry any conviction? If the disparity in dynamics makes no expressive disparity, who cares about it? Why should it make the music inappropriate to the text? Surely it is not just self-evident that if the dynamic of the music is not the same as the dynamic of the text's emotive content, the music will be inappropriate to the emotive expression of the text (or inappropriate to anything else, for that matter.) What does seem evident, and might be the reason why one would let the inference from inappropriateness of dynamic to inappropriateness of music to text go through unchallenged, is that what Hanslick calls the dynamic of an emotion does have a very substantial part to play in making a piece of music expressive of that emotion when the dynamic is also present in the music – it is a, perhaps *the*, major operator, and the presence of a different dynamic from that of a given emotion is often enough in itself to defeat that expressive quality in the music. But the fact remains that it is the expressive quality of the music that is being judged inappropriate to the expression of the text. And if it were possible for a piece of music to be expressive of (say) resigned melancholy, while possessing a dynamic different from the one characteristic of that emotion, I see no reason why anyone would judge it expressively inappropriate to the setting of a text expressing resigned melancholy. If, of course, it is impossible for a musical composition to be expressive of resigned melancholy without possessing the dynamic of that emotion, then that is perfectly consistent with what I am insisting on here, which is that it is the expressivenes of the music, not its dynamic, that is the determining feature of its expressive appropriateness to a text. In either case, the position I have tentatively imputed to Hanslick, in my attempt to save him from contradiction, just will not wash.

So we are faced with the unhappy choice of reading Hanslick as inconsistent, in believing both that music can be expressively inappropriate to its text and that music cannot really be expressive at all; or as very badly confused, in believing that the incongruity we perceive between the expression of a text and the expressiveness of the accompanying music is really an incongruity in dynamics, not expression. My own view is that Hanslick is just inconsistent on this point. But finding inconsistencies is, after all, merely a student exercise and nothing more, unless the inconsistency one discovers has some philosophical lesson to teach, some philosophical point to reveal. And, indeed, I think the present one does; in fact, I think it amounts to a reductio of Hanslick's negative thesis, at least as I interpret it, and even perhaps as Payzant interprets it as well.

To put the thing directly, Hanslick is like a solipsist who can't stop writing letters. He argues that music has no expressive qualities. But when he steps out of the philosopher's closet to face the music, he sings a different tune. The confrontation of music with text forces his hand. It is possible to describe pure instrumental music in many ways, without resorting to emotive predicates, if one has a mind to. However, when faced with the musical setting of a text, if the text has emotive content (which it almost always will), this will compel the listener to perceive either that the music is expressively appropriate to that content, or to perceive that it is not. And in either case, it compels acknowledgment of the incontestable fact that music does possess expressive character. It is to be expected, therefore, and is no surprise, that where Hanslick forgets himself, and lapses into the altogether familiar mode of talking about music in emotive terms, is just where he is talking about the musical setting of texts.

As I said, we can talk about pure instrumental music without describing it in emotive terms; and that is easiest to do, as well as most often done, where experts are talking with experts and can resort to the technical language of music theory and analysis. Where experts talk to laymen, however, it is almost inevitable that emotive descriptions will surface because, in the standard concert repertoire, musical works with palpable expressive properties predominate; and they are perhaps the easiest qualities of the music for laymen to perceive and fasten onto. Hanslick, as is well known, was a professional music critic. Now wouldn't it be a delicious irony to discover that the arch-purist himself, when engaged in his profession of writing for the lay audience, should throw away the book – his book – and talk about music just like the rest of us? And so he does, with a vengeance. It did not take me more than a minute of riffling through the pages of Henry Pleasants' selections from Hanslick's music criticism to find the following egregious example (from a review of 1883).

> Actually, if one were to call Brahms's first symphony the "Appassionata" and the second the "Pastoral," then the new [third] symphony might well be called the "Eroica." The title is, to be sure, not fully applicable, since only the first and last movement strike us as "heroic." In his Symphony in C minor, Brahms plunged with desperate passion into a dark Faustian struggle in the first dissonant measures. The Finale, with its reminiscences of the last movements of Beethoven's Ninth, does not, for all its ultimate achievements, change the

emotional, almost pathological character of the composition. It is the expression of a suffering, abnormally agitated individual. The Symphony No. 2 is a peaceful, almost pastoral counterpart. . . . The Symphony No. 3 is really something new. It repeats neither the unhappy fatalism of the first, nor the cheerful idyll of the second; its foundation is self-confident, rough and ready strength. The "heroic" element in it has nothing to do with anything military, nor does it lead to any tragic dénouement, such as the Funeral March of Beethoven's "Eroica."[8]

And so on. So much for musical purism.

With regard to corny theories of musical expression, Hanslick roused us from our dogmatic slumber – and all credit to him for that. But the deep contradiction in his own work, between the theorist who denies and the critic, who by his actions affirms the expressive character of music, must show us that skepticism is not the answer. Expression is an integral, relevant, essential part of most of the music we listen to. And we had better acknowledge the fact *before* we start theorizing.[9]

8 Eduard Hanslick, *Music Criticisms 1846–99*, ed. and trans. Henry Pleasants (Baltimore, 1950), p. 211.

9 Geoffrey Payzant has suggested to me, in a private communication, that the apparent contradiction I am worried about might easily be resolved by translating *Töne* as "keys," rather than "tones," which is also correct. For, he points out, Hanslick, like many of his predecessors and contemporaries, associated various emotions and moods with particular keys, and thus might merely be saying that Gluck could have chosen a *key* for *Che farò* more appropriate for grief than the key of C major. But two things strike me as very implausible about this "quick fix." First, intuitively, I find it beyond belief that the *only* thing Hanslick is talking about here, and finds inappropriate to grief is the *key*. There are just too many other inappropriate elements. I cannot believe Hanslick, any more than the rest of us, could have thought merely changing the key of the aria would repair its expressive inappropriateness. Second, if one substitutes "keys" for "tones" in Payzant's own translation, the result is an absurdity, to wit: "Music certainly possesses far more specific keys for the expression of passionate grief." This has Hanslick saying, in effect, that the trouble with *Che farò* is that its key, C major, is not "specific" enough. What in the world could that mean? It just seems downright nonsense: a "category mistake."

Chapter XVI

What was Hanslick denying?

It is generally known in musical circles that Eduard Hanslick was skeptical of the claim that music has anything to do with "expressing" the emotions: that he believed, in a word, music doesn't do it. But problems surface as soon as one tries to spell out the skeptical view in any detail, which is to say, to unpack the concept of "expression," and to pin down exactly what Hanslick is denying (and why) when he denies the concept to music. Hanslick refers to his denial (of whatever it is he is denying) as the negative thesis. My object in the present essay, simply stated, will be to spell out as precisely as I can (given the sketchy character of Hanslicks' little book) just what the negative thesis is (and isn't). And I will rely, for the most part, in this reexamination of the negative thesis, on Geoffrey Payzant's excellent new translation of *Vom Musikalisch-Schöonen* (which he renders *On the Musically Beautiful*). It has, is in fact, inspired my renewed interest in what Hanslick was really up to.

Only one thing about the negative thesis seems absolutely clear and beyond dispute: Hanslick was denying that music is essentially an expression of the emotions; denying that music is beautiful or valuable to the extent that it successfully expresses the emotions and lacking beauty or value to the extent that it fails. Payzant thinks that this is all that Hanslick was doing: that this is the sum total of the negative thesis. In his view Hanslick is not denying that music can, for example, arouse or portray human emotions. "He merely says that to do so is not the defining *purpose* of music."[1] It is my view, on the other hand, that Hanslick went far beyond this in the negative thesis: that he in fact denied music can arouse or portray or in any other way "embody" what I shall henceforth call the garden variety emotions, such as love, hope, fear, joy, sorrow, anger, and the like. However, I want to dissociate myself from those "detractors" of Hanslick who Payzant characterizes as having "us believe that he wanted to stamp out every vestige of feeling in music, leaving nothing but the architechtonic, the abstract formal arrangement of tones." Payzant insists that Hanslick "is not guilty of such an absurdity."[2] And I am quite willing, indeed anxious to concur in that if I can. For it is not incompatible with Hanslick's (as I claim) having banished expression of the garden variety emotions from music that he did not, as Payzant puts it, intend to stamp out every vestige of feeling in music altogether. The conflation of the one banishment with the other is, as I have argued elsewhere, a common fallacy.[3] And there is no compelling reason to think Hanslick committed it, although as I shall claim later on, he failed to provide the emotive moment to music that I am confident he did not want to eradicate.

II

Now a word about the word "expression." I have begun in a purposely vague way and characterized the negative thesis as the thesis that music does not "express" emotions. That part of the negative thesis that is *incontroversially* what Hanslick is claiming is that music is not *essentially* the "expression" of emotions. It is yet to be determined just what Han-

---

1 Eduard Hanslick, *On the Musically Beautiful: A Contribution towards the Revision of the Aesthetics of Music*, trans. Geoffrey Payzant (Indianapolis: Hacket, 1986), p. xvi (Translator's Preface).
2 Geoffrey Payzant, "Hanslick on Music as Product of Feeling," *Bruckner-Jahrbuch* (forthcoming), typescript p. 1.
3 See Peter Kivy, "How Music Moves," *What is Music?: An Introduction to the Philosophy of Music* (New York: Haven Publications, 1988).

slick might be denying to music by denying that it "expresses" emotions "essentially" (or in any other way). Here are some possibilities. He might be denying:

(1) that composers express their felt (garden variety) emotions in their music; (2) that music arouses (the garden variety) emotions in listeners; (3) that music represents (the garden variety) emotions (the way a still life represents fruits and flowers); (4) that music possesses (the garden variety) emotions the way an apple possesses redness as a perceptual property.

The notion that composers express their garden variety emotions by writing music (1) is, of course, a version of the "Self-expression" theory of art; and it is compatible with each and all of the rest: for a composer might be thought, I suppose, to express his garden variety emotions by fashioning music that arouses them in others (2), or by fashioning music that represents them (3), or by fashioning music that embodies them in some other way (4), or perhaps all at once. It also is compatible with a denial of the rest, as they do not, clearly, exhaust the possible ways in which someone might be thought to express his or her emotions by writing music. It will be one of the main purposes of this essay to state as clearly and unequivocally as possible which of these meanings of "express" Hanslick has in mind when he denies that music "expresses" the emotions, and what his arguments are.

III

I said that one thing about the negative thesis is clear. Hanslick was denying that music expresses the emotions in the sense that I might deny it is the essential character of something to do something. Here is what Hanslick says in this regard; or, rather, two of the things he says. In the Foreword he writes: "The thesis first and foremost opposes the widespread view that music is supposed to 'represent feelings.' "[4] And in the first chapter he writes:

4 Hanslick, *On the Musically Beautiful*, p. xxii.

in the prevailing view of music the feelings play a double role.

Of music in the first of these two roles, it is claimed that to arouse the delicate feelings, is the defining purpose of music. In the second, the feelings are designated as the content of music, that which musical art presents in its works.

The two are similar in that both are false.[5]

Now as I see the plan of Hanslick's book, via-à-vis the negative thesis, it takes the following course. Hanslick begins by denying, as quoted above, that to express the emotions is the defining purpose of music. And it is clear from the above quotations that he interprets "express" in two different ways: sometimes as "arouse" and sometimes "contain" in the sense of "represent." As far as I can make out, he never entertains the third possibility: that music might "contain" emotions in the sense of possessing them as perceptual properties the way objects possess (say) colors. Nor is that surprising. For the thesis is of fairly recent vintage, the product mainly of contemporary analytic philosophy.

Having denied that it is the essential nature of music to "express" the emotions either by arousing them or by representing them, Hanslick defends his claim by trying to show that music is *incapable* of doing either. That is to say, Hanslick is arguing that it cannot be the essential nature of music to "express" the emotions because music is unable to do it all; it cannot be the essential nature of music to arouse or represent the emotions because it is impotent to do either.

The first two chapters are fairly consistent in this regard (although with some questions already apparent in Chapter 1); and I shall get to the details of the arguments in a moment. The third chapter is devoted to what Hanslick calls his positive thesis: that (in his famous phrase) "The content of music is tonally moving forms."[6] And that will not be my concern in the present essay.

Troubles arise in earnest in the fourth chapter, where lapses from orthodoxy seem to occur. It is these apparent lapses that, I believe, have led Payzant, quite understandably, to

5 Ibid., p. 3. 6 Ibid., p. 29.

conclude that Hanslick could not possibly have meant to deny the power of music to arouse or represent or otherwise "express" the garden variety emotions, but must have intended only to deny their essentiality to the musical enterprise. In Section V of my essay I shall try to bring the most obvious of these apparent lapses into conformity with my interpretation of the negative thesis.

My major tasks, then, are to spell out more fully the negative thesis and its supporting arguments, and to try to make my interpretations of them consistent, as much as is possible, with the rest of Hanslick's views. To these tasks, then, I now turn my attention.

IV

I shall have, perhaps not surprisingly, little new to say in spelling out the nuts and bolts of the negative thesis, as it develops in Chapter 2: not surprisingly, and little new, because although it is Hanslick's most valuable and lasting contribution to the philosophy of music, it is also the best known and best understood. What I have to offer that is new is not a new interpretation of why Hanslick thought music could not express the emotions but, I hope, a clearer way of seeing how this fits in with the general argument of the negative thesis and the apparent lapses from it.

There are three clearly discernible arguments in Chapter 3 that weave in and out of Hanslick's negative thesis, although, because of the vagaries of Hanslick's style, I would not want to claim that they are the only ones and that others cannot be teased out of the text. All of them are directed specifically against the notion that music can "represent" the garden variety emotions; arousal is not spoken of here at all, except for one passing reference, although it is clear, I think, both from the tenor of Chapter 1, as well as from other considerations that I will allude to presently that these arguments are meant to be directed against the arousal notion as well. Together, these three arguments provide the main reason that Hanslick believed *music cannot express the garden va-*

riety emotions: and it is this belief that Hanslick adduces to support the negative thesis that *the expression of emotions is not the (or a) defining property, essence or purpose of music,* just as the proven inability of the Kiwi to fly is sufficient refutation of the claim that flying is its *raison d'être.*

The argument best remembered and, unfortunately, most often adduced by those who are of Hanslick's party in this regard is a very bad one: what I will call the *argument from disagreement.* It is simply that music cannot represent the emotions because if it could then there would be general agreement about what, in any given instance, a piece or passage of music represents. But since, Hanslick avers, there is quite the opposite, complete, chaotic disagreement, music cannot sensibly be thought to represent emotions. Here is the argument in one of Hanslick's characteristic formulations. Speaking of the "mainstream" concert repertoire – Mozart, Haydn, Beethoven, Mendelssohn, Schumann, Chopin – as well as of "the most popular themes from overtures by Auber, Donizetti, Flotow," Hanslick throws up this familiar challenge:

> Who will come forward and venture to declare that some specific feeling is the content of one of these themes? One person will say "love." Possibly. Another thinks "yearning." Perhaps. A third feels "piety." Nobody can refute any of them. And so it goes. Can we call it the representation of a specific feeling when nobody knows what feeling was actually represented. . . . How then can we designate something as what an art represents, when the very dubious and ambiguous elements of that art themselves are perpetually the subject of debate?[7]

I say this is a bad argument, and its continual recurrence in the literature unfortunate, therefore, because anyone who has ever performed the simple experiment of playing brief expressive passages of the kind of music Hanslick is talking about to a group of quite ordinary listeners, with little experience or knowledge of "classical" music, knows quite well

7 Ibid., p. 14.

that the responses, far from being chaotic and random, are actually predictable and consistent. I was about to say *surprisingly* consistent; but it will be a surprise only to those who, in thrall to some theory or other, have prejudged the results. All this is, however, beside the point; for I have not come to argue a point in the philosophy of music – I have argued this one at length elsewhere[8] – but to explicate Hanslick. So I will get on with it directly.

A second argument of Hanslick's intended to show that music cannot represent emotions – an equally bad one, I am distressed to say – concerns the reuse of music by composers to set texts of disparate emotive content or tone. If music really were capable of representing emotions, so the argument goes, then music written to express the emotion of one text could not be reused to set another, because in the second setting we would perceive a disparity between the emotive tone of the old music and the new text. But no such disparities are perceived. Therefore music must be emotively "neutral" (so to say). Hanslick writes:

> In an operatic melody, e.g., one which had very effectively expressed anger, you will find no other intrinsically psychical expression than that of a rapid, impulsive motion. The same melody might just as effectively render words expressing the exact opposite, namely, passionate love.[9]

Or again:

> Our greatest masters of sacred music, Handel in particular, offer abundant examples in support of what we are saying here. He proceeded in this with great nonchalance. Winterfeld has shown that many of the most famous pieces in *Messiah*, including some of the ones most admired for their godly sentiments, are for the most part transcribed from the secular and mainly erotic duets which Handel composed in 1711–12 for Princess Caroline of Hanover to madrigal texts by Marrio Ortensio.[10]

8 Peter Kivy, *The Corded Shell: Reflections on Musical Expression* (Princeton: Princeton University Press, 1980).
9 Hanslick, p. 17. 10 Ibid., p. 19.

The problem with this argument is that it works only if one either ascribes an excessive degree of specificity to musical expression, or adduces excessively vague and unexamined examples – both of which Hanslick seems to do. A vigorous passage may, of course, accompany an expression of passionate anger or passionate love equally well, if there is nothing else in the passage that counts against either of these emotive qualities, and nothing else emotively expressive but the vigor. But that hardly proves Hanslick's point: that a vigorous passage well suited (on that account) to passionate anger is always well suited (on that account) to passionate love. And to convince yourself of that, if it is not obvious at once, just try to imagine the angry music of Pizarro's "Ha! Welch ein Augenblick!" in the first act of *Fidelio,* as accompaniment to Florestan's and Leonore's passionate expressions of love in "O namenlöse Freude" in the second act. As for Handel's reuse of music originally composed for an erotic love poem to accompany the joy of "For unto us a child is born," it need only be pointed out that the joy of love and the joy of the Nativity are both *joy.* (Does that *need* pointing out?) If one were to claim that music is capable of distinguishing between the expression of the fear of snakes and fear of flying, I suppose Hanslick would have a point; since, I dare say, music composed for the one could not do service for the other as well. But no sane upholder of music's power to be expressive holds that. I certainly don't.

However, as I have already said, it is merely my purpose to explicate Hanslick, not to damn him. So it will be well, at this point, to pause to ask just what varieties of the expression theory these two arguments, whatever their merits or demerits, might be potent against if good. The answer would seem to be both the arousal and the representation versions, even though Hanslick is consistent in Chapter 2 in speaking always of representing the emotions, not arousing them. For whether you think music is sad in virtue of arousing sadness in listeners, or in virtue of representing sadness that listeners recognize in music, it would be a serious difficulty for you if there were no agreement among listeners about whether the music was sad or not, and if any music at all could seem emotively appropriate to any text at all.

Hanslick's third argument – by far the most intriguing of the three – is based on a solid, forward-looking knowledge of what an emotion is, and how it is ordinarily aroused. His view in this regard clearly anticipates recent, so-called "cognitive" analyses of the emotions that have, so far, prevailed in contemporary analytic philosophy.[11]

Ask yourself how the garden variety emotions are aroused. What makes you angry, for example? Well, you experience some situation in which you form a belief about something: let us say, you are led to believe that your business partner is cheating you, and you become angry with him. Three obvious components of your anger and its arousal are these: some "facts" which you have become apprised of (either correctly or incorrectly), a belief (that your partner is cheating you) which we can intelligibly understand as arousing your emotion (of anger), and an object of your emotion (you become angry with your partner). All these things, Hanslick wisely observed, are absent from the listening experience. The question is, what are we supposed to conclude from this? Hanslick's answer, consistent with everything else in Chapter 2, is that music cannot "represent" the emotions. The emotions "depend upon ideas, judgments, and (in brief) the whole range of intelligible and rational thought, to which some people so easily oppose feeling." That is just why "The representation of a specific feeling or emotional state is not at all among the characteristic powers of music"; for "the definiteness of feelings lies precisely in the conceptual essence," and this "conceptual essence" music is powerless to provide.[12]

There is a good deal that is murky here. But I suppose what Hanslick is claiming is that since music cannot represent in sufficient detail the situations in which emotions are

11 See, for example, Anthony Kenny, *Action, Emotion and Will* (London: Routledge and Kegan Paul, 1963), and William Lyons, *Emotion* (Cambridge: Cambridge University Press, 1980).
12 Hanslick, p. 9.

normally aroused, it cannot be thought to represent emotions, although the two claims clearly are not equivalent. What, indeed, one would have liked (and expected) him to argue is that since music cannot provide what Hanslick calls the "conceptual essence," the materials that arouse the garden variety emotions, the situations, the "facts," the beliefs, the object, it cannot arouse emotions. (How could "angry" music make me angry? Who or what would I be angry at? And why?) That seems to me to be a good argument. But Hanslick is very clear about what he is doing in Chapter 2: that is to say, arguing against representation.

> How it happens that music can nevertheless excite such feelings as melancholy, gaiety, and the like (*can, not must*) we shall investigate later, when we discuss the subjective impressions made by music. At present we shall merely try to establish theoretically whether or not music is capable of representing a specific feeling. The question must be answered in the negative, since the specification of feelings cannot be separated from actual representations and concepts, which latter lie beyond the scope of music.[13]

But this passage must give us serious pause. Did I not claim that Hanslick was denying both representation and arousal to music? Yet here he seems to be saying that although music cannot represent the garden variety emotions, it *can* arouse them. And, indeed, in Chapters 1 and (especially) 4 he seems to suggest *how* it can arouse them.

Further, the parenthetical phrase, *can, not must*, seems to support Payzant's interpretation of the negative thesis. In Payzant's view, as we saw, Hanslick is not banishing emotion from music, not denying that music can express emotions, only denying that the expression of emotions is the defining, essential function of music. (Indeed, in Chapter 1 he argues that the arousing of emotions cannot be the defining property of music, as distinguished from the other arts, because music is not alone among them in being capable of emotive arousal.) The phrase *can, not must* suggests that mu-

13 Ibid., pp. 9–10. My italics.

285

sic can sometimes express emotions, but need not to remain music, since expression is not its defining property. We also now seem to know in what sense of "express" music can, not must "express" emotions. It cannot represent them, but it can, not must, arouse them.

There is no doubt that this is an attractive interpretation. It seems to account for all the facts: the denial that music is, by definition, expression, the denial that it can represent emotions, and the assertion in Chapters 1 and 2, expanded in Chapter 4, that the arousal of emotions is a familiar, undeniable phenomenon. It also makes room in Hanslick's account for an emotional reaction on the listener's part to the music that he or she enjoys; and this makes what Hanslick is saying far more palatable to common musical sense. For it seems hard to believe that our musical listening is a purely intellectual experience, like examining a bug on a pin. (Even examining a bug on a pin isn't.) Surely we find music not just fascinating, but deeply moving as well. And the present interpretation suggests what is moving about music: it moves us to the garden variety emotions: "music can . . . excite such feelings as melancholy, gaiety, and the like (*can, not must*)."

But as attractive as this interpretation may seem on the face of it, it is dead wrong. However it may seem to go with the letter of Hanslick's text, it violently contradicts its spirit. Further, it would make an utter fool of Hanslick. For it is perfectly clear that all the arguments Hanslick adduces in Chapter 2 against the representation theory of musical expression are, if good, good against the arousal theory as well. Surely Hanslick must have seen this; and although "express" and "represent" are the terms that occur throughout the chapter, I think we must read the argument in Chapter 2 as tacitly assuming "arouse" as well: It is an argument against the notion that music can either represent or arouse – which is to say express – the garden variety emotions. That leaves us with the seemingly formidable task of explaining why, in this very chapter, as well as in Chapters 1 and 4, Hanslick so obviously contradicts what I am saying. So – into the breach . . . but it is not so formidable a task as it might appear.

V

The fourth chapter deals with two separate topics: emotions in the composer and emotions in the listener, I shall talk about the latter first.

I begin by quoting a passage that appears to be a blatant contradiction of my interpretation of the negative thesis but which contains, within it, as well, the means of resolution. Hanslick writes:

> we often see the listener deeply stirred by a piece of music, moved to joy or melancholy, transported in his innermost being far beyond mere aesthetical pleasure, or disturbed. The existence of these effects is undeniable, actual and genuine, often reaching the greatest intensity. It is so well known that we need not tarry over it. Here we are concerned with only two of its aspects: in what way this specifically musical arousal of feeling is distinct from others and to what extent this effect is aesthetical.[14]

The escape clause, for our purposes, is provided by the question Hanslick poses at the end as "to what extent this [emotive] effect [of music] is aesthetical." The answer he seems to be giving, although as much else in Hanslick it is not so clear as one might wish, is that the emotional effect of music of which he is speaking – the arousal of the garden variety emotions – is not "aesthetical" to any extent at all. When we understand how Hanslick believes music does arouse the garden variety emotions, we will understand why he does not believe the arousal of these emotions is "aesthetical." And when we understand what being or not being "aesthetical" means for Hanslick we will understand why his admission that music can arouse the garden variety emotions is perfectly consistent with my interpretation of the negative thesis as denying both the representation and the arousal of the garden variety emotions to music.

How is it that, in Hanslick's view, music can arouse the garden variety emotions? Apparently, by direct effects of

14 Ibid., pp. 49–50.

musical sound on the nervous system. But it can only have these effects, he thinks, if the nervous system is in some abnormal, overwrought state or other, owing to personal circumstances. "We experience this, its unique power over the spirit, at its most powerful, when we are severely agitated or depressed." But if this is so, then there is no aesthetical significance to the emotive arousal:

> in musical effects upon feeling, often an extraneous, not purely aesthetical element may be involved. A purely aesthetical effect addresses itself to a healthy nervous system and does not rely upon any degree of psychological abnormality.[15]

What Hanslick is suggesting, then, is that the propensity of music for arousing such emotions as joy, or sorrow, or anger, or whatever is a function of music qua sound, not qua aesthetical object or qua music; and a necessary condition for the effect is some special – Hanslick thinks "pathological" – state of the listener's nervous system. Thus, if I am depressed over the death of my aunt, the slow movement of Mozart's "Jupiter" symphony may make me sad, while if you are elated over a successful business deal it may make you happy. But the very fact that the emotive effect relies on such extraneous circumstances as these implies that it is not part of the art-object itself – no part of its "aesthetical" effects, any more than it is an "aesthetical" property of a painting that gazing upon it hurts my eyes because of a bad case of conjunctivitis.

But now we can see directly that the power music has of emotive arousal, according to Hanslick, is perfectly consistent with my interpretation of his negative thesis. For when I say that, according to the negative thesis, music cannot arouse the garden variety emotions, I mean, of course, that music, qua music, qua art, qua aesthetical object cannot do so. And what Hanslick is at pains to insist on in Chapter 4, where the mechanism of musical arousal is spelled out, is that when "music" does arouse the garden variety emotions, it is not *music* but *sound*, which has acquired the power be-

---

15 Ibid., p. 50.

cause of the peculiar, "abnormal" psychological state of the listener. So what seems at first blush to be a glaring inconsistency with my interpretation of the negative thesis turns out to be entirely consistent with it, and, in my view, by the way, basically correct in spirit, if not in letter. So far, then, my interpretation works.

VI

I said at the outset that the "expression" theory of music might take the form of the "self-expression" theory. So before I close it would be well to consider the question of what role the self-expression theory might play in the negative thesis, in order to determine whether my interpretation of the negative thesis is consistent with that role. The negative thesis, remember, is the thesis that to express the emotions is not the (or an) essential function of music. My interpretation of Hanslick's position has it that he attempts to prove the negative thesis by proving the inability to express the emotions. That inability has, so far, been cashed out in terms of music's inability to represent the garden variety emotions and its inability to arouse them. But it still might be that music is capable of "expressing" emotions in virtue of expressing the emotions of the composer. And if Hanslick believes that, then I cannot be correct in claiming that he denies "expression" to music *tout court*.

But we can make quick work of that possibility. For where Hanslick does talk about anything resembling self-expression in music, it is only to dismiss it as true but trivial, or importantly false.

It is true, of course – and who would want to deny it – that the made bears the mark of the maker; and this is as true of the making of music as of the signing of one's name. But if that is all the self-expression theory of musical composition amounts to, it has no significance at all, any more than does the true but trivial claim that my fondness for sour pickles "expresses" something, but I know not what, about my personality. "Of course there is a connection between the character of every piece of music and that of its author, but for the aesthetician that is not open to view."[16]

Of much more potential significance is the claim that emotion gives birth to musical composition, and that musical composition, including the resultant work is, therefore, the "expression" of that emotion. The problem is to pin down just what that would mean if true; what significance it would have beyond the platitudinous. Hanslick believes two things that appear relevant. First, he believes that composition is (or may be) initiated by deep feeling. "During the creative activity, an exaltation will fill him [the composer] such as can scarcely be thought superfluous for the release of the beautiful from the depths of the imagination." Second, quite consistent with the emotive thesis (as so far understood), he believes that "Even when a powerful, specific emotion possesses him totally, so that it becomes the cause and inauguration of many an artwork, yet that emotion never becomes the subject of the work." For, as Hanslick reminds us, "This we know from the nature of musical art, which has neither the ability nor the vocation to represent a specific feeling."[17]

The question I want to put is simply, Do these two claims together allow for what might reasonably be thought of as a nontrivial version of the "self-expression" theory? The answer seems to me to be a resounding "No."

In order for something to be an "expression" of an emotion, it seems to me that at least two conditions must be satisfied. If it is my emotion we are talking about, I must at some *appropriate* time, be, or have been in the emotional state in question; and the "something" that is said to be the expression of my emotion must somehow "reflect," in some appropriate manner or other, depending on what kind of "something" we are talking about, the emotion so expressed. My clenched fist under your nose is an expression of my anger – but only if I am angry; and the rash on the back of my neck, although it may be recognized by someone who knows me well as a symptom of my anger, is not an

[16] Ibid., p. 29. [17] Ibid., pp. 45–6.

expression of it because (among other things) it does not reflect my anger in an appropriate way, as the clenched fist does. Now the first of these conditions, the emotion felt, does indeed seem to obtain some of the time in musical composition, according to Hanslick. But the second he seems clearly to be denying in his insistence that the emotion which might give birth to the musical composition is never embodied in it. For how can the composition be "read" as an "expression" of the emotion that impels its production if the work bears no appropriately identifiable mark of the emotion? It perhaps is the rash, but never the clenched fist. It would seem, then, that although Hanslick does allow one of the conditions for self-expression to sometimes obtain in musical composition, he does not subscribe to anything like what I have been calling the "self-expression" theory.

This conclusion becomes even more certain when we consider an ancillary point. Hanslick makes it clear that musical performance, in direct contrast to musical works, is an instance of self-expression; and that he contrasts composition and performance in this regard makes it abundantly clear that he is denying to the former what he is ascribing to the latter: that is to say, self-expression. Hanslick writes, in this regard:

> to the performer it is granted to release directly the feeling which possesses him, through his instrument, and breathe into his performance the wild storms, the passionate fervour, the serene power and joy of his inwardness. . . . Here a personal attitude becomes directly audibly effective in tones, not just silently formative in them. . . . The musical artwork is formed; the performance we experience. Thus the emotionally cathartic and stimulating aspect of music is situated in the reproductive art, which coaxes the electric spark out of its obscure secret place and flashes it across to the listener.[18]

Thus it seems clear that Hanslick could not have embraced anything like the self-expression theory of music. Where he does embrace self-expression, it is self-expression in perfor-

---

[18] Ibid., p. 49.

mance, which he explicitly denies to musical compositions. And even were that not so, he denies, as we have seen, one of the necessary conditions for any self-expression theory of art, namely, the embodiment of the emotion expressed, in some intelligible way or other, in the work of art. We can reasonably conclude, therefore, that the negative thesis denies not only that music can "express" emotions in the senses of "arouse" or "represent" them, but in the sense of "self-expression" as well.

VII

There is one further point that must be pursued briefly before I press on to my conclusion. I suggested earlier that one motive, a very commendable one, for the insistence that Hanslick could not possibly have been denying, in the negative thesis, that music can arouse the garden variety emotions, is that such a denial makes of the musical experience, as Hanslick would then seem to be construing it, a completely arid intellectual affair, denuded of all emotional investment whatever. We would all be, in Hanslick's view, a bunch of musical zombies, or very much like the Hollywood caricature of the cold, dispassionate scientist, unmoved by the cries of his victims, who sees, like the true Cartesian, motion but not expression on the vivisectionist's table.

I said that I saw nothing incompatible in maintaining, as Hanslick does, that music cannot arouse the garden variety emotions, and maintaining, nevertheless, that music is deeply moving: and I have tried to outline such a view myself elsewhere. It involves seeing that the experience of musical structure – of Hanslick's tonally moving forms – is itself a deeply moving experience. We are moved, excited by, passionately interested in the various formal and sensuous beauties of music. Therein lies our emotional investment.

But, alas, I have search in vain for any hint in Hanslick that he saw such a possibility. The closest he comes is acknowledging that the musical *performance* can embody and stimulate emotion; but it is the *act* of performance, not the musical work in the performance that does these things; and that will not suffice. Indeed, that is why, I suspect, Hanslick on occasion, spoke about arousal of the garden variety emotions of music in a somewhat loose and unguarded way, easily misinterpreted. He surely must have had some inkling that there was this lacuna in his theory; and there are times, I think, when he forgot himself and left the impression that the arousal of the garden variety emotions by musical sound – which he recognized as a bona fide phenomenon – might fill the lack. In his official doctrine, however, this phenomenon cannot do duty for a true emotive dimension in music because the garden variety emotions are aroused, as he quite correctly maintained, in aesthetically irrelevant ways. And where Hanslick described the aesthetically relevant listening experience, it is in terms of a dispassionate cognition that is obviously patterned after the Kantian model of disinterested perception, as, for example, where he writes:

> The beauty of a self-subsistent, simple theme makes itself known in aesthetical awareness with an immediacy which permits no other explanation than the inner appropriateness of the phenomenon, the harmony of its parts, without reference to any external third factor. It pleases us in itself, like the arabesque, the ornamental column, or like products of natural beauty such as leaves and flowers.[19]

The supreme irony is that where Hanslick describes the beauties of music, particularly in his music criticism, his descriptions are so rich in feeling tone that they plainly reveal a man who was deeply moved by his own musical experiences. But he could find no place in his theory for his own palpable emotive investment in music. His keen philosophical intelligence got him as far as recognizing that the traditional accounts of listener emotion had to be wrong. But neither intelligence nor emotion could take him any further than that.

[19] Ibid., p. 32.

VIII

It is time now to make a conclusion, in the form of a review of what Hanslick is denying and, if I may, an "appreciation" of what Hanslick has done.

Hanslick denies that it is the defining function of music to "express" the emotions in any of the following three senses of "express." He denies that it is the defining function of music to (1) arouse emotions in listeners; (2) to represent emotions in music; or (3) to express the emotions of composers. He argues for this denial by claiming that since music *cannot* express the emotions in any of these senses of "express," it cannot, plainly, be the defining function of music to express the emotions in any of these three senses of "express."

Hanslick indeed thinks that people sometimes do have emotions aroused in them when they listen to music. But when this happens, it is not, strictly speaking, the music that arouses such emotions; rather, it is completely extraneous, nonaesthetical aspects of musical sound, which acquire this arousal power, usually by virtue of the abnormal emotional states of the listeners so affected.

Hanslick also thinks that although musical works are not instances of self-expression, musical performances are. However, in neither of these cases – musical arousal or musical self-expression in performance – is a *musical work* the expression of a garden variety emotion in any of the senses of "express" recognized by Hanslick. Hence, both are consistent with the interpretation given here of Hanslick's denial: namely, that Hanslick denies "expression" in any of the senses recognized by him to *musical works.*

What of Hanslick's negative thesis remains valid for us after well over a century of criticism and speculation? I can now only give my own view, based on my own conclusions about the many vexed questions of music and emotion. But here, for what it is worth, is what I think. Hanslick was dead right in denying that emotive "expression" in any sense is a or the defining function of music. He was dead right in denying

294

that music can arouse the garden variety emotions in any aesthetically significant way, and very much on the right track in explaining how it arouses them – which of course it does – in various musically irrelevant ways. He was dead right in denying that music "represents" emotions, but dead wrong in thinking that representation and arousal exhaust the possibilities of musical expressiveness. Music does "embody" emotions, and is expressive of them, but in a way unimagined by Hanslick.

Finally, it must be acknowledged that in denying the arousal of the garden variety emotions to music, Hanslick failed to provide any other expedient for explaining how we are emotionally moved by it. For it is obvious that we are; and obvious that if we weren't, music would scarcely have the attraction for us that it obviously does.

It seems to me that Hanslick's little book, for all its vagaries and mistakes, shines out like a beacon of musical clarity and truth in a century that saw the writing of more nonsense about music than any other period in history that I can think of. That of course is why musicians, musicologists, and philosophers today continue to be drawn to it. I think we are now in a position to provide a satisfactory account of how music can be expressive *and* moving *and* "pure" in *something* like Hanslick's sense of formalism. But any such account will have Hanslick to thank for its possibility.

Chapter XVII

A new music criticism?

I

By "criticism" I understand here the discussion of works of art in any and all ways that might be considered relevant to their understanding and appreciation. By "interpretation" I understand the discussion of works of art purporting to explicate their meaning. By "analysis" I understand the discussion of works of art that concentrates solely on their phenomenological, syntactic, and formal properties.

People have been writing about music, or things with at least strong family resemblances to what we recognize as music, for a very long time: since Plato, anyway. And at least some of this writing can, I think, be plausibly described as "criticism." But musical criticism in the modern model – as an identifiable, more or less self-contained discipline – is of fairly recent vintage, its emergence closely associated with the rise and emancipation of instrumental music in the late eighteenth and early nineteenth centuries.

It is surprising neither that musical criticism gained its autonomy in lock step with the emerging autonomy of pure instrumental music, nor (which is also the case) that the philosophical problems we associate with it were defined in just that process. For while music remained predominantly vocal, and a text, therefore, all but omnipresent, musical criticism was never *merely* musical criticism, the problem of talking intelligibly and informatively about music *alone* never clearly perceived or articulated.

My subject is music criticism in its modern, emancipated form. And I shall be dealing exclusively with the discipline of writing about music that is "pure": that possesses, in other words, neither text nor title nor program nor any other extra-musical elements; what I like to call "music alone." Thus, whenever, from now on, I refer to musical criticism, or musical analysis, or musical interpretation, I should be taken, unless it is otherwise apparent, to be talking about the criticism or the analysis or the interpretation of pure instrumental music; of music alone.

Taking 1854, the year Eduard Hanslick's *Vom Musikalisch-Schönen* first appeared, as a convenient though by no means infallible reference point, it seems fair to say that musical criticism up to that time was not perhaps wholly, but nevertheless *importantly* interpretive, and only gradually becoming importantly analytic, whereas from that time onward it was to become increasingly analytic, to the extent that presently what most of the learned think of as responsible, professional criticism is wholly analytic, and technically analytic at that, while interpretation is consigned to the outer darkness inhabited by program annotators and those reviewers in the daily press that have not yet been replaced by the new generation of musicologicaly trained scholar-journalists.

Twenty years ago this attitude toward music criticism, I would think, all but universally prevailed among professional musicians, theorists, and scholars. But today the monolith is beginning to show some cracks. And Joseph Kerman is not alone in observing: "As a kind of formalistic criticism, analysis does not address all or even many of the problems that must be faced if music is to be studied in its integrity."[1]

General statements from above, however, are not the only sign of professional discontent with the exclusively analytic approach to musical criticism. For there is to be discerned, as well, what might justifiably be called a "new musical criticism," pursued neither by amateurs nor popularizers, but by

---

1 Joseph Kerman, *Contemplating Music: Challenges to Musicology* (Cambridge, Mass.: Harvard University Press, 1985), p. 115.

hardened professionals, fully equipped with the analytic tools of the trade, and quite self-consciously aware of the directional change they are attempting to initiate. That change, in a word, is the reintroduction of interpretation into the criticism of music, not as a substitute for analysis but as a companion to it. In spirit I am wholly with the innovators; in letter I am not.

In what follows I shall first present two "case studies" of the kind of approach I take to exemplify the new criticism, and then register some objections, *founded on philosophical considerations*. (I emphasize that my objections have a philosophical foundation because I am in no position, qua philosopher, to press *musical* objections against practical criticism.) Finally, given that I share with those I criticize in the desire for a new music criticism, to supplement analysis (as we know it) while emphatically *not* replacing it, I shall conclude with a sketch, consistent with my own philosophical conclusions about music, of how such a new criticism should proceed.

II

1. The case for music as emotive autobiography

Anthony Newcomb observes, in his article of 1984 on Schumann's Second Symphony: "While the nineteenth century judged it to be one of his highest achievements, the twentieth is generally puzzled by it and tends to reject it as defective." Newcomb shares the nineteenth-century evaluation of the work, and makes the tentative inference that "our problems with the piece may be rooted in current analytical tools for absolute music."[2] He aims, then, at a reevaluation, an up-grade of Schumann's Second Symphony. His means to that end is the application of a critical method that relies on something other than (although not excluding) the "current analytical tools for absolute music." The reevaluation is not a new evaluation but a return to the evaluation – the high

2 Anthony Newcomb, "Once More 'Between Absolute and Program Music': Schumann's Second Symphony," *19th-Century Music* 7 (1984), p. 233.

evaluation – that Schumann's contemporaries placed on the symphony; and the critical method aimed at achieving this reevaluation is a revival, therefore, of the critical method by which Schumann's contemporaries achieved that evaluation.

Further, there is the underlying assumption in all this, I believe, that Schumann's contemporaries were in a particularly privileged position to possess both the correct method of criticizing Schumann's symphony, and, by consequence, the correct evaluation of it, because of their temporal and ideological closeness to the composer. I hope to have something more to say about this assumption on another occasion; but for the present I must, regrettably, put it aside.

From what I said in my introductory remarks, it should come as no surprise to the reader that Newcomb wishes to redeem interpretation for musical criticism: "for these early critics, Schumann's Second had a 'content' of what they called 'thoughts' or 'ideas.' "[3]

The basic "content" that these early writers, and Newcomb himself discern in Schumann's work is what literary critics call a "plot archetype." Newcomb explains: "The plot achetype may be indicated by reference to a specific work of world literature (*Hamlet, Romeo and Juliet, Faust,*) or it may be left unexplicit, in which case it must be a relatively standard fable that is not over-particularized and is easily recognized." In the case of Schumann's Second "contemporary reviews agree overwhelmingly in lining up Schumann's new symphony of 1846 with Beethovan's Fifth (and sometimes with his Ninth as well, which was heard as belonging to the same plot archetype)."[4] That plot archetype was "suffering leading to healing or redemption."[5]

Of course, a plot archetype without "content" is a mere abstraction – a point which I will expatiate upon later on. But the plot archetype that the early critics perceived in the Second Symphony, namely, "suffering leading to healing or

3 Ibid., p. 236.   4 Ibid., p. 234.
5 Ibid., p. 237.

redemption," Newcomb finds not lacking in content, being, so he thinks, amply fleshed out by the psychological events of Schumann's own life. The content, in a word, so Newcomb thinks, is autobiographical.

To begin with, the work narrates its own composing.

> We have seen that Schumann's Second Symphony was from the beginning interpreted by critics and commentators according to the plot archetype of Beethoven's Fifth: i.e., suffering leading to healing or redemption. As it happens, the same archetype can be connected with the personal circumstances surrounding the genesis of the work, for the same evolution of mental states appears in Schumann's brief and moving entries in his *Haushaltbuch,* as he sketched the symphony in less than three weeks.[6]

Beyond, however, being "about" itself, as it were, in being about the process of its own composing, Schumann's Second Symphony is, more generally, about Schumann's overall psychological history during its creation. That is to say, on Newcomb's view the psychological story the work tells is not merely of the composer's inner struggle with the creative process but an inner struggle of far broader scope. "Schumann's often-quoted letter to D. G. Otten of April 1849 offers another specific and personal exemplification of the same plot archetype, as he talks of his struggle through to mental and physical health during his actual work on the symphony." Newcomb concludes: "The struggle in the symphony from suffering to healing and redemption seems also to have been Schumann's own."[7]

Here, then, is a general idea of how Newcomb views Schumann's Second Symphony, and how this constitutes a new direction – or, rather, the revival of an old direction – in musical criticism. I cannot have done justice, in this very brief sketch, to either the range or detail of Newcomb's historical and critical remarks. In particular, I have omitted his discussion of musical "allusions," which deserves a separate hearing. But I hope to have captured the structure of his ar-

6 Ibid.   7 Ibid.

gument, which is the essential thing for my purposes. And I will move on now to the second of my "case studies," with the same end in view: to lay out the bare bones of method, inference, and conclusions.

2. *The case for music as emotive exploration*

The immediate motivation for the attempt of Robin Wallace to, as it were, "reform" music criticism is somewhat different from Newcomb's. For whereas Newcomb wished to restore the tarnished reputation of a once-admired work, Wallace, rather, is intent on accounting for the greatness of a work that is considered on all hands, today, to be one of the musical monuments, Beethoven's A-minor Quartet, of which he remarks: "Few works of chamber music have attracted as much reverential commentary."[8]

But beneath this superficial difference lies a foundation of substantial agreement. Like Newcomb, Wallace wishes to restore to criticism what I called in my introductory remarks the interpretive dimension. And also like Newcomb, he sees this as a return to earlier critical methods rather than the invention of new ones.

It is something Wallace calls the "spiritual" (following J. W. N. Sullivan, one supposes) that he wishes to recognize, at least in Beethoven's case, even though "the idea of spirituality in music still seems too remote and metaphysical for all but the most 'charismatic' classroom teaches to discuss."[9] For, Wallace believes, "it is possible to say more than has yet been said about the spiritual side of Beethoven's music in ways that are relevant to contemporary life." And, he points out, in a remark that is obviously intended as support for his critical methods: "Such an approach would agree with the attitudes of Beethoven's contemporaries toward his music."[10]

---

8 Robin Wallace, "Background and Expression in the First Movement of Beethoven's Op. 132," *The Journal of Musicology* 7 (1989), p. 3.
9 Ibid.   10 Ibid., p. 5.

The object of Wallace's "experiment" in the "new music criticism" – or the "old music criticism," if you prefer – is the first movement of Beethoven's A-minor Quartet. Wallace's general characterization of the work as a whole, and the first movement in particular is that they are in an important sense "ambiguous." Of the whole work he writes: "As a test case I would like to explore the idea that in a piece like Op. 132, deliberate ambiguity, which is an expression of music's potential for diversity rather than organic coherence is an essential part of the work's content, and hence of its message."[11]

This deliberate ambiguity is realized in the first movement of Op. 132 in a number of ways, according to Wallace. Most important, the structure of the movement – in fairly palpable sonata form – seems to have two recapitulations. "Though written in a form which makes reference to the traditional sonata, the movement appears to have two unique and self-sufficient recapitulations: the first beginning in the dominant, E minor, and proceeding through the mediant, C major, while the second begins in the tonic, A minor, and proceeds through the tonic major, A major." What Wallace suggests is that the question of which *is* the recapitulation be given up in favor of the conclusions that the structure is inherently ambiguous in that regard, and intentionally so. "Instead of trying to resolve these alternatives," Wallace writes, "I would like to approach the problem of which is the true recapitulation by posing another question: might not Beethoven, in this movement, have deliberately played upon the structural ambiguity inherent in the form which he created, in order to impress the listener with the possibility of divergent expressive interpretations?"[12]

A second ambiguity is suggested, on Wallace's view, by the constant shift between minor and major; and a third devolves on the extreme emotive contrast between first and second subjects.

11 Ibid.   12 Ibid., p. 9.

In addition to the obvious conflict between the rival recapitulations, there is the tonal plan of the movement, which vacillates constantly between major and minor keys before concluding resolutely with the march-like section in A minor. Superimposed, as it were, onto this contrast is the opposition of the pleading first theme with the relaxed, lyrical second theme – perhaps a deliberate exaggeration for rhetorical purposes of the sort of contrast which by this time had become fairly standard in sonata form.[13]

Finally: "To the ambiguities already observed in this may be added one which concerns its tonality: it appears to be in A minor, but in a very real sense it is in A major as well."[14]

So we may list four ambiguities of the first movement of Op. 132: (1) it is ambiguous as to which of two possible recapitulations is "the" recapitulation; (2) it is ambiguous as to predominant mode: (3) it is ambiguous as to predominant mood; (4) it is ambiguous as to key.

What further can we make of these "ambiguities"? Or, as Wallace puts the question, "What may we conclude about the expressive content of this work?"[15]

One would have supposed the answer would be that the work is expressive of ambiguity. But Wallace apparently does not want that conclusion, even though he has, it seems, presented at least strong, if not convincing evidence for it. Rather, Wallace would have it that "by making the music deliberately ambiguous in as many ways as possible," Beethoven was "thus challenging the listener to bring personal emotional interpretations to the process of listening." Which is to say, I take it, that the movement is expressive of whatever the listener is stimulated to hear in the expressive vacuum Beethoven has created for just that purpose. And this, Wallace adds, is sufficient answer to those (myself particularly, I suspect) "that assume that the expressive content of a work must be objectively verifiable in order to be taken seriously." For: "The unique content of Op. 132's first movement," Wal-

13 Ibid., pp. 9–10.   14 Ibid., p. 11.
15 Ibid., p. 15.

303

lace assures us, "is an assertion of the opposite conviction – that an emotional message which is deliberately ambiguous is nevertheless significant and may generate strength and assurance rather than confusion."[16]

Wallace's article ends in somewhat murky fashion. As we have seen, he believes that in some important sense Beethoven's late works are "spiritual"; but it never becomes clear exactly what that means, beyond merely that the music is expressive in the ways that, for example, Wallace has maintained the first movement of the A-minor Quartet is. At the close there is a suggestion that Beethoven is working out childhood conflicts and neuroses in some kind of Freudian way. However, the dominant theme seems to be, rather, one of emotive exploration and revelation, connected perhaps to therapeutic benefits for the listener. We can see a little bit of all these things in the following passage:

> Children who are idealized by their parents are forced to suppress their own feelings in order to live up to those parents' expectations, and Beethoven consequently arrived in Vienna an extremely ambitious but somewhat crude and boorish individual. In his more ambitious works, he then proceeded to explore thoroughly and systematically the emotions of anger, fear and sorrow which his far-reaching imagination found within his own psyche. Those who are frightened by Beethoven's music, then, might be apprehending not a primeval and uncontrollable force in musical expression, but simply their own carefully hidden emotions, a full awareness of which is difficult if not impossible for many adults (particularly men) to face.[17]

It is not very clear to me what the connection is exactly between this rather grandiose vision of music's "content" and the analysis and interpretation of the first movement of Op. 132 that has preceded it. One must presume the latter is a specific instance of what the former describes in more general terms. And yet that conjecture I find very difficult to accept, given what seems to me to be the very wide gap be-

16 Ibid., pp. 16–17.   17 Ibid., pp. 19–20.

tween the instance and the generality. But such considerations bring us directly to my critique of these two "case studies." So, I will postpone them for their proper place in that critique, to which I now turn.

III

1. *Music as emotive autobiography:*
The case against

The leading thought behind Newcomb's version of what I have been calling the "new music criticism" is the idea that works of "pure" instrumental music may contain or exhibit what he calls, after the literary critics, "plot archetypes." I intend to go straight to that idea and concentrate on it. Because of its centrality, concentrating on the plot archetype idea will, as a matter of course, bring out just about everything else of importance I have to say about the general outline of Newcomb's position.

I begin with a very simple example. I suppose – although you don't have to agree with me to catch my drift – that the *Odyssey* and the *Aeneid* share at least one plot archetype, *the long voyage home* (even though in the case of Aeneas the "return" is a metaphorical one, since he is reconstituting his home somewhere else). Now what should be abundantly clear straightaway is that one cannot determine what plot archetype either of these two poems exemplifies, or, a fortiori, that they exemplify the *same* one, without *first* knowing the content and details of the stories and *then* abstracting from those particulars to the plot archetype which they may exhibit. But Newcomb, in his discussion of Schumann's Second Symphony, has things exactly the other way around; and this is very odd indeed. For instead of first determining what the details of the story are, in the Second Symphony, and *then* trying to figure out what plot archetype they might instantiate, he *first* determines what plot archetype characterizes the work and *then* looks around for the particulars to fill out that plot archetype. It is a procedure every bit as metaphysically impossible as six characters in search of an author.

Put another way, a work of art cannot have a plot archetype without having a plot; and we cannot know what its plot archetype is without first determining its plot. This is no less true if the work of art is a musical work. In order to determine what the plot archetype is of Schumann's Second Symphony, we must *first* determine *its* plot. But the mere suggestion, at the outset, that the Second Symphony has a plot, is certain to be greeted with extreme skepticism by many, including myself. What makes Newcomb's whole argument even initially plausible, to the unwary, is that he has begged the question of plot right from the start by introducing the notion *first* that the work exemplifies a plot archetype. For it follows that if it has a plot archetype, it has a plot. And since the description of a plot archetype is so empty, as compared with the description of a plot, a plot archetype seems like the kind of thing a musical work might contain. But accept the one and you must accept the other. Schumann's Second Symphony cannot *just* contain a plot archetype without a plot. So you have now been manipulated, by acquiescing in the notion that the work has a plot archetype, into a receptive attitude toward suggestions for a plot. And Newcomb's psychobiographical suggestions for such a plot seem, I suppose, as good (or as bad) as any others. However, this whole procedure of first identifying the plot archetype, and then finding a plot to instantiate it is totally fallacious. It is like finding a smile, and then looking for the face that goes with it.

As I have said, the leading thought in Newcomb's discussion is the idea of musical works like Schumann's Second Symphony being instances of or possessing (if you like) plot archetypes. And that idea only has appeal if one can, *per impossible*, first identify the plot archetype, and then find a plot, or plots to fill it out. That, I have tried to show, is a kind of metaphysical impossibility. In a word, first the plot, *then* the plot archetype.

But, it might be objected, perhaps I am putting too much weight on the notion of plot archetype. Certainly Newcomb has discovered *something* in Schumann's Second Symphony that seems to "match" (I am trying to choose an innocuous, non-question-begging word) the psychological events in Schumann's life that he adduces. He misdescribes this "something" as a plot archetype; but whatever it is, it's there. So let's just call it by the right name and forget about plot archetypes altogether.

With this assessment I heartily concur. But once one does call things by their right names, it will readily be seen that what Newcomb has "discovered" (or "rediscovered") in Schumann's Second Symphony is not some fancy new literary entity whose hitherto unsuspected presence will now finally reveal the hidden layers of content in "pure" instrumental music. Rather, what he is talking about turns out to be the familiar expressive properties that, Hanslick et al, notwithstanding, so many of us continue to believe music possesses. And the "plot archetype" (so called) is simply the general statement of how these expressive (and other phenomenological) properties are temporally strung out. What Newcomb calls the "plot archetype" of Schumann's Second Symphony, "suffering leading to healing or redemption," is, I submit, nothing but the pattern of expressive properties appropriate to suffering, leading eventually, in the last movement, to expressive properties appropriate to healing or redemption. The "plot archetype" is simply the expressive plan of the work.

This being said, it now becomes quite obvious that the rest of Newcomb's critical program, namely, establishing this expressive pattern as a psychological autobiography, fails in an old and familiar way. For all that his argument amounts to, it would seem, is a version of this familiar inference:

The work is expressive of ϕ.
The composer was feeling ϕ while composing the work.
Therefore, the work is about or represents the composer's ϕ.

As we all should know by now, there is a logical gap between these premises and their conclusion. It requires more to make Schumann's Second Symphony about or a representation of his suffering and redemption than that the work is expressive of them and Schumann experienced them. And that being the case, there seems little more to say.

2. *Music as emotive exploration:*
The case against

The notion that music somehow offers us "insight" into the emotions recurs perennially – or perhaps it is omnipresent, always finding some advocate or other no matter how skeptical the age. The problem for any advocate is to show that music is capable of embodying or representing (or whatever) any "interesting" emotions, or failing that, to show us how music can tell us anything interesting about the rather ordinary emotions it can embody or represent. There are two things (at least) someone might have in mind in maintaining that music provides emotional "insights." He or she might mean that music – *great* music, of course – is capable of embodying novel and interesting emotions which people have never perhaps thought of or experienced before, thus providing them with fresh psychological materials, in that sense providing psychological "insights." Or, of course, the advocate of music as a source of psychological insight might actually mean that music reveals things to us – tells us things about – our emotions, the way Freud or Dostoyevski, St. Augustine or the Greek playwrights did.

The latter notion seems, on the face of it, monstrously implausible. For conveying such insight requires all the resources of articulate language, unavailable to the composer. Music, at least as we know (and have) it, cannot say "boo," let alone make statements about the nature of the emotions.

The former notion, then, emerges, if only by default, as the only one even remotely plausible. But the merest scrutiny uncovers problems. Let us suppose it granted – I grant it as do many others – that music can embody (the phrase I will use is "be expressive of") the emotions. *What* emotions? Well it would seem that the ones customarily ascribed to music, and the ones there is a fairly well agreed on evidential base for, are far from astounding or out of the ordinary. One says a stretch of music is sad or joyful, amorous or yearning, serious or light-hearted, funereal or anguished, and so on. And one points to altogether familiar melodic, harmonic, rhythmic, contrapuntal, and orchestral elements in support of such ascriptions with the reasonable expectation of something like consensus.

But as soon as one ventures into exotic territory, where the emotions become curious or esoteric enough to be "interesting discoveries," it becomes impossible to understand how, or believe that music can be expressive in those curious and esoteric ways. All sense of a rational universe of discourse, of a reasoned consensus vanishes.

Thus we are in a dilemma. The emotions music can be expressive of are not interesting enough in themselves to constitute anything remotely resembling a psychological revelation. And those that might be, music is impotent to embody. If, therefore, one wishes to claim music provides "insight" into our emotive life by giving expression to subtle and fascinating new emotions, one must grasp the second horn of the dilemma and provide an account of how, appearances to the contrary, music *can* be expressive of "interesting" emotions.

I would suggest that Wallace, in his discussion of Beethoven's Op. 132, has failed to make clear to his readers (or to himself) which horn of this dilemma he has chosen to grasp. At the close of his essay he says that Beethoven "proceeded to explore thoroughly and systematically the emotions of anger, fear and sorrow which his far-reaching imagination found within his own psyche." Now clearly there is nothing unusual or prima facie interesting about anger, fear, and sorrow. They are perfectly familiar emotions that we have all experienced at one time or another. They are also, to be sure, emotions that music can be expressive of in obvious ways. But if Beethoven is to be praised for his emotive "insights," it cannot be just for managing to make his music expressive of these garden variety emotions. They provide, merely in the contemplation, nothing that could be described as a discovery or revelation. It must be, then, that what Beethoven reveals to us *about* them constitutes the discovery or revelation: and that seems strongly suggested by Wallace's claim that Beethoven "explore[d]" them "thoroughly and systematically." Thus it would appear from this passage that Wallace has grasped the first horn of the dilemma. If that is the case, however, he has utterly failed in his project. For we are at a loss to understand how music can tell us things about anger, fear, sorrow, and the other garden variety emotions. We are at a loss, indeed, to understand how it can even tell us trivial things about them, let alone profound and interesting things. And Wallace, so far as I can see, makes no attempt to show us how music might accomplish such a task of thorough and systematic exploration.

What Wallace *has* tried to do, I think, is show us how music can be expressive of emotions more interesting and esoteric than anger, fear, and sorrow. That is why, I suggested earlier, there seems to be some difficulty connecting Wallace's specific discussion of Op. 132 with the general conclusions at the end of his essay, and why I have suggested here that Wallace is not clear which version of the "revelation" theory he is espousing. For the meat of his paper can be understood as a spirited, if unsuccessful, attempt to defend the notion that great music can embody "interesting" and esoteric emotions, thus constituting at least an implicit defense of the notion that great music provides psychological insight by displaying forth emotions strange and wondrous to contemplate. Whereas the conclusion is consistent, rather, with the notion that great music provides psychological insight by conveying to us new information about emotions we are already well acquainted with: anger, fear, sorrow, and the like.

I say we might understand Wallace as attempting to explain how great music can be expressive of emotions more "interesting" than the garden variety ones, providing thereby psychological discovery. He does not say that that is what he is doing. But if it isn't, I am puzzled as to what he does intend. Anyway, it is a worthwhile endeavor and, if successful, would certainly open up new vistas for music criticism. So let us pursue the idea for a moment.

It will be recalled that Wallace reads the first movement of Beethoven's A-minor Quartet as expressively "ambiguous." But this expressive ambiguity, he claims, is there for a further expressive purpose: to occasion in the listener emotive responses that will fill this "ambiguity" which the composer has intentionally put there to that very end. The listener, at Beethoven's behest, is challenged, as Wallace puts it, "to bring personal emotional interpretations to the process of listening."

Why Wallace should want to go from the reasonable and well argued conclusion that Beethoven's A-minor Quartet is expressively ambiguous to the very questionable one that it is expressive (apparently) of any "personal emotional interpretation" the listener is stimulated to in his or her encounter with it is difficult, at first, to understand. But viewed as an attempt to broaden the canvas of emotions music can embody from the ordinary to the "interesting" and "exotic," it immediately becomes intelligible. For the only limit, after all, to what emotions Beethoven's A-minor Quartet might suggest to the listener, given an elaborate enough train of associations, and a neurotic enough listener, would be whatever limit there is to the emotions human beings are capable of experiencing or cognizing. And if emotions so deviously occasioned in the listener's consciousness by a musical work are to be legitimately ascribed to that work as *its* expressive properties, the claim that great music is psychologically insightful has been made good, at least in one of its forms.

We now have a mechanism that does indeed explain how music can be expressive of even the most esoteric and bizarre emotional states, from those of the Underground Man to those of the Wolf Man. In burgeoning forth these newly discovered and novel emotional states, great music "explores" the terra incognita of the human psyche.

But that Wallace's sophisticated reflections on the first movement of Beethoven's A-minor Quartet should have led him to what turns out to be, really, the most naive and blatant form of "expression by free association," is a distressing outcome. Further, it is very difficult to understand what possible justification we would have for ascribing a psychological "insight" that might be so occasioned by a work of Beethoven's to *Beethoven*, or an emotion so arrived at to Beethoven's work. Nietzsche and Dostoyevski may have given Freud valuable insights into the emotional life by the content of their writings. But if Freud got such an insight through a laborious train of though initiated by a chance remark of his tobacconist, it would seem very odd to ascribe it to the tobacconist and not to Freud. Is there any more justification in ascribing such an insight to a composer, if his music does not possess the "content" of the insight, but merely stimulates a thought process that, in the event, produces an insight in someone else?

It seems to me that Wallace has badly misused or misconstrued the concept of "ambiguity" which he so persuasively applies to the first movement of Op. 132. To be "ambiguous" is not to be, on that account, a blank check. Semantically, to be ambiguous is to have more than one possible meaning, not to be of indeterminate meaning, to have any meaning you like. "Bear" is ambiguous: it means "to carry" or "to give birth" or "heavy thick-furred quadruped." But it does mean one of those things. Ambiguity is not a license to reverie and free association.

If the first movement of Beethoven's A-minor Quartet is, as Wallace argues, ambiguous between the mood "of the pleading first theme and the relaxed, lyrical second theme," then it cannot simply be expressive of *anything* that it may suggest to the impressionable listener. It might be irretrievably ambiguous between those two moods, in which case it would be expressive of neither (or both?), but not, on that account, open for any interpretation whatever. Perhaps further scrutiny of the context – for context, after all, is what disambiguates – might make one plump either for "pleading" or "relaxed" as the predominant mood. Perhaps, given the other ambiguities Wallace has pointed out in the movement, one might want to conclude that *ambiguity* is what it is expressive of. But what one *cannot* conclude on the basis of the movement's ambiguity is that it is expressive of light-hearted frivolity, just because it is ambiguous, and light-hearted frivolity is what it made one think of, by a process of association, unconscious suggestion, or whatever. Ambiguity is not pure potential, but discrete and determinate, within the relevant range of alternatives.

Wallace's parting shot with regard to his claim that because the first movement of Op. 132 is ambiguous, it is open to "personal emotional interpretations," chides those foolish enough to "assume that the expressive content of a work be objectively verifiable in order to be taken seriously." This seems to me more like a reductio than like a defense. Why on earth *should* I take a claim about the expressiveness of music seriously if I am not only offered no evidential support whatever for it but am assured, into the bargain, that none will ever be forthcoming and none can be? That seems to me to be just about the standard case of a claim that *shouldn't* be taken seriously. Why should claims about the expressiveness of music be somehow free of the rational and evidential constraints we put on claims about other things? Are the claims incorrigible? Are those that make them infallible? Are we dealing here with mystical experience?

I do not suggest that the evidential base for the ascriptions of expressive properties to music has the rigor (if that is the right word) of the evidential base for ascribing mass to subatomic particles. But to suggest that we need be bothered with no evidential base at all seems a hard saying indeed. And in the face of it, I remind myself, and those who espouse the view, of Socrates' warning to his disciples in face of an argument gone bad:

> It would be pitiable, Phaedo, he said, when there is a true and reliable argument and one that can be understood, if a man who has dealt with such arguments as appear at one time true, at another time untrue, should not blame himself or his own lack of skill but, because of his distress, in the end gladly shift the blame away from himself to the arguments, and spend the rest of his life hating and reviling reasonable

discussion and so be deprived of truth and knowledge of reality.[18]

IV

So far, the thrust of my paper has been largely negative. But critic-bashing is not my intent. Indeed, as I said at the very first, I share the perceptions of Newcomb and Wallace that a "new music criticism" is wanted, if a full picture of the musical work is ever to be achieved in critical writing. Further, as I have said before, there is something in the spirit of Newcomb's and Wallace's criticism with which I am in harmony, even though there is something very important in the letter with which I am at odds. It is time now to put all these things on the table.

The regnant view of responsible, professional criticism is that it consists solely in analysis: that is to say, the understanding of music purely in terms of syntax, structure, and what other aesthetically significant sonic properties musical works might be legitimately thought to have. But there is something deficient in practice, if not in theory, in such a criticism. On this Newcomb and Wallace and I agree.

Newcomb and Wallace, as can be inferred from their own critical practice, must believe that what is lacking in criticism as analysis is *interpretation*. Analysis tells us how music is, but not what it is about. The criticism of Newcomb and Wallace attempts to go from how music is to what it is about. That is to say, Newcomb and Wallace do not wish to substitute interpretation for analysis, but infer interpretation from analysis.

Both Newcomb and Wallace offer what might be called "psychological" interpretations. For Newcomb, Schumann's Second Symphony is "about" Schumann's feeling states, for Wallace the first movement of Beethoven's A-minor Quartet is "about" feeling states in general: that is, an exploration of

18 Plato, *Phaedo*, trans. G. M. A. Grube, (2d ed.; Indianapolis, Ind.: Hackett, 1977), p. 41 (90c–d).

feeling states. In both critics, there is an inference from the expressive properties of music to psychological interpretations of the music. Or, if not that, then it is simply taken for granted that by discovering expressive properties of music one is discovering semantic properties: that is, to discover that a segment of music is ϕ, where ϕ names an expressive property, is to discover, *eo ipso*, that it is about ϕ. In any case, the articles of both Newcomb and Wallace are peppered with phrases that imply expressiveness is being taken semantically, taken as semantic "content."

Now it is quite understandable that Newcomb and Wallace should be concerned to emphasize the expressive qualities of music. For it is the expressiveness of music that analysis most conspicuously ignores, by design and not by accident. This attitude of complete theoretical disdain for the expressive in music, on the part of contemporary analysis, reminds one of nothing so much as the corpuscularians' disdain for secondary qualities. What truck has geometry with the color or warmth of the universe? These are in the eye of the beholder (whatever that may mean) and not objects of scientific knowledge (or perhaps any knowledge at all worthy of the name). Even so the expressive qualities of music to the musical "geometers" and "physicists." Would one require Euclid to address the color of triangles in his theorems? No more should one require the Schenkerians to bother about whether the music is angry or yearning.

This is not to say that either the corpuscularians or the contemporary analysts are wrong-headed in ignoring secondary qualities and expressive qualities respectively. Ignoring things is frequently necessary for studying other things. In the case of the musical analyst, the mistake lies in claiming or assuming implicitly that "this is all there is" rather than the more modest "this is all I am interested in right now." But the music critic who wishes to give a fuller, if in some respects less detailed account of a musical work cannot say, with the analyst, "this is all I am interested in right now." Nor, unless contemporary aesthetic theory is to be completely ignored, can the critic say, with Hanslick, "this is all there is" – not, at least, without a pretty persuasive argument.

It may not be the last step a "new music criticism" must take – but there is little doubt that the first step must be to reconstitute serious discussion of musical expressiveness as a responsible, "professional" part of its method. On this Newcomb, Wallace, and I agree. Where we part company is in the way we see this happening. For Newcomb and Wallace think, judging from their critical practice, that the expressive is to be made part of criticism by adding interpretation to analysis. Whereas I am of the opinion, as can be gathered from my criticism of their criticism, that expressive interpretation is impossible. This impossibility has nothing to do with its being *expressive* interpretation, but has everything to do with its being expressive *interpretation*. For on my view, *any* interpretation of pure music is impossible, simply because it requires of pure music that which it cannot possess: *semantic* or *representational properties*.

But if the "new music criticism" is not to introduce discussion of expressiveness by way of interpretation, what avenue is left? Well, why don't we take the "new" in "new music criticism" seriously? What Newcomb and Wallace both see themselves doing, after all, is reviving an old (and discredited) kind of music criticism rather than inventing a new one. The new way is not to amplify criticism by adding interpretation to analysis but, rather, by amplifying analysis itself. For once one ceases to see expressive properties of music as semantic or representational properties, it becomes clear that they are simply *musical* properties: they are phenomenological properties of music, and as such a proper subject of musical analysis. Musical analysis, as I stated at the outset, I take to be solely concerned with the structural, phenomenological and syntactical properties of music. The new music criticism is, as I conceive of it, true to the insights, the faith (if you prefer) of contemporary analysis, which insists on construing pure instrumental music, music alone, as a structure without a content. But it rejects the implicit, some-

times explicit assumption of most contemporary music analysts and theorists that music does not possess expressive
properties at all, either because expressive properties must
be semantic properties and music alone is, by hypothesis, a
syntax without a semantics, or because the criteria by which
conclusions are reached about the expressive properties of
music are irretrievably subjective, the "conclusions" themselves completely lacking in consensus.

Now it may seem something of an exaggeration to characterize a music criticism of the kind I am outlining above as
"new." One can, after all, find stretches of music criticism in
which the structure of music is discussed, and expressive
predicates employed, where no suggestion is made that the
music must have an expressive "content": that it must be
"about" what it is expressive of. Tovey's *Essays in Musical
Analysis* provide many such examples.

But where music criticism has been both expressive and
"pure," that is, nonsemantic, it has been, so to say, by accident rather than by design. And because of that, the same
critic who, in one place, uses expressive predicates nonse-
mantically will, in another, fall into the semantic or representational heresy, thus causing suspicion that the semantic-free
instances are not what they seem but implied expressive
"interpretations" after all. The "new music criticism," however, will not be virtuous merely by accident. It will explicitly, and self-consciously be analysis – but analysis that includes in its catalogue of *purely musical properties* the *expressive*
ones as well as those more common to the discipline.

The "new music criticism," however, must be new in another respect as well. It must not only be analysis-with-a-
difference in that it is an analysis recognizing expressive
properties as part of the purely musical fabric. It must also
treat those properties in a more serious and functional manner than heretofore. Where music criticism has taken expressive properties seriously, and tried to explore their functions
within a musical composition, it has, in my experience, always been in interpretational terms. And where it has treated
expressive properties in purely musical terms, it has not taken

them seriously at all, which is to say, not attempted to understand them as important structural or syntactic parts of the musical composition in which they occur. Rather, they are used as a convenient means of identifying themes or other musical elements to the lay person, the critic's interest in them ending there. Or, it is simply observed that some theme or other is "tinged" with this or that emotion, as if that were sufficient: rather like an art critic who points out that a portion of a painter's canvas is "tinged" with orange while providing no account at all of what role that distinctively orange element plays in the composition of the painting. We would find that unacceptable in an art critic, and should find it no less so in a critic of music.

The issue is a crucially important one. For if the expressive properties of music do not play a functionally interesting and vital role in musical syntax and structure, then musical analysis has been right all along in ignoring them; and a new music criticism will have to gain its purchase elsewhere.

As a philosopher, I cannot tell music critics and analysts their business. The safe course, therefore, is to make an end here with a simple admonition to those in the business of talking about music: "Talk about the structural and syntactic function of expressive properties as well." Were I to do that, however, I think I would be suspected, and with some justification, of merely mouthing words without meaning. "It is all very well," I can hear the analysts and critics saying, "for a philosopher to tell us to investigate the function in musical syntax and structure of musical expressiveness. But unless the philosopher can give us at least some assurance that such a function is plausible, or even intelligible, we are not about to commit ourselves to what looks much like a wild goose chase." Fair enough: so I am going to conclude with two examples of what I have in mind when I speak of the syntactic or structural function of musical expressiveness: when I speak, in other words, of taking musical expressiveness seriously.

V

I want to discuss two kinds of what might simply be called musical "resolution." They are familiar kinds. I don't know what others call them but I will call them "resolution by arrival" and "resolution by return." I will give two contrasting instances of each kind of resolution, the contrast being, among other things, an *expressive* one. The point of the exercise is to argue that an analysis of the respective "resolutions," in structural or syntactic terms, that leaves out the expressive contrast, is incomplete in a musically nontrivial way.

1. Resolution by arrival

The first movement of both Mozart's Symphony No. 39 in E flat (K. 543) and his String Quartet in C (K. 465) begin with slow (Adagio) introductions of similar lengths, leading into the main Allegro sections. In both cases, clearly, some of the functions of the slow introduction are to create tension, ambiguity, and expectation, all of which are resolved with the arrival of the opening sonata theme.

There are, however, marked differences between the introductions as well. The introduction to the E flat Symphony is, for the most part, diatonic, stays in major keys, with only a suggestion here and there of minor keys and chromaticism. It is, as a result, predominantly sunny rather than sad, and in that respect offers little or no contrast to the sunny (though sedate) first theme of the Allegro. The famous introduction to K. 465, on the other hand, is, at the outset, dissonant to the extreme limits of the style (giving the work, of course, its nickname, the "Dissonant" Quartet), highly chromatic, and predominantly in minor tonalities, all of which contribute to a palpably dark, anguished character, in sharp contrast to the sunny (though yearning) character of its sonata-allegro first theme.

Now in comparing these first movements, it seems fair to say that the sense of release, of resolution when we arrive at the main theme in the "Dissonant" Quartet is stronger than that which we experience on arriving at the main theme in the E flat Symphony. A lot of this, of course, is due to the greater dissonance, harmonic ambiguity, and so forth, of the "Dissonant" Quartet's slow introduction, as well as to the coming to temporary rest out of minor into major. But it does also seem to be the case that the expressive resolution from darkness to light, from melancholy and anguish to the happier, more contented end of the emotive spectrum provides a stronger resolution than a passage from darkness to darkness, or, as in the case of the E flat Symphony, from brightness to brightness. My point is that in describing and comparing these two instances of "resolution by arrival" (at the main theme of the sonata-allegro section), descriptions and comparisons that do not take into account the syntactic or structural contributions the expressive properties make to the resolution are, thereby, syntactically or structurally incomplete. A number of musical elements contribute to making the resolution stronger in the case of K. 465 than in the case of K. 543. But one element is the expressive. And the expressive element, by the way, is probably going to play a far greater role in the lay person's conscious experience of musical resolution than any of the others, at least in the instances cited.

Let this stand, then, for a case of taking expressive properties seriously as musically syntactic or structural ones. For if musical resolution is a syntactic or structural concept, then, surely, since expressive properties contribute to, or detract from musical resolution, they must be understood as doing so syntactically or structurally. I hope another example will make this point secure.

2. Resolution by return

It is something of a music-critical cliché by now that the basic principle of classical sonata form is the principle of resolution. It is a "resolution of return" in that there is a return of themes, or at least key areas in the recapitulation. One of the roles expressive properties can play in the long-term resolutions that sonata form affords is observed in the ways Mozart and Haydn manage sonata movements in minor mode.

In the sonata movements of Haydn's Symphony No. 49 in F-minor ("La Passione"), the expositions follow the key scheme: first theme in the tonic, second and closing themes in the relative major; and the recapitulations: all three themes in the tonic. In contrast, the first movement of his Symphony No. 83 in G-minor ("La Poule") follows the same key scheme in the exposition, but a different one in the recapitulation, namely: first theme in the tonic, second and closing themes (along with a coda) in the tonic major, a strategy obviously employed to avoid ending in the minor.

If we now ask which key scheme, that of "La Passione" or that of "La Poule" affords, in the recapitulation, a stronger resolution, the answer we get is not altogether clear, but interestingly complex and (crucial for our purposes) requires serious consideration of the movements' respective expressive properties.

It will be convenient to compare the first movement of the G-minor Symphony with just one of the movements of the F-minor: the second, Allegro di molto.[19] The returns of the first themes, at the beginnings of the recapitulations, should provide resolutions of equal satisfaction in the two movements: both are returns to the tonic, to the home keys of the respective first themes, and to the original moods of somber seriousness and passion. But when the second themes come around, the waters begin to muddy. Is the return of the second theme in the tonic major (in "La Poule") a weaker or stronger resolution than the return of the second theme to the tonic (in "La Passione")? And which of the movements makes the stronger close?

I will not venture an answer to either of these questions here. What I do want to establish is that these questions cannot be answered without serious consideration of the expressive properties of the respective movements. There are, it

19 "La Passione" has the usual four movements of the Classical symphony, two fast, one slow, and a minuet, but is unusual in the order of movements: slow, fast, minuet, fast, rather than fast, slow, minuet, fast.

seems to me, various musical forces pulling in different directions in each recapitulation, some toward and some at least obliquely away from resolution. And the expressive properties are very much a part of these complex "parallelograms" of musical forces.

For example, the passage from light to dark emotions in "La Passione," from the end of the exposition to the recapitulation, should make for a less perfect resolution than the passage from light to dark and then to light again in "La Poule," from the end of the exposition to the first theme of the recapitulation to the second, closing theme and coda. On the other hand, the full and complete return to the home key, in "La Passione," should pull strongly in the direction of repose, whereas the last forty-eight measures of recapitulation in "La Poule" – second theme, closing theme, and coda – are in the tonic major, and thus do not constitute a full return home.

I have not, needless to say, mentioned various other syntactic and structural parameters, pulling in one direction or the other. All I wish to underscore by these remarks is that whatever conclusions the analyst draws about the resolutions of these two sonata movements, their expressive properties must at least be a subject of serious consideration in drawing them, even if the final verdict, in these particular cases, is that their presence is irrelevant (a verdict, by the way, which I would think highly implausible).

VI

There is, as I have tried to show, a fresh breeze blowing across the music-critical landscape. Various practitioners of the art have felt, as I do, that that breeze blows in the direction of musical expressiveness – a subject that has been off limits to "responsible" criticism in our time. My own fear, as expressed in this essay, is that the "new music critics" will allow themselves to be blown onto the shoals of interpretation. What I have tried to argue here is that there is a middle way between the Scylla of "expressionless" analysis and the

Charybdis of interpretational criticism. Contemporary philosophical analysis has gone a long way toward answering the skepticism that, since Hanslick, has been felt by music professionals in contemplating emotive descriptions of pure instrumental music. It has also gone a long way toward making intelligible, and even attractive, the notion that music possesses expressive properties neither dispositionally, as powers to arouse, nor semantically, as psychological scenarios, but, rather, as a part of the heard musical soundstructure. These philosophical conclusions, tentative and developing as they may be, must be taken seriously by music critics. They point to a new musical criticism that will be analysis pure and simple: but analysis, as we have seen, with a difference. Perhaps they point in the wrong direction. But the way, wherever it leads, is a complicated one. It cannot be seen from here. It must be explored.

Music alone

Chapter XVIII

The fine art of repetition

Our understanding of musical technique would
have advanced much further if only someone had
asked: Where, when, and how did music first develop its most striking and distinctive characteristic – repetition?

Heinrich Schenker

I

The growth of pure instrumental music in the late eighteenth
and early nineteenth centuries, both in production and in
importance, as practice and as "idea," was an event of some
moment in the history of art and its philosophy. "Absolute
music," as this music came to be called in the Romantic era,
music, that is, without program, text, or title – what I like to
call "music alone" – posed, and still poses a pressing problem for aestheticians. It is the problem of providing a ratio-
nale for such music that is both faithful to its at least apparent lack of either representational or propositional "content,"
and adequate to its more than just apparent position of
prominence in the lives of great numbers of persons who
place a value and significance on it in no way lower than the
value and significance traditionally placed on the "content-
laden" arts of sculpture, painting, and literature.

The present attempt to nibble away at this problem (for I
cannot hope to do any more than that here) arises out of
what I perceive to be a kind of paradoxical situation. For,

strangely so it seems to me, starting in the late eighteenth century, theories of absolute music that are seen to do fullest justice to the growing importance and felt significance of such music, are in direct conflict with a fact about pure instrumental music so obvious and elementary as to make nonsense of the theories straightaway, whereas, conversely, the only theory I know about that does full justice, at least implicitly, to this obvious and elementary fact, is seen as doing so little justice to the importance and significance of music alone as to make the music an utterly trivial confection, and the theory, from the point of view of either the mere enthusiast or the hardened professional, a palpable nonstarter.

The obvious and elementary fact, to which the title of this essay alludes, is simply that music alone, from Bach to Brahms, and before and beyond, consists to a large, although of course varying degree, in quite literal repetition of what has been heard before. Indeed, because quite frequently the repetition is literally *literal*, there is no need for the notes to be written down or printed a second time. So musicians have devised instructions, such as double dots in front of a double bar, or *da capo*, or *dal segno*, all of which tell the performer to go back to some designated place in the score or part and simply play the thing over again. Everyone knows this obvious and elementary fact. It is almost embarrassing to point it out. Yet for the most part it remains unremarked and unexplained both by philosophers and by others who write on musical aesthetics in a philosophical vein. Where, infrequently, it has been noticed by those whose theories it confutes, the phenomenon has been dealt with, in my experience, either by simply sweeping it under the rug, or by giving accounts of it that are so desultory as to be open to the most obvious objections. Ironically, the theory that does have the potential for accommodating the musical repeat has, to my knowledge, been seriously suggested only twice in modern times, by a thinker of importance, and in neither instance has that thinker paid the slightest attention to the musical repeat or (therefore) martialed the potential of the theory for dealing with it.

The importance of this question of the musical repeat is not to be underestimated. If, for example, the performer omitted the repeats that J. S. Bach has written into the *Goldberg Variations*, for example, the work would be almost half the length the composer obviously intended it to be: almost half the music would be up the spout. And to take a notorious, not to say crucial case, if the instruction to repeat that Beethoven has put at the close of the exposition of the *Eroica's* monumental first movement is ignored, as it frequently is by modern conductors, fully 150 measures are lost, about one-fifth of the movement as Beethoven originally conceived it. In both cases, the relation of part to whole is seriously compromised. And, one is forced to believe, a theory of absolute music that cannot account, or will not account, for the aesthetic significance of almost one-half of the music of the *Goldberg Variations* as conceived by Bach, or fully one-fifth of the music of the *Eroica's* first movement as conceived by Beethoven, is a theory hardly worth considering.

I propose, then, in what follows, to address seriously, as a problem in the philosophy of art, the function of repeats in absolute music. My task will be three-fold: first, to demonstrate the inadequacy of the dominant theories; second, to demonstrate the potential for success of the theory that has fallen by the wayside, apparently because it fails to do justice to the aesthetic value and importance of music alone; and, finally, to answer the charge that the "fallen" theory does really trivialize what it explains, by trying to rehabilitate it in that regard. I say that I can only begin this rehabilitation here because, on my view, we are in no position, in the present incomplete state of our knowledge, to fully understand all the things that the "fallen" theory, in the fullness of time, is capable of telling us about the experience of absolute music. And it is my position that it is the sum total of all these things that the theory can tell us, not merely one crucial thing, that will, if anything can, tell us what makes music alone valuable and important to us, and why.

II

Since serious philosophical speculation about the nature of absolute music began to gain momentum in musical and philosophical circles in the second half of the eighteenth century, three basic kinds of models have been proposed: I call them the "literary" model, the "organism" model, and the "wallpaper" model. The literary model can itself be subdivided into at least three clearly discernible varieties: the "discourse" model, which likens music alone to a kind of discursive argument, the "dramatic" model, which likens it to a kind of emotive stage play, and the "narrative" model, which likens it to a kind of recited emotive story. But as my remarks with regard to the literary model will be at a level of generality at which there is no need to make these further distinctions, I shall simply talk, for the most part, throughout this essay, of the "literary" model *sans phrase*.

The literary model seems to have been by far the most vigorously pursued in the eighteenth century, and understandably so. To begin with, it had the obvious virtue of being a temporal model. For a piece of music, like a play, narrative, or discourse, is experienced as a series of *ordered* events. I underscore "ordered" to distinguish the experience of literary and musical works from the experience (say) of paintings, which is also, to be sure, an experience of a series of perceptual events, the crucial difference being, however, that each time we experience a given piece of music, or a play, a story, or a written discourse, the parts we experience are always ordered in the same way: first the main theme, then the second theme, first chapter one, then chapter two, and so on; whereas today I might begin looking at the left panel of an altarpiece, tomorrow the right, today the lower part of a large fresco, tomorrow the upper, and still be viewing these works "properly."

Second, the literary model seems to give to music alone a dimension that assures something like the high status that its enthusiasts and practitioners ascribe to it. That dimension is the dimension of meaning or content that linguistic models are bound to carry with them, albeit in this case in the highly suspect form of the conceptually inexpressible. As Carl Dalhaus put the point in his brief history, *The Idea of Absolute Music*,

> [I]nstrumental music's claim to be taken seriously as a manifestation of "pure art," rather than being dismissed as empty sound, was nourished by literary models that grounded a new musical consensus to its formulations. . . . The metaphysical prestige of absolute music came about via a transfer of the poetic idea of unspeakability.[1]

The organism model, which gained impetus perhaps somewhat later, also had the virtue of a built-in temporality. For it was the perceived phenomenon of development, of direction and progress toward a goal, in symphonic music particularly, that called it forth as a metaphor. And so it was the aspect of growth in living systems, the progress from infancy to adulthood, or, better, the gradual unfolding of the embryo that was the aesthetically operative idea. It is for this reason that I have chosen, quite self-consciously, to call what I am talking about the "organism" model rather than the "organic" model, which is the more usual locution. When a work of art is called "organic" these days, it means not much more than well organized in some way, unified, as the parts of a living system are. And one can just as well call a static object "organic" in this sense, as a series of events in some temporal progression or other. But it was the teleological progress of musical events that the life-metaphor was contrived to describe in terms of biological growth or development. It is just that specific metaphor of biological development or growth, not merely the concept of organic unity, that I wish to single out by calling it the "organism" rather than the "organic" model.

What might immediately strike one as a weakness in the organism model, as opposed to the literary ones, is that there is no very obvious support in the former, where, as we have

1 Carl Dalhaus, *The Idea of Absolute Music*, trans. Roger Lustig (Chicago and London: University of Chicago Press, 1989), p. 146.

seen, there is in the latter, for the prestigious place that instrumental music occupies in the Pantheon of the arts and sciences. Literary models bring with them at least the promise of content and (therefore) truth: They give absolute music, so to say, epistemic status. But it is hard to know why any particularly exalted status should be forthcoming by way of the organism model. Why should pleasant but empty noise that seems (phenomenally) to "develop" or "grow" as a living organism does be more valuable than pleasant but empty noise that lacks that appearance? Wherein lies the status-bestowing power of the organism model? And if it lacks such power, why was it a successful contender in the crucial period of theorizing that surrounded the growth of absolute music and its ideology?

My tentative suggestion would be that the model of organic growth or development seemed to assure status to music alone because the apparent success of the model made it seem plausible to look upon such music as itself a metaphor for living things, as, for example, in A. W. von Schlegel's remark that "The harmony made up of simultaneously sounding notes that are concordant with each other, and which, though diverse, form a unity, may well, in fact, represent in audible terms the internal structure of life."[2] And since a high value was placed on living things, the art that seemed (and may still seem to some) the most powerful metaphor of life became (and still remains) a highly valued enterprise.

And now, at last, it is time to briefly introduce the third candidate, the pitiful wallpaper model of music alone: pitiful because it seems such a palpable nonstarter, bestowing no status at all on the enterprise, except that possessed by any "mere" decoration or adornment. What perfume is to the nose, or wallpaper to the eyes, music is to the ears. Indeed, those who have wished to denigrate absolute music have used the charge of "mere decoration" as their bill of indictment.

---

2 *Music and Aesthetics in the Eighteenth and Early-Nineteenth Centuries*, ed. Peter le Huray and James Day (Cambridge: Cambridge University Press, 1981), p. 266.

All that music alone amounts to, they say, is pleasant but empty noise. Surely that cannot be all the mighty Beethoven was involved in, its defenders reply.

Now I hold no brief for either the status-bestowing power of the literary model or that of the organism one. I think in the end that they both come to nothing: the former because it promises meaning or content but can never really deliver the goods, the latter because it is simply a nonsequitur, since it no more follows that music is a metaphor of life because it may resemble life than that any X is a representation of any Y – to take the more general form of the fallacy – just because the relation of resemblance may hold between them. But that is not my concern here: Rather, it is to argue that both are totally defeated straightaway by the obvious fact of the musical repeat, and so the question of their power to bestow value, or lack thereof, need never come up in the first place. In fact, it is, as I shall argue, the pitiful wallpaper model that makes sense of the fine art of repetition. And it is *that* model, therefore, the value-bestowing power of which I will at last have to defend, being the model most obviously deficient in that regard, without even prima facie respectability. However, I have yet to make good my initial claim, that the literary and organism models do not make sense of the musical repeat. To that claim I now turn.

III

I said that the lowly, common repeat sign in instrumental music, and the simple musical fact of literal repetition that it bestows, have been given little attention by philosophically minded writers on music. However, there is a notorious repeat sign in vocal music, that of the so-called *da capo* aria, over which a good deal of talk was generated in the eighteenth century, of considerable aesthetic importance. I think we can learn something about the present topic from a brief discussion of that one.

The basic kind of *da capo* aria about which eighteenth-century theorists of the opera were exercised was that in which a leading emotion is expressed in the first, main section of the aria, a contrasted or related emotion is expressed in the usually less elaborate second section, with an instruction to repeat the first section appended to the end, thus making a symmetrical three-part form: ABA. The major objection voiced against this mainstay of the Baroque *opera seria* was that it did not make dramatic sense, it lacked dramatic verisimilitude. Folks don't do that sort of thing. They don't repeat verbatim what they have just said a minute after they have said it, which is, essentially, what the *da capo* aria makes everyone in an opera do for hours on end. As one of the leading critics of the Baroque Italian opera, Francesco Algarotti, put the point in 1755:

> Words are to be treated in no other manner but according as the passion dictates; and when the sense of an air is finished, the first part of it ought never to be sung over again, which is one of our modern innovations and quite repugnant to the natural process of our speech and passions, that are not accustomed to thus turn about and recoil upon themselves.[3]

Of course it was recognized on all hands that whatever the dramatic imperfections, or even absurdities of the *da capo* aria, as a purely musical form it was perfection itself: the ideal embodiment of the neoclassical principle of unity in variety. The instrumental music of the same period fully exploited the *da capo* principle. And even Gluck, to whom it was dramatically repugnant, could not help, as a musician, almost wistfully referring to "those symmetrical forms, those periodic repetitions which give the arias a piquant and pleasant effect,"[4] bidding them a reluctant farewell, almost as Plato did to certain morally repugnant forms of poetry in Book X of the *Republic:* "For we are conscious of being enchanted by

---

3 Oliver Strunk (ed.), *Source Readings in Music History* (New York: Norton, 1950), p. 669.
4 *The Collected Correspondence and Papers of Christoph Willibald Gluck,* ed. Hedwig and E. H. Mueller von Asow (New York: St. Martin's Press, 1962), p. 117.

such poetry ourselves; though it would be a sin to betray what seems to us the cause of truth."[5]

Thus the judgment read on the *da capo* aria, which, in the event, turned out to be its epitaph as well, was: perfect as music, absurd as musical speech, because musical repetition makes sense where linguistic repetition does not.

One would have thought, then, that a music liberated from speech, as the Viennese classical style became, would have been a music thereby fortified against the charge that *its* repetitions were absurd. Ironically, such was not the case. For if the words did not survive, their memory lingered on in the literary model of music alone. And it did not escape notice that if music without words is, nevertheless, to be understood along textual lines, its repeats are every bit as absurd as those of the *da capo* aria. Sonata movements, in the late eighteenth century, frequently repeated both the exposition *and* the development cum recapitulation. Of this practice the composer Grétry remarked:

> A sonata is a discourse. What would one think of a man who, after cutting his discourse in two, would repeat each half? . . . That is just about the effect repeats in music have on me.[6]

What Grétry apparently failed to realize is that even if the repeats of a movement in sonata form were to be omitted in performance, as they frequently are nowadays, and even if future composers were to write sonata movements without the traditional repeats, as they increasingly did in the nineteenth century, the problem for sonata form, seen as literary discourse, would hardly have been avoided. For the very sonata principle, as Grétry should have known, is a principle of repetition, of return. The point of the recapitulation, as its name implies, is to return, to review, to repeat what was first given in the exposition, albeit with different key relation-

5 Plato, *The Republic,* trans. John Llewelyn Davies and David James Vaughan (London: Macmillan, 1950), pp. 352–3.
6 Quoted in Michael Broyles, "Organic Form and the Binary Repeat," *The Musical Quarterly* 66 (1980), p. 343.

ships and, as the nineteenth century wore on, more and more extensive variation of the thematic material. The sonata-allegro, in its most pristine form, in Haydn, Mozart and Beethoven, is, indeed, a palpable *da capo* form, and remained so as long as it remained intact.

The point is made abundantly clear in the familiar difficulties that were felt with regard to the *Leonore* overtures, particularly the third. Gluck had stated in the Dedication to *Alceste* that the purpose of the opera overture is to present the "argument" of the drama to come.[7] And it seems apparent that that indeed was what Beethoven tried to do in *Leonore* No. 3, the thematic plan giving us a musical representation of the main plot of *Leonore*, later *Fidelio*, from Don Florestan in his dungeon cell through the struggle of the sonata exposition to the triumphant trumpet flourishes that signal his rescue. The problem is that, from the dramatic standpoint, the overture should have ended with a coda to the trumpet call, as the opera ends with the grand chorus of rejoicing. But from the musical point of view, the movement, being in sonata form, required a recapitulation; and Beethoven being the composer he was, gave us one, thus essentially telling the whole story over again, which is dramatically absurd. I do not know who first remarked on this dramatic anomaly, but Wagner is undoubtedly its most famous and most incisive critic. What he says is well worth quoting, as it states as well as anything I can think of the difficulty of reading sonata form as a literary text. Wagner writes:

> But he who has eyes, may see precisely by this overture how detrimental to the master the maintenance of the traditional [sonata] form was bound to be. For who, at all capable of understanding such a work, will not agree with me when I assert that the repetition of the first part after the middle section, is a weakness which distorts the idea of the work almost past all understanding; and that the more, as everywhere else, and particularly in the coda, the master is obviously governed by nothing but the dramatic development? But whoso has

7 Strunk, *Source Readings*, p. 674.

brains and lack of prejudice enough to see this, will have to admit that the evil could only have been avoided by entirely giving up the repetition; an abandonment, however, which would have done away with the overture [sonata]-form.[8]

Nor will it do to say that the problem of *Leonore* No. 3 is simply the problem of sonata form when its "program" is a statable one, when, that is, we know the "story" in some of its particulars. For if the literary model is to have any content at all, and not be just an empty phrase, it must be ascribing some generally accepted property of literary discourse to pure instrumental music, and that property seems to be its directionality: its progress through a story, or through a rational argument, from beginning to end. And no matter how vague we are about the "content," so long as we retain this essential directionality, the literary model will be incompatible with the sonata-allegro principle, or any of the other repeats in instrumental music. As Heinrich Schenker long ago observed, "language . . . prefers exactly the opposite strategy [to music] – that is, a continuous flow, without repetition."[9] Give up this principle of directionality, this "continuous flow," however, and you simply give up the literary model altogether.

Well, in point of fact, the literary model was pretty much given up by many in favor of the organism model, at least as regards the sonata principle. So let us turn to the rival account and see if it has anything better to offer in the face of the musical repeat.

8 Richard Wagner, "On Franz Liszt's Symphonic Poems," *Richard Wagner's Prose Works*, trans. William Ashton Ellis (London: William Reeves, 1907), Vol. 3, pp. 245–6. I am assuming that it is *Leonore* No. 3 that Wagner is talking about here, although he does not explicitly say so, referring to it merely as "the great Overture to Leonora" (ibid., p. 245).

9 Henrich Schenker, "The Spirit of Musical Technique," trans. William Pastille, *Theoria* 3 (1988), p. 88. I am most grateful to Kevin Kosyn for drawing my attention to this essay, after hearing me deliver an earlier version of the present essay.

IV

I guess it is fairly clear that the "development" section of the sonata movement provides the principal musical analogy for the organism model. Indeed at least the English term itself, "development," seems as if it might be, *au fond*, a biological term, or at least express, right from the start, a biological metaphor. Everywhere we look, among the life forms of the planet, we see processes of "development" to some biological end taking place, exemplified most vividly, I would think, by the maturation of the embryo. Such development seems to us like an unfolding, a revelation of potential; and it is just this unfolding or revelation of potential that the biological metaphor is supposed to illuminate in the exposition and development sections of the sonata movement.

But thus stated, it should be abundantly clear that the organism model is just as decisively defeated by the musical repeat as is the literary model in all its forms. I will not even speak here of such obviously recalcitrant forms as the minuet-and-trio, scherzo, and the binary dance forms of the Baroque, with their plethora of repeats. Consider only sonata form, which really gave rise to the organism model in the first place, and has always been its most favored case.

An embryo which followed the plan of a sonata movement, even where neither the exposition nor the development were repeated (which would omit some of the most imposing and well-known examples in the repertoire), when it got to the point in its progress to term analogous to the sonate recapitulation, would have to go right back to conception and start the process all over again. This in itself, it seems to me, renders the organism model inapplicable to and unilluminating of what is agreed on all hands to be its best case in the traditional repertoire.

Music is what it is, repeats and all. The literary and organism models are what they are: "process" models that do not allow of their doubling back on themselves. Either these models must be given up, or the musical repeat must somehow come to be understood in a way that makes it compatible with them. Let us take a look at one possible strategy for accomplishing the latter before we declare the literary and organism models defunct.

V

I take my departure from some sage remarks on musical repeats made by Edward T. Cone. But I hasten to add that Cone's remarks were not intended for the purpose to which I shall try to put them here, and he is, therefore, in no way responsible for the fact that they fail of this purpose, which, indeed, they do. Cone asks: "Is there such a thing as literal repetition in music?" In partial reply to his question, Cone cites an example, Chopin's Polonaise in A major, of which he writes:

> This is a piece notable for the six-fold statement of its opening period, each time literally repeated: AABABA Trio, ABA – thus six A's in all. But the second A is already different from the first. The first was preceded by silence and followed by its repetition; the second is preceded by the first and followed by B. The third is now preceded and followed by B, and the fourth is preceded by B but followed by the Trio, and so on. My contention is that each statement is influenced by its position, by what precedes and what follows it, so that each is, in important respects, different from all the others.

Cone concludes from such considerations: "In general, there is no such thing as true redundancy in music."[10]

But if Cone is right, do we not have here a perfect defense of both the literary and organism models against the charge that they are incompatible with the palpable fact of repetition in music? For what Cone seems to be saying is that there is no repetition in music: The palpable fact turns out to be a palpable fiction.

The view can be stated more clearly by introducing the familiar concept of the intentional object. What we can de-

10 Edward T. Cone, *Musical Form and Musical Performance* (New York and London: Norton, 1968), p. 46.

rive from Cone's analysis is that, although the physical sounds are indeed duplicated in music when the repeat signs are observed, the intentional object, which is the music heard, is not; and it is the intentional object, after all, the music as heard, that we are talking about when we analogize *music* to discourse or to living organisms. Thus, when the exposition is repeated, because we are hearing a different intentional object, we are hearing different music; we are not going back but going on, as both the literary and organism models require.

But surely this seems too good to be true, the victory too easy. We know in our hearts that music does repeat itself a great deal; and no metaphysical sleight of hand, based on what appears to be a rather overly strict notion of identity, is going to dislodge this belief. Cone himself wisely cautions that, as he puts it, "I mean to imply nothing so profound as the Heraclitian impossibility of stepping into the same river twice"[11] Our task, as I see it, is to preserve our intuition that music does, in a strong, full-blooded sense, repeat itself, while preserving as well the important implication of Cone's remarks which I take to be that, each time a musical section is repeated, the intentional object is nontrivially different, different, that is, beyond the Heraclitian sense of merely not being numerically identical.

Let us work from Cone's conclusion: "There is no such thing as true redundancy in music." In the present instance I take this to mean, *minimally,* that we cannot just leave off the repeats in *any* composition without leaving out something in the music: Repeats are not expendable. At the very least, one changes a composition's proportions in ignoring the repeat sign, even if, *per impossibile,* one were leaving out merely an intentional object type-identical to the intentional object of which it is the literal repetition. And with this minimal sense of not being redundant I am scarcely in disagreement, as it is, in fact, the premise with which I began.

But Cone means more by his denial of redundancy to the

---

11 Ibid.

repeated material in music than that it is nonexpendable in this minimal sense. He is, to put it my way, denying that, in what we call literal repeats, the intentional objects are type-identical. For the repeated material is perceived as coming after and before music different from that which the original material is perceived as succeeding and preceding. And that makes the respective intentional objects tokens of different types. Nor do I demur from this conclusion of Cone's. It is part of Cone's point that we do, or should, hear music differently when it appears the second, or third (or whatever) time from the way we did the first, and that the performer should play it differently. With that any sensitive (and sensible) listener or musician must agree.

The intentional objects that result from the type-identical repeats of the physical sounds are, in Cone's words, "in important respects different from" one another. And the full weight of the argument would seem to fall on the word "important." My question is this. Does the fact, which one must grant, that the intentional objects are in important respects different imply that they are tokens of different types? Here we have to be careful.

It is, of course, a very important fact about the ten-dollar bill in my pocket that it is mine, and a very important fact about the ten-dollar bill in your pocket that it is yours. But, of course, they are both tokens of the same type: namely, the type "ten-dollar bill." Similarly, it is an important fact about the first playing of the exposition of Mozart's A-minor Piano Sonata that it is preceded by silence and precedes the second playing; and it is an equally important fact about the second playing that it is preceded by the first playing and precedes the development. But they are still intentional tokens of the same type. Indeed, it is just because they are heard as tokens of the same type that they can, one would presume, have the aesthetic effect they are supposed to have, of being the same *except for* their relationships to what they precede and what they succeed.

But look, someone might reply: The intentional object you should be talking about is not just the sounding of the notes

341

as heard; rather, that plus its preceding and succeeding relations as heard. And that whole intentional object is a type-different one for the first hearing of the exposition from the whole intentional object for the second.

Well, that is a perfectly intelligible way to talk, but it can't evade the fact that imbedded in each larger intentional object is another that, in both first and second hearings, is a different token of the same type, and so heard. And the repetition – the type-identity – of *these* intentional objects is trouble enough for either the literary or the organism models, as not much reflection will reveal.

Suppose you were to attend the performance of a fairly conventional play, not some bizarre effusion of the *avant garde,* in which the first act was repeated, verbatim. If you were to express the view that such a performance was absurd, that it was absurd to get to the first act curtain and then start the plot all over again before getting on with it, and if the response was that the first act wasn't literally repeated at all, since the second time it was a different intentional object, namely the first-act-coming-after-the-first-act, I think you would think the reply absurd. It is reduncancy enough, and destructive enough of the usual notion of a plot or a story or a narrative, that the two acts, minus the preceder and successor relations, are type-identical. And this is exactly the absurdity musical repeats present when music is understood on the literary model.

Now here, I suppose, the defender of the literary model is going to chide me to the effect that it is unfair, after all, to compare the palpable absurdity of repeating the first act of *School for Scandal* with repeating the exposition of Mozart's A-minor Piano Sonata. For *School for Scandal* has a statable, describable plot, whereas, on the literary model, the exposition of the sonata has plot, or argument, or narrative structure that is ineffable. And wherein lies the absurdity of hearing the first part of an ineffable story twice before getting to the second part (which will also, in this case, be heard twice)?

But, as I have had occasion to remark before, either the literary model is going to have explanatory content, or it is just a mouthing of words. Grétry took its explanatory content to imply that hearing the exposition of a sonata movement twice before getting on with it would be absurd. If, however, you so denude the literary model of explanatory content that it imputes a plot or argument to music in only a phantom, Pickwickian sense, then it ceases to be illuminating to call a musical composition a discourse. I suggest that having an ineffable plot or argument, which, because of its ineffability, sustains repeated experiencing of its parts without any hint of absurdity, is tantamount to not having a plot or argument in the first place; and, further, that a literary model with such a phantom, bodiless concept of plot or argument, is a *literary* model in name only, completely empty of meaning and unilluminating of the musical experience.

The organism model fares no better. Perhaps indeed it fares worse, for one can hardly fall back on the notion of ineffability in applying it. If a musical composition is to be illuminatingly described as an organism, we must, I would think, show how, *in its musical particulars*, it exhibits the character of an organism. And as a musical composition proceeds temporally from a beginning to an end, it is the growth, the goal-directed development of an organism, particularly an embryo, that provides the over-arching metaphor, as we have seen. But that metaphor is simply contradicted by the musical repeat, even with the understanding that the successor and predecessor relations are changed the second time around. An embryo that repeated the first third of its development all over again before continuing to term would be seen as doing something biologically absurd, at least as biological organisms have developed on planet earth, even if it were pointed out that the second coming of the first stage bore relations to what came before and after it different from those of the initial first stage. The whole thing is biological nonsense. But it is not *musical* nonsense. And one can only conclude from that that the biological metaphor, like the literary one, fails to be revelatory of the character of musical experience, and for much the same reason. As attractive as these metaphors have been, it is time at last to admit their bankruptcy and seek for another. The wallpaper model awaits us. As unpromising as it may seem on first reflection, it was first hinted at by a philosopher of genius, and flirted with by a musical writer of great talent. So far that is merely an argument from authority. Let us see, then, if there is more to it than what may simply have been the folly of two gifted thinkers.

VI

In §16 of the third *Critique*, Kant, during one of his rare, example-giving moods, suggested some of the things that exhibit what he called "free beauty" and that, by consequence, satisfy the stringent requirements of a "pure judgment of taste." Kant wrote:

> So designs *à la grecque*, foliage for framework or on wallpapers, &c., have no intrinsic meaning; they represent nothing – no Object under a definite concept – and are free beauties. We may also rank in the same class what in music are called fantasias (without a theme), and, indeed, all music that is not set to words.[12]

Kant, I take it, was placing all pure instrumental music – both that which he perceived as being without determinate themes, toccata-like improvisations, and written out things of that kind, and music which he perceived as having thematic character – among what he called free beauties.[13] And

12 Immanuel Kant, *Critique of Aesthetic Judgment*, trans. James Creed Meredith (Oxford: Clarendon Press, 1911), p. 72.

13 H. H. Bernard, in his earlier translation of 1892, agrees with Meredith in translating the German word *Thema* as "theme" (in the musical sense). *Critique of Judgment* (New York: Hafner, 1951), p. 66. But Werner S. Pluhar, in his new translation, renders the word "topic," thus making the contrast here between instrumental music without, and instrumental music with a program or represented subject. *Critique of Judgment* (Indianapolis: Hackett, 1987), p. 77. Pluhar's translation seems to me wildly implausible. For Kant is clearly saying here that *all* music without words, whether or not it has a *Thema*, is an example of free beauty. However, music with a topic, either representational or narrative, would have an object, a content, and would thus *not* be a *free beauty*. Pluhar's translation would make Kant contradict himself in one breath, over a rather simple matter. It hardly seems likely.

that it was placed in that class of things cheek by jowl with "wallpapers" and "designs *à la grecque*" strongly suggests those decorative images were uppermost in his mind in characterizing music as an art.

Kant was apparently quite untroubled by the implication for the status of absolute music that placing it among the minor decorative arts of wallpaper and designs *à la grecque* carried with it. For music ranked very low in his estimation, and as §54 of the *Critique of Judgement* amply testifies, he saw absolute music as a bodily rather than a mental pleasure – indeed, nothing more than a sonic *digestif*, if we are to take his remarks seriously.[14]

The decorative image that Kant projected onto music with such complacency surfaced again, no doubt under his influence, in the second great purveyor of musical wallpaper, Eduard Hanslick. But Hanslick, unlike Kant, was not untroubled by the seeming trivialization of music that such an image implied. This is not surprising, since Hanslick was a musician, and Kant musically untutored.

Music as sonic decoration is graphically described by Hanslick in two striking passages, right after he has delivered his famous *bon mot* to the effect that "The content of music is tonally moving forms." He writes:

> How music is able to produce beautiful forms without specific feelings as its content is already to some extent illustrated for us by a branch of ornamentation in the visual arts, namely arabesque. We follow sweeping lines, here dipping gently, there boldly soaring, approaching and separating, corresponding curves large and small, seemingly incommensurable yet always well connected together, to every part a counterpart, a collection of small details but yet a whole. Now let us think of an arabesque not dead and static, but coming into being in continuous self-formation before our eyes. . . . Does this mental impression not come close to that of music?

And again:

14 *Critique of Aesthetic Judgment*, trans. Meredith, pp. 196–203. For a detailed discussion of this section, see Peter Kivy, "Kant and the *Affektenlehre*," Chapter XIV in this volume.

As children all of us have much enjoyed the play of colour and shape in a kaleidoscope. Music is a kind of kaleidoscope, although it manifests itself on an incomparably higher level of ideality. Music produces beautiful forms and colours in ever more elaborate diversity, gently overflowing, sharply contrasted, always coherent and yet always new, self-contained and self-fulfilled.[15]

I said that Hanslick, unlike Kant, could not easily accept the trivialization of music these decorative models – wallpaper, arabesque, kaleidoscope – seemed to imply. Two things make this apparent: first, Hanslick's rather lame attempt to counter the implication early on; and, second, the retreat from the position to a form of the literary model as the argument progresses. Both deserve notice.

I purposely omitted a crucial sentence from each of the above quoted passages, sentences, as I see it, that represent attempts to upgrade the status of music in light of its purely decorative character. I will quote them now. With regard to *music as arabesque*, Hanslick remarks: "Finally, let us think of this lively arabesque as the dynamic emanation of an artistic spirit who unceasingly pours the whole abundance of his inventiveness into the arteries of this dynamism." And with regard to *music as a kaleidoscope of sound*, Hanslick has this to say: "The main difference between such a musical, audible kaleidoscope and the familiar visible one is that the former presents itself as a direct emanation of an artistically creative spirit, while the latter is no more than a mechanically ingenious plaything."[16]

There is an argument lurking here something to this effect. Music is a sonic arabesque or kaleidoscope. But music emanates from artistic, creative minds and they do not; this explains why, although they are trivial, decorative arts, music,

---

15 Eduard Hanslick, *On the Musically Beautiful: A Contribution towards the Revision of the Aesthetics of Music,* trans. Geoffrey Payzant (Indianapolis: Hackett, 1986), p. 29.
16 Ibid.

on the contrary, is an exalted one: "on an incomparably higher level of ideality."[17]

Now I described this argument initially as a lame one; and with it thus spelled out, we can see where the problem lies. The argument seems to be circular. To put it somewhat crudely: The answer to the question, What makes visual wallpaper trivial and sonic wallpaper an exalted human accomplishment? is that visual wallpaper emanates from ordinary minds and sonic wallpaper from creative, artistic minds. But if one goes on to ask the question, How do we know sonic wallpaper emanates from creative, artistic minds, and visual wallpaper from ordinary minds? the answer seems to be that we know this because sonic wallpaper is an exalted human accomplishment (that only creative, artistic minds can have achieved) whereas visual wallpaper is trivial decoration that the ordinary mind can produce with ease. It is clear that Hanslick has things the wrong way around. We do not, after all, know the *Hammerklavier* Sonata is an exalted work because it was written by an artistically creative mind but we know Beethoven's was an artistically creative mind because we know first that the *Hammerklavier* Sonata is an exalted work. And we need some reason independent of Beethoven possessing an artistically creative mind, and having been the composer of the *Hammerklavier* Sonata, for thinking the *Hammerklavier* an exalted work, or we fall into vicious circularity.

But Hanslick's second attempt to avoid the taint of trivialization that the wallpaper model seems to transmit to music is not better: It simply evades the question by changing the model. Hanslick writes:

> [B]y contrast with arabesque, music is actually a picture, but one whose subject we cannot grasp in words and subsume under concepts. . . . It is a kind of language which we speak and understand yet cannot translate.[18]

17 I omit as irrelevant to my discussion here the obvious intent, also, in the second quotation, to separate music from the "mechanical" aspects of the kaleidoscope: the random motion of the colored glass pieces and the multiplication of the image by mirrors to achieve symmetry.
18 Hanslick, *On the Musically Beautiful*, p. 30.

Hanslick's second answer, then, to the question, What makes sonic wallpaper important and visual wallpaper trivial? is that sonic wallpaper has a content, is a discourse, and visual wallpaper is contentless. Kant had more philosophical nerve. His high estimation of poetry, and low estimation of music alone, were based on the premise that poetry had content, particularly moral content, and music, being sonic wallpaper, had none. Hanslick obviously shared Kant's belief that content makes the difference, but could not follow Kant in demoting music to the social and intellectual status of the decorative arts; so he gave his "wallpaper" a content, albeit, of necessity, the usual ineffable one. In so doing, he no longer had a wallpaper model at all. He had a literary model with all the sins on its head against the musical repeat that I have been inveighing against. With Hanslick we are back where we started.

I propose to regain Kant's original insight and try to match his nerve: to follow, as Socrates would urge, where the argument leads. The original insight, that the comparison with wallpaper means to uncompromisingly make plain, is that music, indeed, possesses no content. It is pure, empty decoration: arabesque. I have put the point in a way as damaging as possible to the reputation of music as an exalted human endeavor. For what I shall now try to show is that in following the wallpaper model of music, in its most ruthless form, to where it leads us, we will find that the more we understand it, the less we will fear its apparent trivialization of the musical experience. Instead of seeing the identification of music with the decorative arts as a trivialization of the former, perhaps, rather, we will come to see it as an ennobling of the latter: the redeeming of the decorative arts from the Western prejudice for knowing as the only goal worthy of the human intellect. This is a formidable task that I cannot hope to complete here. I can only make a beginning.

VII

Let us begin with Kant's insight. Pure music, music alone, possesses no content whatever. The wallpaper model does simple justice to this simple assumption, as Kant was, so far as I know, the first to discover.

But let us recognize straightaway, as well, that the wallpaper model also does simple justice to the simple fact of the musical repeat, in all its varieties, which neither of the competing and more favored models could do. This latter point requires elaboration, as it is, of course, the central point of my discussion. And to make this point adequately it is time to move on, now, to a more sophisticated, and more concrete example of visual design than terms like "wallpaper" or "arabesque" or "kaleidoscope" usually connote. They have, after all, so far been nothing more than names for a model and have given that model only the barest of outlines.

I have on my floor an old and rather worn, but, nevertheless, I am told, fine example of a certain kind of Persian carpet, quite familiar to the connoisseurs. I have spent many idle and enjoyable moments in what I think of as "exploring" this carpet.

If I begin my exploration on one of the outer edges, what I find is a small repeated pattern, varying only in an occasional color. What happens, quite simply, is that I begin discovering a pattern of repetition; or, if you want to look at it passively, a pattern of repetition is discovered to me. This, of course, requires some small time to accomplish, and a repeated pattern to be there in the first place for me to discover, or for me to be discovered to. In his wonderful book on the decorative arts E. H. Gombrich has aptly characterized what I am thinking about here as a process in which "groping comes before grasping or seeking before seeing."[19]

Now, having groped for and grasped the pattern of one outermost border of my carpet, I have many choices. I may

19 E. H. Gombrich, *The Sense of Order: A Study in the Psychology of Decorative Art* (Ithaca: Cornell University Press, 1979), p. 5.

follow it to the end, or swerve into the next border – the longitudinal sides of my carpet actually have six border patterns of varying widths – or, perhaps, I may plunge deep into the interior of my carpet where the larger but shorter patterns lie. If I follow the outermost border pedantically to the end, then I may turn the corner to follow a latitudinal border; or I may take the step inward at this point. In all these cases I will, of course, cease momentarily experiencing repetition, and experience instead a contrast. There will be a new groping and a new grasping, as another pattern is made out.

One thing very obvious about my carpet is that both longitudinal borders are of the same pattern, as are both latitudinal ones. I can find this out in at least two ways: either by completely circumnavigating the carpet, turning the corners seriatim until I am back where I started, or by stepping back far enough so that my eye can take in the whole pattern at a glance. The former way of doing the business, I want to suggest, is a perfect visual analogue of experiencing the musical repeat. Indeed, the border of my carpet is the exposition, repeated, of a visual sonata movement with two themes. If I pursue the longitudinal North to South I get the first theme. When I turn the corner and pursue the latitudinal West to East I get the second theme, and turning the corner to follow the opposite longitudinal border South to North I have reached the double bar and begun the repeat of the exposition.

Having reached this stage of enlightenment with regard to my carpet, I think I now know exactly what I would say to Grétry's suggestion that the repeats in a sonata movement are absurd. I should say that, to the contrary, to leave them out would be an act of vandalism in spirit, if not in fact, as gross as cutting off two borders of my Persian carpet because they are "just the same old thing." A sonata movement is a sonic carpet, its repeats the burgeoning forth of its pattern. And so of any other musical form in which instructions to literally repeat appear. This point requires some elaboration.

It is sometimes said that music is a temporal art while such visual arts as painting and sculpture and decoration are not.

This, of course, is not literally true. For as we have seen in the simple case of my Persian carpet, the experience is an experience in time. How could it be otherwise? But what does seem to be true – and perhaps this is at the heart of the oft-repeated formula – is that the sequence of perceptual events in music is much more rigidly determined by the composer than is the sequence of perceptual events in my experience of the carpet by its creator. For I can pursue many directions, as we have seen, in my perusal of my carpet, and still be correctly described as having perceived that very carpet. But I cannot listen to the movements of a symphony out of sequence, or the development first and the exposition last, of a sonata movement and still be correctly described as having heard that very work. That would be tantamount to cutting up my carpet and putting it together in a different combination of patterns. It would be a different carpet. The composer of a symphony has composed it such that the Minuet must be heard after the Adagio and before the Finale, much as the creator of my carpet had composed it such that the outermost longitudinal border must be spatially contiguous to the next outermost one and not to any other.[20]

Thus repeats, both the external ones, in which whole sections of works are literally played again, or internal ones, where small musical figures or patterns are reiterated, are the means by which the composer of the sonic carpet makes his design, in the large and in detail. Now something very important emerges from this conclusion, when we contrast the way I attend to music with the way I attend to my Persian carpet. Because I am not under the composer's military discipline in looking at my carpet, I can fix the pattern in my mind with little trouble: I have the luxury, as Gombrich might say, of groping until I grasp. However, I have no such luxury

20 I suppose it is possible to devise a way of looking at my carpet that is so sequentially bizarre as to prevent me from ever grasping any of the patterns, in which case I have not really perceived the carpet at all, even though I may have perceived every square inch of it, if, for example, I look at it through a peephole that never lets me see two contiguous elements at once, and I never manage to see any two in sequence. So in that sense even the carpet has built into it some prescription for looking; call it a condition of "normal" looking.

when listening to music. I cannot go back to linger over a pattern I have missed, unless, of course, I am reading a score, or playing the piece on the piano, or in some other way "studying" it. In other words, the prescribed way of listening to a musical composition, to experience it as intended, is in an unbroken temporal sequence from prescribed beginning to prescribed end, in prescribed order, whereas the prescribed way of looking at my Persian carpet, to experience it as intended, allows a freedom to wander, to linger, to begin where one pleases, and to retrace one's steps as desired. Musical repeats, then, perform an obvious and vital function in that they are the composer's way of allowing us, indeed compelling us to linger; to retrace our steps so that we can fix the fleeting sonic pattern; they allow us to grope so that we can grasp.

What I am saying here, I must caution, can be easily misunderstood and lead to the following objectionable conclusion. If the function of repeats is simply to enable us to grasp a pattern, then they would seem to be dispensable in any circumstances in which we have reason to believe the audience is capable of grasping the pattern without them: for example, if it is an audience of very musical people, or an audience of concert goers who have heard the *Eroica* enough times to be familiar with the themes. But this seems absurd. The repeats are no more dispensable aids to listening than are the reiterated patterns of my carpet dispensable aids to grasping the pattern. If I can grasp the pattern of the outermost longitudinal border of my carpet after seeing three instances of the basic squiggly figure, does that mean the other seventeen are redundant and can be cut away to save space?

The trap here lies in the problem-solving idiom – Gombrich's groping and grasping – that we so naturally (and quite correctly) fall into. It makes it sound as if the carpet has, as its purpose, the posing of problems, and the providing of clues to their solution, with the goal being solely the solving of the problems. And if you solve the problems with fewer clues than are given, then you put down the puzzle and pick up a new one. Why bother with the other clues? Likewise with musical repeats. Once the pattern is grasped, why go back again? Repeats are for dullards.

What has happened is that a means-ends distinction has been imposed, quite inappropriately, on alien territory by the problem-solving idiom, innocent enough in itself. Groping and grasping are, indeed, part of the musical experience, as they are part of properly experiencing my carpet. But groping, although a means to grasping, is an end in itself as well. And grasping, although the end of groping, is not a termination, but part of an ongoing experience. To grasp a pattern is to solve a problem, to be sure. However, the grasping of the pattern is just a part of the process in which we experience the whole composition that that particular piece of pattern inhabits and enhances. There is no denying that musical repeats are an aid in grasping patterns, but they are, at the same time, part of what constitutes musical patterns in the first place. Or, in other words, quite generally, repetition is the means of grasping pattern; but, by definition, pattern is that very repetition, and to dispense with the remainder after it has been grasped would be to dispense with *it*, whereas *it*, the *pattern*, is the whole point of the exercise.

At this juncture I think I can fairly claim to have accomplished the first positive task I set myself in this essay, which was to show that the lowly wallpaper model of pure music could succeed, where the more highly touted literary and organism models could not, in accommodating the simple and incontrovertible fact of the musical repeat. I could well go on from here to exploit what I see to be other intriguing possibilities of the wallpaper model for enhancing our understanding of the musical experience, but this essay grows apace, and I will have to leave many things for future times and other occasions. I certainly cannot close, though, without attempting to deflect the charge that the wallpaper model cannot account for the high status in the Pantheon of the arts occupied by pure instrumental music, at least since the time Viennese classical style reached its maturity. To make of such music "mere" decoration many would say is reason enough to reject the wallpaper model out of hand. And that is just what seems to have been done. I conclude, therefore, with at least the beginning of an attempt to answer this charge. Beginnings, however, as I have said often enough, are all the conclusion I can give. The problem is just too large for more than that.

VIII

I begin with a basic assumption for which I can offer no proof whatever. It seems to me that there is no single incantation I can recite over the wallpaper model to at once make it obviously secure against the charge of trivializing music. There is no such anodyne, no magic bullet. Success in this regard can lie, I believe, only in more fully understanding all those things about the sonic patterns we call absolute music that make them intriguing to human beings, and capture their attention; that make music orders of magnitude more compelling than what customarily decorates our walls and floors. I shall enumerate and discuss briefly four such elevating characteristics of music. I must be brief, and can, because none of these characteristics is newly discovered, but all are familiar and much discussed in the musical literature; all I need do is remind you of their existence, and suggest their relevance to the present question.

First, music is a multidimensional pattern. This follows from the obvious fact that Western music is, unlike, I believe, any other of the world's musics, polyphonic.

Since the sixteenth century, the norm for polyphonic music has been four-part texture. This means that, by and large, instrumental music presents to the listener at least four sonic layers: the outer voices of bass and soprano, the inner voices of tenor and alto. These voices, even where the writing is basically harmonic rather than contrapuntal, never entirely blend, nor are they meant to. We hear the particular qualities of chords as the emergent qualities of the individual tones, but they never blend as do the ingredients in foods and mixed drinks. We hear a chord as one *and* as many; and when we hear the progression of chords in four-part writing, we hear

354

– or should hear – the simultaneous progression of melodies as well.

But if four-part writing is the norm, four-layered music is not, by any means, its maximum effect. For when one adds orchestration to four-part writing, one adds further layers to the four-part texture. An oboe playing the same tune as the violins produces a newly emergent tone-color, to be sure; yet the line never ceases to be two layers of sound, particularly so if the oboe is playing an octave above or an octave below the violins, rather than in unison. And when orchestration reaches the dimensions of a Berlioz or a Mahler, the layers of sound present a texture of enormous complexity, compared with the four-layered texture of a string quartet. And yet the four-layered texture of the strings is itself far in excess of the visually decorative.

Wallpaper and Persian carpets are not, to be sure, two-dimensional, for they display figure and ground. But the part which polyphonic texture plays in the musical experience lifts instrumental music far above even such true art works as Persian carpets in respect of dimensionality. If absolute music is wallpaper for the ears, it is a many-dimensioned wallpaper that offers intrigues and complications far beyond its visual counterparts.

Second, music is a quasi-syntactic pattern. Its structure is "grammatical."

Perhaps this "grammatical" dimension of music, above anything else, has fueled the linguistic metaphor. And because of that we must be careful here. I have always observed the convention, when referring to this aspect of music, of putting "grammar" or "syntax" in quotation marks, to suggest a problematic or attenuated sense. For the syntax of natural languages is not completely separable from semantics, since a test for correct syntax seems to be whether a purported sentence "makes sense." Music is separated from that dimension of natural language syntax by its total lack of semantic properties. Nor is musical "syntax" exactly analogous to the syntax of such artificial structures as symbolic logic either, since its "syntactical" rules are never stated, nor can they be, with the logical rigor of these mathematical disciplines.

Nevertheless, I take it as something there is no real need to argue for here, that even the layperson with no explicit knowledge of musical "syntax" at all experiences music not merely as a sonic pattern but as a sonic pattern susceptible of "grammatical" error.[21] Because of this the composer can play, so to speak, with "grammaticality" as a structural parameter. Thus, to take but two trivial examples, a deceptive cadence is experienced not merely as an unexpected event but as a "syntactically" jarring one that eventually will be put to rights. The final "cadence" of Mozart's *Musical Joke* (K. 522), twenty-four "grammatically" impossible measures of it, and the final "grammatical" howler at the finish, is one big "syntactical" put on, as is so much else in this work – a work indeed made possible by the well-known "syntactical" turn that music took in mature Viennese classical style.

Thus the parameter of musical "syntax" puts another complication into absolute music that separates it from its visual counterparts, even while keeping it well within the wallpaper model. Absolute music, we can now add, is not merely multidimensional wallpaper for the ears, but multidimensional wallpaper with a quasi-syntactical structure: It is a pattern with a "grammar."

Third, absolute music is, in most of its traditional manifestations in the last two hundred years, a highly expressive pattern of sound. It possesses emotive properties as part of its perceived structure. In this, I dare say, it is not unique among the decorative arts. My Persian carpet, for all its loss of color over the years, still has suggestions of expressive tone, and the fine examples of the art in museums leave no doubt about the matter. But to Western ears and eyes, at least, music is the expressive art above all others among the nonrepresentational ones, and has been so considered since time out of mind.

21 For my more detailed views on this matter, see Peter Kivy, *Music Alone: Philosophical Reflections on the Purely Musical Experience* (Ithaca: Cornell University Press, 1990), pp. 109–15.

There is no need to dilate on this well-known, and most thoroughly discussed aspect of music, except to point out the particular way in which I have put the matter here. I am saying that music is expressive of the garden variety emotions – anger, sadness, joy, fear, and the like – not in virtue of arousing those emotions in listeners, as has been traditionally maintained, but in virtue of possessing them as heard musical properties, indeed properties that are part of musical "syntax" and structure.[22] I am not alone in believing that the expressive in music is heard and not aroused, although there is a good deal of disagreement among those that share this view about just how the possession of expressive properties by music is to be explained.[23] Suffice it to say that, however one wishes to understand the claim, there is substantial agreement, both among laypersons and experts, that music is, to a very high degree, an *expressive* texture.

Here, then, is another parameter, that of the expressive, which, if it does not belong uniquely to music among the decorative arts, at least belongs to music in the West so preeminently as to make it a distinguishing mark. Why sound patterns should exhibit such a saturation of expressive quality, over and above that which abstract visual patterns seem to possess, I do not know. But that they do seems to be generally acknowledged. So we may now expand our characterization of absolute music, in contrast to the other arts of decoration, and state that if music is merely sonic wallpaper, it is not only multidimensional and quasi-syntactic, but deeply expressive wallpaper as well.

Finally, absolute music is, as we all are well aware, deeply moving. It provides a profoundly emotional experience to its devotees.

Now this power of music to move us emotionally has been traditionally taken to mean that sad music moves us to sadness, happy music to happiness, and so on. But that is not what I am saying at all. Music does, indeed, possess such

22 For details see ibid., Chapter 9.
23 For my own views on this, see Peter Kivy, *Sound Sentiment: An Essay on the Musical Emotions* (Philadelphia: Temple University Press, 1989).

357

emotions as sadness, happiness, anger, and the like, as I have already pointed out, in the form of heard musical properties. However, it moves us in quite another way than by making us sad or happy or angry. I have written elsewhere about how music moves us emotionally, and will not go into the details here.[24] All I can say to those, of whom there are many, who believe that music moves us by raising the garden variety emotions, is: We at least all agree on this vital point, that music is deeply moving of the emotions, and that is all the agreement I require for present purposes. For it appears to me that in its capacity to move, absolute music is far beyond the other arts of decoration, however that capacity and its results are ultimately to be understood, just so long as they are understood within the conceptual limits of the decorative arts. And we can, then, add this capacity to move us to the arsenal of music's weapons as a decorative art.

So music, I am arguing, is "merely" sonic wallpaper, but it is wallpaper with some pretty impressive features. It is multidimensional wallpaper. It is quasi-syntactical wallpaper. It is deeply expressive wallpaper. And it is deeply moving wallpaper. These features, I urge, help redeem music from the charge that as a decorative art, it is somehow demoted to the status of the trivial. But if you are still not convinced, then forget about music for a moment and take a good long look at the Alhambra. Unlike the Sistine Ceiling's, its adornments are "merely" decorative. They are also "merely" breathtaking, "merely" exalted, "merely" magnificent, "merely" sublime. Perhaps after all that is not only the shortest but the best argument of all for the wallpaper model of absolute music. If I call Beethoven's C sharp-minor Quartet "merely decorative," and the Alhambra is my paradigm, "decorative" hardly seems a put down, and Beethoven still retains his well deserved place in the Pantheon of arts and letters.

24 On this, see Kivy, *Music Alone*, Chapter 8.

IX

But I close on a cautionary note. This is not a theory for all seasons. It is a theory about a certain kind of music, that has flourished for a certain short period of time, in a certain circumscribed region of the world. That music, unlike almost all the other musics of other periods and other places, was written without verbal text, and without any further function in human society than to be an object of rapt attention. The importance of the repeat, both external and internal, in the music of this tradition cannot be overestimated, and has been not merely underestimated, but almost totally ignored by those who have tried to write "philosophically" about such music. Indeed, I would put it this strongly: The music which I have been discussing does not merely contain repetition as an important feature, but as a defining feature.

It may well be asked, does musical repetition have to be? Is it written in the book of nature that music must be based on the principle of repetition? And the answer clearly is *no*. For this is a normative as well as a descriptive principle, and the composer is free to observe it, or to rebel against it, as he or she sees fit. Rebel against it indeed certain composers of the twentieth century have done in trying to create what Cone calls "a music of continuous mutation."[25] Of such music the account I have given says nothing at all.

25 Cone, *Musical Form and Musical Performance*, p. 54.

Chapter XIX

Is music an art?

Goethe ridicules the grouping together of all the
arts which are so different from each other in
their aims and means of expression.

Paul Oskar Kristeller

I

Since about the middle of the eighteenth century, but not
before, the term "Art" – Art with a capital "A" – has been
taken to comprise "above all the five major arts of painting,
sculpture, architecture, music and poetry." As Paul O. Kristeller, discoverer and principal expositor of this important
historical event, observes: "These five [now] constitute the
irreducible members of the modern system of the arts, on
which all writers and thinkers seem to agree."[1] In light of
Kristeller's discovery, my thesis in the present essay can be
very concisely put. It is simply that music is *not* one of the
Arts with a capital "A," which is to say, *not* one of the fine
arts.

Now it might be objected straightaway that this is, on the
very face of it, an utterly absurd, completely indefensible
thesis, since music just is, as a matter of fact, now classified
as one of the Arts with a capital "A," one of the fine arts,

---

1 Paul Oskar Kristeller, "The Modern System of the Arts," reprinted in Kristeller,
  Renaissance Thought and the Arts: Collected Essays (Princeton: Princeton University
  Press, 1980), pp. 164–5.

and has been since 1746 to be exact, so there's an end on't. Whatever is so classified is that very thing, just as whatever is sold in a grocery store is groceries, regardless of what philosophical analysis or marketing research might reveal.

Well, of course, I am not denying that music is now classified as a fine art. But that it is a fairly recent historical event. And we customarily represent the event not as *constituting* music Art with a capital "A" from then on but as drawing our attention to the fact – getting us to see that – music was Art with a capital "A" all along, at least as far back as one wishes to push the repertory of Western art music. But if it makes sense to claim that before the eighteenth century people didn't know that what they called music was Art with a capital "A," and mistakenly thought it was something else, then it would seem also to make sense to at least suggest that they may have been right all along and the eighteenth-century philosophers mistaken in reclassifying music as one of the fine arts. The claim, though perhaps dead wrong, is not unintelligible or silly.

II

My thesis, then, is that music is not Art with a capital "A." But things are not quite so simply put. Specifically, what I am saying is that pure instrumental music, music without text, title, program, or plot – what the nineteenth century came to call "absolute music" – is not Art with a capital "A." Further, I am going to claim that Renaissance polyphony (I will not push my argument further back than that) is also best understood, prior to the middle of the sixteenth century, as not one of the fine arts. And this claim is meant to include not merely what was then the more or less minor genre of pure instrumental music, but, more important, the musical setting of sacred texts as well. Finally, I am going to claim that, beginning in the second half of the sixteenth century, the musical setting of texts – which is agreed on all hands to have undergone a profound change, under the influence of the Counter Reformation, the Council of Trent

(1545–1563), and, at the end of the century, the invention of opera – presents the clearest case for a kind of music that *is* Art with a capital "A."

So I am arguing that prior to the middle of the sixteenth century, music is best understood not as a fine art but as something else, to be specified shortly. After that, it undergoes a profound change that encourages thinking of it as Art with a capital "A." And, ironically, in the eighteenth century, just when it is finally swallowed up into the system of the fine arts, it gives birth to pure instrumental music in its modern, imposing form: just the very music that immediately comes to mind when the art of music is mentioned – and just the very music that has been most difficult to place in a theoretical framework capable of enfranchising *it* as Art with a capital "A" while at the same time enfranchising the visual arts and literature as well.

The solution to this dilemma lies simply in recognizing that the eighteenth century passed on to us a problem intractable because based on a false premise. More exactly, the modern system of the arts was formed before absolute music in its later, imposing form was an issue. What the eighteenth-century theorists had in mind, in these formative years, when they baptized "music" Art with a capital "A" was always, essentially, music that accompanied a text. As we shall see, the baptism was not implausible, given that absolute music was barely a consideration at all. And when it became an issue, as the age of Haydn, Mozart, and Beethoven rolled around, the die was already cast. Music was now in the modern system – Art with a capital "A" – and absolute music must be gathered in, recalcitrant though it was. It is time now to correct that original false step, by recapturing for absolute music the pre-Tridentine concept of what music is, which the eighteenth century never completely gave up where absolute music was concerned.

What place, then, did music occupy, among human institutions, in the Renaissance, before the momentous events that so transformed it at the end of the sixteenth century? If we confine ourselves to composing, performing, and the experience of listening to music, to the exclusion of music theory, it seems obvious enough to be a truism that music was seen as a craft. But what *kind* of craft?

In answering this question, let me appeal not to historical texts but, rather, to the contemporary musical ear. Listen, for example, to the superb mass settings of the great fifteenth-century master, Johannes Ockeghem. Compare them to the more familiar polyphony of Palestrina a century later. What must strike one immediately is a kind of remoteness in the earlier composer – not so much an other worldly quality but something, it seems to me, removed in some way from the "human," if I may so put it. Worldly, then, but not human.

Pressed a bit further, the comparison can, I think, fix this impression more clearly. What is "human" about Palestrina? To my ear it is the quality of being a human "utterance"; and in a moment we will have some historical backing for this claim. Palestrina's text sounds as if it is being declaimed, enunciated by a persona, or, better, personae whose intention it is to convey the meaning of the text. I get no such impression from Ockeghem's sacred works, which seem to me, rather, not to be utterances at all but opulent decorative structures: not expressions of the sacred words but *settings* of them in the very sense in which a goldsmith might make a setting for a precious gem.[2] (One wonders, indeed, if our very idiom for describing what composers do with texts, namely, that they "set" them, might not be a vestigial reminder of this earlier compositional attitude.)

But if my impression is correct, then we can now say just what kind of craft music was prior to the middle of the six-

2 I have expressed this thought previously in *Osmin's Rage: Philosophical Reflections on Opera, Drama and Text* (Princeton: Princeton University Press, 1988), Chapter 1.

teenth century. It was akin to the jeweler's craft, or, as we might call it now, being in possession of the modern system of the arts, one of the *decorative* arts, to distinguish it from Art with a capital "A." The composer was a jeweler, and the sacred texts were his precious gems, to be placed in ever more elaborate and dazzling settings, until the words became dwarfed by their frames, like relics in their golden and crystal reliquaries. This is not to say that the words became disvalued. Quite to the contrary, the overpowering, complex beauty of their musical settings is a direct and ample expression of the value beyond price that was placed on them by the composers and their world.

Sacred polyphony, in the first half of the fifteenth century, just because it was a supremely decorative art, displays, I think, an exuberant freedom of the musical imagination that is still impressive today, even to an age familiar with the concept and reality of absolute music. But this freedom entailed, as the spokesmen for the Counter Reformation and the Council of Trent made abundantly clear, a sacrifice to the intelligibility of the text that finally became unacceptable. It is a more than twice-told tale that polyphony was in jeopardy at the Council of Trent because it was seen as the villain of the piece. How can you understand the message when everyone is saying something different, simultaneously? But sacred polyphony survived, Palestrina its supreme master in the post-Tridentine period, with the imprimatur of the Church. This in itself should suggest that polyphony was not really the perpetrator at all, rather, as it turns out, merely an accessory before the fact. As an eminent authority on the relation between tone and text in the early history of Western music observes: "Composers contemporary with and preceding Josquin may at times have been too preoccupied with technical considerations, particularly those attendant upon a polyphonic coordination of voices, to pay attention to individual word stress."[3] Thus, apparently, it was not polyphony

---

3 Don Harrán, *World-Tone Relations in Musical Thought: From Antiquity to the Seventeenth Century* (Neuhausen-Stuttgart: Hänssler-Verlag, 1986), p. 335.

per se that obscured the text, but the pre-Tridentine poly-phonists' preoccupation with the musical setting itself as pure decorative or structural art. It was not the many-voiced structure that obscured the text but what the individual voices were doing, namely, weaving long, sinuous, melismatic threads that spread the syllables so far apart as to make them unintelligible as words and sentences. To quote the same eminent authority once again, "the recommendations of the Council of Trent . . . were engendered by the concern of the ecclesiastics lest music prevail over words and prevent their understanding"; and the leading recommendation of all to composers was "to curtail melody for the sake of verbal clarification."[4]

To say that composers of Catholic sacred music, in obedience to the directives of the Council of Trent, *curtailed* melody for the sake of verbal clarification, although true, is to place what they did in an unnecessarily negative light. Melody was indeed curtailed; but, as I view what happened, it was curtailed not in the sense of sacrificed in obedience to authority, contrary to any aesthetic inclination whatever, but, rather, given a different, certainly less flamboyant character, in pursuit of a new, *positive* aesthetic program aimed at achieving the desired objective of textual intelligibility. And, again, I think we can make this clear with a comparison, this time between the polyphony of Palestrina and what can be looked on as the culmination of the movement toward textual intelligibility in the invention at the end of the century of operatic declamation: the so-called *stile rappresentativo*. Operatic monody, both in theory and in practice, makes unmistakably clear what has been going on. Music has been transformed from the decorative craft of text-setting into the fine art of utterance-representation. The first composers of opera, as one of their spokesmen put it, "found a way of imitating familiar speech."[5]

4 Ibid., pp. 345–6.
5 Pietro de' Bardi, "Letter to G. B. Doni," in Oliver Strunk, *Source Readings in Music History: From Classical Antiquity through the Romantic Era* (New York: Norton, 1950), p. 364.

Thus it was through the positive aesthetic program of artistically representing human utterance, not the negative one of simply trimming their melodic sails, that the inventors of opera achieved, to whatever extent they did, the intelligibility of the text. And in seeing their explicitly stated program, as well as their musical results as the culmination of a historical process already in progress during the Counter Reformation and immediately after the Council of Trent, it becomes abundantly clear that such representation of human utterance was already in place in post-Tridentine sacred polyphony – which is precisely why Palestrina possesses that "human" quality of expression that the music of Ockeghem does not. The stage was now set for music to be initiated into the modern system of the arts, for it now was squarely within the category of the representational, which of course would eventually be the defining property of the fine arts when they received their capital "A" in the eighteenth century. For vocal music it was already, essentially, a *fait accompli* at the end of the sixteenth.

IV

"The decisive step toward a system of the fine arts was taken by the Abbé Batteux," Kristeller tells us: "he was the first to set forth a clearcut system of the fine arts in a treatise devoted exclusively to this subject."[6] Batteux' leading idea – his *même principe*, as the title of his work calls it – was, of course, the Platonic and Aristotelian concept of "imitation." And it remained the leading idea of almost all writers throughout the eighteenth century. As Batteux put the momentous conclusion: "We can define Painting, Sculpture, Dance, as an imitation of beautiful Nature, expressed by colors, by relief, by attitudes. And music and Poetry an imitation of beautiful Nature expressed by sounds, or by measured discourses."[7]

Music, as we have seen, was ready for this development,

6 Kristeller, "The Modern System of the Arts," p. 199.
7 [Charles] Batteux, *Les beaux arts reduits a un même principe* (Paris, 1747), p. 43.

and had been since the late sixteenth century. For it already was by that time, both by practice and by precept, an "imitation of beautiful nature" in the form of a representation of human vocal utterance. And it is as the representation of human utterance, and other forms and mechanisms of human emotive expression in general that the *même principe* in Batteux and the rest was almost invariably understood, where music was concerned, throughout the eighteenth century.

But it is absolutely crucial to remember – I have been guilty of forgetting it myself, at times – that what was being talked about almost exclusively during the formative years of the modern system of the arts when music was the subject was *music with a sung text,* most particularly the controversial arts of opera and music drama. And it is not at all clear that pure instrumental music even as late as Kant's third *Critique* – which is to say, the 1790's – was yet *firmly* in place as Art with a capital "A."

The classification of pure instrumental music, it is also important to note, was inextricably entangled in the closely related activity of *evaluating* it, throughout the eighteenth century and well into the nineteenth; for in classifying absolute music as Art with a capital "A," one was, in effect, elevating it as well. Thus it is fairly safe to read the low esteem in which philosophers and critics tended to hold pure instrumental music, at least in the eighteenth century, even as late as mature Haydn and Mozart, as, ipso facto, a reluctance as well to classify it with the fine arts. That almost universally held evaluation is a familiar and well established fact. As a recent commentator on this aspect of the musical scene concludes: "Until near the end of the eighteenth century, the overwhelming majority of critics held the opinion that instrumental music was vastly inferior to vocal music, and for many the reason lay in the apparent inability of instrumental music to convey moral instruction or, indeed, to attain any level of intelligibility."[8] Indeed, even as late as Hegel, music

8 David P. Schroeder, *Haydn and the Enlightenment: The Late Symphonies and their Audience* (Oxford: The Clarendon Press, 1990), p. 64.

without a text still had, in spite of the towering figure of Beethoven behind it, an only grudging acceptance on the part of many, including Hegel himself, who insisted that "music must, on account of its one-sidedness, call on the help of the more exact meaning of words and, in order to become more firmly conjoined with the detail and characteristic expression of the subject matter, it demands a text which alone gives a content to the subjective life's outpouring in the notes."[9]

Kant had, indeed, nominally classified pure music as one of the fine arts. But in the end he held open the distinct possibility that although pure musical pleasure might be "the effect of an estimate of form in the play of a number of sensations," it might also be a pleasure afforded by "mere sense-impressions"; and he concluded: "According to the former interpretation, alone, would music be represented out and out as a *fine art*, whereas according to the latter it would be represented as (in part at least) an *agreeable* art."[10] Thus, in the work that is agreed on all hands to represent the culmination of aesthetic thought in the eighteenth century – the most profound contribution up to that time to the philosophy of art as we understand it – the issue of absolute music as Art with a capital "A" was still in the balance.

For absolute music, the balance was only tipped decisively in the direction of the fine arts in the Romantic era. And it is of particular significance to my argument that this is the very period in which instrumental music underwent the greatest pressure in its history in the direction of the literary and pictorial arts, eventuating in the development of the tone poem, programmatic symphony, and various other forms of illustrational music: surely a case of Mohammed coming to the mountain. The failure of theory to produce the desired result of conceptually connecting absolute music with the firmly established and clearly representational fine arts of literature, painting, and sculpture led instead to an alteration in

9 G. W. F. Hegel, *Aesthetics: Lectures on Fine Art,* trans. T. M. Knox (Oxford: The Clarendon Press, 1975), Vol. 2, p. 960.
10 Immanuel Kant, *Critique of Aesthetic Judgement,* trans. James Creed Meredith (Oxford: The Clarendon Press, 1911), p. 190 (§51).

musical practice itself, thus producing a plethora of "literary" and "painterly" works for instruments alone that could readily be seen as of a kind with poems, novels, plays, paintings, and statues. But, of course, what they could *not* any longer be seen as was works of absolute music. And the reverse side of this coin was, deplorably, an increased tendency to put literary or painterly interpretations on the pure musical canon. The strategy then consisted in both transforming present musical practice to accord with theory and misinterpreting past musical practice to the same end. The result for the philosophy of art was no progress at all with the question.

Here endeth my historical tale. What can we learn from it?

V

Philosophers of art, for a long time, have accepted it as an established historical fact that "music," *sans phrase,* came to be seen as one of the fine arts in the early eighteenth century, with Batteaux finally, but *merely,* dotting the "i" in 1746. In addition, we have come to realize that aesthetics and the philosophy of art also took on their modern, philosophically autonomous character during the very same crucial period; and so, like epistemologists, philosophers of mind, philosophical psychologists, and various others, philosophers of art tend to see the sources, primal formulations, and initial solutions of their problems as coming in the early modern period. The heavy hand of a nearly three-hundred-year history, then, as well as the whole philosophical weight of the Enlightenment, has laid on aestheticians the firm conviction that the membership of music, including absolute music, in the modern system of the arts is an established, long-standing, and incontrovertible fact. In consequence, it has also laid on them what they perceive as the unavoidable task of finding, where three centuries of predecessors have failed, a theory to conceptually knit absolute music to the rest of the fine arts. The task has proved intractable. The question then forces itself upon us: Is the task really unavoidable?

One thing we can certainly accomplish by a fresh and un-biased look at the history of musical thought and practice is to lift that heavy historical hand and philosophical weight. It simply is not the case that absolute music ever became firmly established in the eighteenth century as one of the fine arts. The question was not settled then, even as late as Kant's third *Critique*. The firm historical tradition is far shorter and more problematical than we have tended to think. And if you are intimidated by the authority of history, and the weight of Enlightenment thought from Shaftesbury through Kant, ease your mind. Neither is nearly so imposing as we have been led to believe.

I have come firmly to believe that the history of thinking about the nature of music as an art, and the practice of music itself, from the pre-Tridentine Renaissance through the third *Critique*, has an important philosophical truth to tell us, or, at least, an important philosophical hypothesis to propose, worth considering seriously. I have come to this truth, or this hypothesis (if you prefer) on independent, ahistorical grounds, in my thinking about absolute music, but I am con-vinced that the history of musical thought lends it support. Prior to the Counter Reformation, music was generally per-ceived as among the crafts, and in its primary function, as the setting of religious texts, seems rather analogous to the particular craft of setting precious jewels. It is, in short, what we would call now one of the decorative arts. Various intel-lectual movements in the second half of the sixteenth cen-tury, notably the Counter Reformation and the rise of opera, transformed the musical setting of texts – still, and for a long time to come, the major work of composers – into a palpably representational art, recognized as such, that is, as *represen-tational*, although not yet as Art with a capital "A," since, as Kristeller observes, "the Renaissance . . . was still far from establishing the modern system of the arts."[11]

In the eighteenth century the musical setting of texts –

11 Kristeller, "The Modern System of the Arts," p. 186.

usually still all that "music" meant – was emphatically recognized as one of the fine (that is imitative or representational) arts. But pure instrumental music was never, as I now read the historical record, firmly established as one of the Arts with a capital "A," for the obvious reason that it was, and remains impossible to construe as "representational" in any full-blooded sense of that concept. Kant was not alone in his century in harboring doubts, recognizing the distinct possibility that the art of absolute music might well be more akin to the decorative arts than to the arts of the modern system.

I suggest that philosophical thinkers about music until the end of the eighteenth century had things exactly right, and that the nineteenth century began to get them exactly wrong. Since the end of the sixteenth century there have been *two* arts of music: the fine art of musical text setting, which is basically the art of representing human expression in musical tones, and the decorative art of absolute music. Recognizing this simple fact frees us from the impossible philosophical task of finding a theory or some other kind of conceptual analysis that can enable us to understand absolute music as one of the fine arts. In a word, it *isn't*.

But although liberating us from a pseudoproblem we should never have become involved with in the first place, the recognition of absolute music as a decorative rather than a fine art opens up to us a host of new and, to me, both exciting and important problems that may have implications quite beyond the confines of musical aesthetics. These problems are all special cases or implications of what might be called the "prestige" question.

Absolute music until the end of the eighteenth century was, as we have seen, far from the center of attention, the setting of religious and dramatic texts being the main business of composers. It was held in low esteem, compared with vocal music, well into the nineteenth century, particularly among philosophers of art. Nevertheless, in spite of reluctance clearly born of a pronounced bias toward the content-laden arts, ab-

solute music did finally achieve an exalted place in the Pantheon. That place is now an incontrovertible fact of the art
world. And the mere suggestion that absolute music be
understood as a decorative rather than a fine art is bound to
be seen as a demotion, an affront to the dignity and intellectual stature of the discipline, indeed, an impossible suggestion, a nonstarter just because it cannot account for the prestige pure instrumental music now enjoys in our intellectual
lives.

But I would suggest that such a response both evades the
issue, and at the same time expresses a deeply held Western
prejudice in favor of the arts of representation that absolutely demands examination. I say it is an evasion of the issue because, as philosophers of art, we have failed to take
seriously the possibility that absolute music is as it appears,
an art of pure sonic design which, for that very reason, has
called forth such terms as "absolute" and "pure" to describe
it, and to distinguish it from other musical kinds. Instead of
accepting this, at least tentatively, as a working hypothesis,
so that we can explore its implications and possible foundations, we have persistently applied our philosophical ingenuity to the task of transforming absolute music into one kind
or another of crypto-representation, on the sometimes explicit but all too frequently unexpressed premise that only as
representation can it really be taken seriously, which, manifestly, it is.

The question we should be asking is not, How does absolute music, appearances to the contrary, manage to represent? That is the evasion. Rather, we should be asking, What
is it about *us*, and about our world, that has made the pure
contentless art of musical design so important for our lives
in the past one hundred and fifty years, but not before? What
needs of ours does it serve? And why have other people not
felt those needs? What distinguishes sonic from visual design that seems to make the former play a role in our lives so
different from the latter? What does it all *mean* – but not in
the semantic sense?

I have only just begun to address such questions in my

own work[12] and I urge other philosophers of art to take up the task as well. It is a hard task, because we have paid little attention to the decorative arts in our philosophies, tend to disvalue them in comparison to the arts of content, and are, at present, ill equipped to talk about them.

It will be important, I think, to look to others for help: to the cognitive psychologists, perhaps; the philosophers of mind, structural linguists, and to people like E. H. Gombrich, who has written so brilliantly about the decorative arts of visual design and who, by the way, quite naturally ends his book on the decorative arts with a chapter on *music*.[13]

I think this is a great challenge, and will spare us another dreary round of philosophical books and papers trying to understand absolute music as a representational or linguistic art. The books and papers get more and more clever, more and more philosophically sophisticated, and, for me at least, less and less plausible. The lady doth protest too much, methinks. I believe that until we meet this challenge head on, and try to philosohpically understand pure music on its own terms – which is to say as a pure decorative art – we will remain with an important and, to date, mysterious aspect of our artistic natures unexplained and, worse still, unexamined.

12 Peter Kivy, "The Fine Art of Repetition." Chapter XVII in this volume.
13 E. H. Gombrich, *The Sense of Order: A Study in the Psychology of Decorative Art* (Ithaca: Cornell University Press, 1979), Epilogue: *Some Musical Analogues.*